S0-AGF-893

Talking Murder

TALKING MURDER

INTERVIEWS WITH 20 MYSTERY WRITERS

CHARLES L. P. SILET

Ontario Review Press + Princeton

Copyright © 1999 by The Ontario Review, Inc.
All rights reserved.
Printed in the U.S.A.

Ontario Review Press
9 Honey Brook Dr.
Princeton, NJ 08540

Distributed by W. W. Norton & Company, Inc.
500 Fifth Avenue, New York, NY 10110

Library of Congress Cataloging-in-Publication Data

Silet, Charles L. P.
   Talking murder : interviews with 20 mystery writers / Charles L.P. Silet. — 1st ed.
      p.   cm.
   ISBN 0-86538-096-1 (pbk. : alk. paper)
   1. Detective and mystery stories, American—History and criticism—
Theory, etc. 2. Detective and mystery stories, English—History and criticism—
Theory, etc. 3. Authors, American—20th century—Interviews. 4. Authors,
English—20th century—Interviews. 5. Detective and mystery stories—
Authorship. I. Title.
   PS374.D4S535 1999
   813'.087209'09045—dc21   99-18501
                                                                       CIP

First Edition

Acknowledgments

I would like to thank the following publications for originally publishing, in whole or in part, some of the interviews included in this book.

"Edna Buchanan" in *Mystery Scene*, No. 62 (1999), 54–59.

"Eva Wylie, Anna Lee, and the Contemporary Crime Novel" in *Mystery Scene*, No. 49 (1995), 20, 59, 65–68; and "Liza: An Interview with Liza Cody," *The Armchair Detective*, 25 (Spring 1992), 190–199.

"Drugs, Cash, and Automatic Weapons: An Interview with James Crumley," *The Armchair Detective*, 27:1 (Winter 1994), 9–15.

"Hard Talk: An Interview with Barbara D'Amato," *Clues*, 17:2 (Fall/Winter 1996), 105–131; and "Barb D'Amato," *Mystery Scene*, No. 47 (1995), 26, 28, 60–64.

"The Bone Collector: An Interview with Jeffery Deaver," *The Armchair Detective*, 30:2 (Spring 1997), 142–146.

"The Bookman's Eye," *The Armchair Detective*, 28:2 (Spring 1995), 124–133.

"Mad Dog and Glory: A Conversation with James Ellroy," *The Armchair Detective*, 28:3 (Summer 1995), 236–244.

"Nottingham Noir: An Interview with John Harvey," *The Armchair Detective*, 29:3 (Summer 1996), 272–279.

"An Interview with Laurie King," *The Armchair Detective*, 30:1 (Winter 1997), 77–99.

"Elmore Leonard on the Movies," Mysterynet.com, 1999.

"The Mystery Scene Interview with Peter Lovesey," *Mystery Scene*, No. 49 (1995), 22, 24–26; and "An Interview with Peter Lovesey," *Mean Streets*, Issue 6 (May 1992), 24–30.

"The 87th Precinct and Beyond: An Interview with Ed McBain," *The Armchair Detective*, 27:4 (Fall 1994), 392–399.

"Rosamond Smith: A.K.A. Joyce Carol Oates," in *Mystery Scene*, No. 62 (1999), 60–64.

"What's the Worse That Could Happen?: An Interview with Donald Westlake," *The Armchair Detective*, 29:4 (Winter 1996), 394–401.

I would also like to thank all of those publishers who gave me permission to publish the photographs in this volume which accompany the interviews.

Thanks are also due to Sheryl Kamps who always knows how to fix any computer problem, and to Thomas Kent, Chair of the Department of English, Iowa State University, and to Elizabeth Beck, Director of the Honors Program, Iowa State University, who provided the funds for some much needed research assistance.

I also want to acknowledge my debt to Raymond Smith and Joyce Carol Oates of the Ontario Review Press who originally encouraged me to consider this project, and then agreed to publish it. They have shown remarkable forbearance coping with deadlines and have done a thorough job as editors.

Finally, once again, I want to recognize the support given to me by my wife, Kay. She suffers through my various projects with understanding and love.

Contents

Introduction

I began interviewing crime writers entirely by accident. In the spring of 1989 while living in Glasgow, Scotland, I decided to renew an acquaintance with an old Indianapolis high school chum, Michael Lewin, who after college had taken up mystery writing as an occupation and now lived in Frome, near Bath, in England. I had to travel to London to interview a film director I had been writing about and headed west the following morning to meet Mike for lunch. Over sandwiches we got caught up on our pasts, reminisced about those friends with whom we were still in contact, and generally chatted nostalgically as people do who have not seen one another for some years. After lunch we took our coffee to a terrace out back of the restaurant, and I asked how he began his career as an author of mystery novels.

Mike talked about a creative writing class he had taken at Harvard and then told a story about a poolside chat he had about mystery fiction with Ross Macdonald. As the story unfolded I became more and more intrigued until I realized that I had to get it on tape. I fished my recorder out of my satchel, plunked it down on the table in front of Mike, and asked him to start over with his Macdonald story. We spent the next hour and a half talking about mysteries; I asked questions and Mike responded. When I returned to the states a few months later, I transcribed the interview, sent a copy to Mike for his corrections and additions, and began to shop it around for a publisher. That afternoon I not only renewed a friendship but unknowingly I began something of a second career interviewing crime and mystery writers.

In the following collection are twenty of the fifty some interviews I have since completed over the past ten years. It has been a labor of love. In spite of the fact that the authors I have interviewed have written about all kinds of murder and mayhem, they have been the most considerate, congenial, and cooperative people to interview. They are men and women dedicated to their craft, articulate about their writing, and enthusiastic about discussing it. Without fail they have answered my questions cordially, corrected their responses and returned the manuscripts of the interviews promptly, and suffered my most naive gaffes with good humor.

I have conducted interviews in bars, in hotel lobbies, in motel rooms, at bookstore signings in between customers, in cars to and from airports, even literally on the run, asking questions as we walked from one appointment to another. I have talked with them over the phone at their homes, during hectic book tours, in the early morning and late at night. Some I did by mail, faxing changes over the telephone wires. The circumstances of some of the interviews were as interesting as the final pieces that eventually resulted from them.

Robert Parker spoke to me from his study which was undergoing renovation, and the original tape contains a running commentary about the workmen, his wonder-dog Pearl, and his wife who all at one time or another came into the room while we were on the phone. Walter Mosley was on his way to a literary luncheon and spoke to me by car phone while he was stalled in New York City traffic. I met James Crumley in a secluded hotel bar in Des Moines. Although the place was practically deserted it was difficult to hear the soft-spoken Mr. Crumley over the musak that was piped into the room. After a few minutes struggling to be heard, he got up, walked over to the bartender and asked him to turn it off and the bartender did. Whether he was just being polite or whether Crumley, bearded and large, intimidated him I'll never know. After our interview Crumley went back to the bar and the music began again as we had a congenial drink to round out the afternoon's talk. On another tape I have recorded, interlarded between my questions and her answers, the various conversations a writer was having with her children as she orchestrated both the preparation of dinner and their various after-school activities.

Most of the following interviews first appeared in various magazines from around the world devoted to mystery and crime fiction. After I sold my first interview to *The Armchair Detective*, Kate Stine, the editor, asked me to become *Armchair's* primary interviewer and we worked closely for several years preparing the magazine's cover pieces. Ed Gorman of *Mystery Scene* has used my interviews for years in his journal and has commissioned others for several of the anthologies he has edited with Martin Greenberg. Pat Browne at

Clues has routinely published my interviews as well. Stuart Coupe of the Australian *Mean Streets* both commissioned interviews and reprinted others that had already appeared elsewhere.

Although each stands alone, I have included many of the same questions in the interviews to provide a continuity among the selections. So, for example, I normally asked about the difference between crime writing and the conventional literary novel, included a question about the social impact of crime fiction, and inquired about the influence of other crime writers on their work. Also I wanted to make each interview as comprehensive as possible and not just focus on the author's latest novel, so I usually included several questions about the author's background, why he or she was drawn to writing crime fiction, and the like. I think such material helps to avoid some of the usual datedness of interviews as well as providing the reader with a broader understanding of the author's career.

Anyone who does very much interviewing soon realizes that interviews assume a life of their own. No matter how much preparation one makes or how many probing questions one crafts, inevitably the flow of the interview will take the interviewer in directions he or she had not anticipated. The one rule I have always followed is to ask short, general questions and then let the person being interviewed expand on them. Interviews where the questions are longer than the answers are usually more about the interviewer than the writer being interviewed and they reveal an interview in trouble. Not only was I after information about the writer's career and work, but I also wanted it to be in the author's own voice, to try to capture the immediacy of conversation, so I kept my editing to a minimum. And in order to have these interviews factually accurate, I routinely sent copies of the transcription to the writers for their comments before they went into print.

As well as reprinting previously published interviews for this collection I included several, with Elmore Leonard, Andrew Vachss, Michael Connelly, Walter Mosely, and Robert Parker, that had not appeared before. Some of the authors I also had interviewed more than once: Walter Mosley, Liza Cody, Peter Lovesay, and Ed McBain many times. In those cases I combined the separate interviews into a single one. In a few cases the interview as initially published did not contain all of the material from the final typescript, so I went back to the original version to reprint the complete version here. I also tried to mix the genders, men and women, and nationalities, both American and British, and the varying prominence of the writers.

Through the years I have discovered that interviews with crime writers, if done carefully, can provide a revealing source of literary information for both the casual reader and the serious student of the literature of mystery and suspense. The following collection contains interviews with twenty of the most innovative, significant, and prolific authors now working in the field. The interviews are engaging, informative, and often very funny. It is my hope that the readers of these pieces have as much enjoyment reading them as I did conducting them.

Talking Murder

Grief Street
Thomas Adcock

Photo © Gerardo Somoza

Thomas Adcock was born in Detroit and grew up there and in New York City, in upper Manhattan and at one point in Brooklyn. After briefly attending Michigan State University, he became a newspaper man in the Midwest, primarily in Minneapolis and Detroit, where he worked on the *Detroit Free Press* and for *The New York Times* bureau. In part, his desire to write fiction came from the restrictions of journalism; there was just never enough space to write what he wanted to say within the limits of news reporting.

After a brief stint of on-the-job training writing men's adventure books under a pseudonym, Adcock wrote under his own name *Precinct 19*, a novel based on his research on a NYPD precinct. The first of his Neil Hockaday police series, *Sea of Green*, came out in 1989. The second book, *Dark Maze*, was published by Pocket Books, and won the 1991 Edgar for Best Original Paperback. Since then his Hockaday novels have been garnering rave reviews and a growing readership. The most recent in the series, *Grief Street*, was published in 1997.

Currently, Thomas Adcock lives in the New York City neighborhood "Hell's Kitchen"—which is increasingly featured in his novels—with his wife, actress Kim Sykes.

Silet: Why did you start writing crime fiction?

Adcock: Practically speaking, crime fiction has a market that the publishers know how to deal with. Artistically and politically speaking, we live in a criminal society. What we have is trickle-down crime, from the White House and the Congress down to the street. The politicians, of course, are in charge of making us believe that the only crime is on the street. When I was an eighteen-year-old kid growing up in the city of Detroit, I could walk into any auto plant and get a union job that would support a family. Today, an eighteen-year-old kid in Detroit has three employment choices: minimum wage at McDonald's; the U.S. Army, if it will have him; or else he can sell crack cocaine—which, according to James Mills' extravagantly documented book *Underground Empire*, has replaced General Motors as Detroit's biggest industry. So, who's the criminal here? The kid selling the crack? The kid ripping off the bodega? Or the people responsible for what's happened to a city that throws kids away—like the kids in my book *Thrown-Away Child*?

People say the story today is crime, and I agree. So I write novels about crime. And I happen to agree with George Bernard Shaw that poverty is the essential crime. So who are the criminals? The poor little squeaks we read about in the newspaper crime blotters? Or are the criminals maybe the big shots in Washington who take away money for schools and milk for poor children, who have no shame about doing that in the richest country the world has ever known? Okay, that's my screed for the day.

Silet: When did you start writing fiction?

Adcock: To begin with, I had to learn to write it. I thought if I went into a bookstore and picked out some novel I thought I was capable of writing that maybe that would give me some clues. I found my meat, so to speak, in the "hairy chest" pulps, the so-called male action-adventure novels. They were short, only about sixty to seventy-five thousand words, and I figured I could at least write this stuff. And so I did—quite a number of them, in fact. Learning to be a novelist is O.J.T.—on-the-job training. These early books weren't particularly good, and I had sense enough to use pen names.

But writing pulps taught me the three most valuable lessons of creating a book worth reading: how to maintain the narrative flow, which is how to entertain; how to make action grow in a natural way from the personalities of your characters; how and when to slip in ideas that will stay with a reader for a while, maybe even forever if you're a good enough writer. I had three different pseudonyms in those old days. I'll tell you only this: they all have the initials B.S.

Silet: Was your first book out from under the anonymity *Precinct 19* ?

Adcock: That was the first book under my own name, written as a non-fiction novel about the year I spent hanging around with cops on the Upper East Side of Manhattan. My notion was that whatever happened, happened. It was an open-ended thing. I decided that when I had a collection of stories that kind of wove together, that's when I would stop. Happily enough, the resulting book coincided with the popularity of the "Hill Street Blues" television show. So it sold pretty well, although it's now in book heaven.

Silet: After *Precinct 19*, you wrote *Sea of Green*. That was the first of the Neil Hockaday series.

Adcock: Well, it introduced Neil Hockaday. Remarkably enough, Hockaday lives in my neighborhood, has the same ethnic background, used to have a tremendous drinking problem, and seems to be a square peg in a lot of round holes. He is a philosophical Irish Catholic, New York City-born cop who, unlike other cops, actually lives in the city—specifically the neighborhood where he was born. Hockaday says he's a half-honest cop in the city that's about three-fourths on the take, so he considers that pretty good, valorous almost. As he goes about his adventures he doesn't understand about crime or law very much. As he puts it, he doesn't understand why a rich man and a poor man are equally punished for stealing a loaf of bread. He's more interested in justice than the law.

Silet: So he has a bit of a social conscience?

Adcock: Hockaday is kind of a Dorothy Day Catholic, she being the founder of the Catholic worker movement. He's a bit of a lefty, but I don't think he truly cares about left or right wing. He cares about spirituality not politics. In fact, he doesn't vote, for God's sake.

Silet: Did you think of him initially as a series character?

Adcock: At first, I saw him in only three books. I wanted him struggling through an ugly divorce, in which he recognizes his problems and hers, and returning to the streets of Hell's Kitchen to find people struggling through something far worse than his own trials: namely homelessness. That was *Sea of Green.* Then I wanted him to have an adventure out in Coney Island, which is a deeply strange place. That was *Dark Maze.* And these two novels were the preludes to *Drown All the Dogs,* in which our moody man Hockaday solves the great case of the detective's career: the mystery of his own makings, the mystery of his Irish roots. The novels did well enough so I continued in the series with *Devil's Heaven.* Then we come to *Thrown-Away Child,* and finally my latest, which is called *Grief Street.*

Silet: Tell me a little bit about *Dark Maze.* What did you want to do with that book?

Adcock: One of my clearest boyhood memories is Coney Island in the summertime. There was a spook house on the midway called "Hell Hole." It's still there. It was decorated—and still is—with one of the most depraved, violent, sickest murals I've ever seen. And yet millions of kids over the years had been taken to the place by their parents. For fun! Every year, that terrible mural is repainted. Every year, kids and parents don't seem to notice the horror in the painting. They go into the spook house and come out laughing. Isn't being ignored the worst thing that can happen to an artist?

So, who the hell is the artist? Maybe the guy was once a serious painter, reduced to carnival illustrations. Maybe he takes out his frustrations and anger in his murals. That's what I saw in that mural, way back when I was a kid. So now I'm grown up and writing about the possible meaning of this artist. I made him a homeless guy, with the street name "Picasso" on account of his paintings. Well anyway, *Dark Maze* is about being ignored, which is a kind of failure. And it's about the consequences to us all when somebody fails.

Silet: Tell me about *Drown All the Dogs.*

Adcock: By this point, Neil Hockaday and his girlfriend, Ruby Flagg, are "slow-dancing together," as he puts it. Oddly enough, Ruby's an African-American actress. I say "oddly" because my own wife, oddly enough, is an African-American actress. Anyway, Hockaday gets word that his only living relation, his uncle Liam who lives near Dublin in a place called Dun Laoghaire, is dying. So he decides that his only living relation should meet the woman in his life. In the back of his mind, Hockaday finally wants to know something of the father he never met—Aiden Hockaday, who was lost in World War II. Naturally, Detective Hockaday arrives in Dublin to find himself immediately involved in crimes that have something to do with strange and twisted Irish politics—going back to the little discussed Irish fascist movement during the war, the so-called "blue shirts," aligned with Germany against the common enemy, England.

William Butler Yeats, the poet-politician, was for a time the unwitting conscious of the blue shirts. Yeats wrote a number of poems in celebration of fascism, which he greatly admired from his travels in Italy during the 1920s, an admiration shared by many other prominent European artists and intellectuals. There is also the crime of the Great Hunger, the so-called potato famine of the 1840s, the oppressive consequences of which are with us today—in Ireland, and in the Irish Americans. In fact, the story in *Drown All the Dogs*—a bit of Yeats's poetry, by the way—goes back and forth between Ireland and New York. When Hockaday returns home, he is shaken to the bone by it all—the politics, and the family secrets.

Silet: Hockaday—a guy somewhat like you, oddly enough—goes to Ireland with certain expectations of discovering his roots. But what reality does he find there?

Adcock: On my way to Ireland for the first time, in 1950, I had the mistaken idea that I would find smiling Irish eyes, and charm, and welcoming arms for the likes of me—whose people, the Bradys, had suffered through the Great Hunger and two emigrations, first to South Wales for work in the coal mines, and finally to America. The arrogance of that idea vanished during my first few steps on Irish soil, when I felt a certain weight of sorry Irish history, an articulation of strange things I'd felt inside of me all my life. First of all, the depth of ordinary Irish conversation.

People in Ireland talk of the days of Cromwell, for instance, as if this were last Tuesday. History is very much present, and very important. Included in that history is the fact that we Irish Americans were the ones who left. This was a kind of betrayal, do you see? A betrayal of the ones who stayed, the ones who ate weeds and grass to keep from starving; the ones whose lips turned green, the ones who lost their teeth, but kept the land. I was the one who left.

Silet: *Drown All the Dogs* is very much about the power of genetic memory, specifically Irish Memory. How personal was this book?

Adcock: I didn't know it when I sat down to write the book, but I found out a lot about myself. I think this is part of the novelist's job: to grope for answers, as eloquently as possible, about himself and where he came from. At certain moments, when I would be writing about made-up characters in some little place in Ireland, I would come to a point where I had to stop and ask myself, "How did I know that?" The answer, of course, is that the memory of an ancestor is inside of me. I believe it's true of us all.

In the case of writing *Drown All the Dogs*, I discovered in myself an Irish voice and mythological sense, an understanding that poverty is the greatest of all crimes, an appreciation of the Dorothy Day message: to take some kind of action in life to confront oppression and to resist fear. In my case, that means trying to write novels according to A. J. Liebling's notion of the high purpose of journalism: to comfort the afflicted and afflict the comfortable.

Silet: Hockaday was a boozer. What finally makes him give it up?

Adcock: In an opening chapter of *Devil's Heaven,* he was taken away by the "bodysnatchers." That means fellow New York cops who are likewise alcoholics. They grab somebody like Hock—anywhere, even from home—and physically remove him to a place over in New Jersey where a "pissbum" cop can dry out. This place is real, by the way. It happens to be an old warehouse in Paterson that was operated by Dutch Schultz during prohibition, but is now a center run by Franciscan priests for the benefit of alcoholic cops—and priests. Everybody knows the expression "going the straight and narrow." The warehouse in Paterson where Hock gets dried out is located at the corner of Straight Street and Narrow Street.

At the time Hock gets visited by the bodysnatchers, his relationship with his wife, Ruby, is not so good—because of the drinking and brooding, the vicious cycle drunks get into. So he's receptive to drying out, not that he does so with a great deal of ease. Oh, boy, an Irish Catholic cop with a drinking problem. What will these novelists think of next?

Silet: In *Thrown-Away Child,* Hock goes to New Orleans to meet Ruby's family. Did she travel north to flee the poverty and racism of her youth?

Adcock: Ruby grew up in a public housing project in New Orleans, and certain other things about her background trouble her about going home again. But there's more to the story. For instance, Hock connects with a New Orleans cop named Claude Bougart, who happens to have been one of Ruby's old beaux. Bougart is likewise a disenchanted, square peg kind of a cop. He's black, in a department that is overwhelmingly white and racist in an overwhelmingly black city. So these two disenchanted cops manage to upset things.

Silet: In the book, you also make a harrowing connection between the street children of Brazil and certain children in New Orleans, the thrown-away children of the title.

Adcock: You've read about these shantytown slums on the outskirts of Rio de Janeiro and other Brazilian cities, shantytowns entirely populated by children dumped there because they simply can't be cared for? We see in the papers once in a while how these kids run through the streets and mug tourists and so forth. Well, what do you expect to happen when kids are thrown away? Now it's happening in this country—again. We're repeating sorry chapters of our own American history, we're going back to the days of street waifs. I see it in New York, where it is most visible and most immediate. It's certainly happening in Los Angeles, and it's bound to happen in other cities as well.

Silet: Lets talk about the next Hockaday novel.

Adcock: That's called *Grief Street*. The central plot has to do with homicides during the confluent holidays of Yom Hashoah—the Day of Remembrance for the victims of the Holocaust—and Good Friday. The slayings occur in Hockaday's own neighborhood, and Hock goes up against an extraordinarily evil murderer, someone who believes he is no less than Satan come home to Hell's Kitchen. So—how to go after Satan? Ordinary cop methods are useless. So how do you deal with this? Hock calls up a lot of Celtic spirituality and mythology. He consults an Irish hermit priest, who becomes his rabbi, if you will, in a rather unorthodox police procedure.

Silet: Hock himself thinks about quitting the force and becoming a private investigator.

Adcock: That's a decision Hock needs to make, and he's dreading it. Whether to stay with the NYPD, which is making him crazy on account of a very bad cop called Joseph "King Kong" Kowalski, or to join Mogaill as a peep. Hock and Kowalski locked horns in *Devil's Heaven*, and their unresolved dispute is part of *Grief Street*. That ties in with another element of the new book—the unresolved sorrows of Hell's Kitchen, sorrows visited on that neighborhood as the result of emigration from Ireland during the Great Hunger.

CLPS: So again, your neighborhood is a character in the book?

Adcock: Hell's Kitchen is a very colorful place. For instance, the name. It came from a tenement on West Thirty-Ninth Street, exactly three blocks from where I live. The block isn't there anymore, it's now the Lincoln Tunnel to Jersey. The block was so notorious that it seemed right to blow it to smithereens to build a tunnel. Anyway, that tenement—which at the turn of the century was a whorehouse owned by a madam named Annie—was where the name Hell's Kitchen was coined. All the rooms were occupied by Annie's "girls," who worked as prostitutes except when Annie hired them out during labor disputes—to whichever side was willing to pay the most for muscle, the higher price. The gang was know as Annie's goons. One hot summer night there happened to be a riot at Annie's place, which wasn't unusual. A couple of cops were talking out on the stoop, after things had calmed down. One cop said to the other, "This place, it's hotter than hell." The other cop disagreed and said, "No, it's even hotter—it's hotter than hell's kitchen."

Silet: Why is the crime novel especially good for social commentary?

Adcock: Because readers and writers together are looking for some way to make sense of the crime of our times. We're looking for light in a dark world. And it is a dark, very brutal world. Everybody feels it. Not just poor folks, but middle-class folks—down-sized folks. Everybody feels the pressure, the insecurity, the fear. My God, we have communities under lock and key; we have armed guards patrolling our neighborhoods, like in so-called Third World countries. This is our reality. But that's not enough for us to simply know this reality. In fiction we have our chance for light. A good novel gives us a world of illuminated darkness. Good characters in fiction give us inspiration that we need to face our own reality. That's what I think people are looking for in the better crime novels. I know I am. Also, I'm trying to write the better ones.

Miami, It's Murder
Edna Buchanan

Photo © Jim Virga

Stories have always fascinated Edna Buchanan, and she decided to become a writer even before she could read. Through the years as a journalist, a writer of non-fiction crime books, and now as a novelist and creator of the Britt Montero mystery series, she has worked to perfect her craft.

Edna Buchanan was born in New Jersey and was raised by her mother. She never liked school very much and she dropped out of high school at age sixteen. While holding a number of odd jobs she enrolled in her first creative writing class. There she received encouragement and learned the rudiments of storytelling. When she moved to Miami a few years later a career in journalism was far from her mind, but her success (first on a Miami Beach local paper, *The Sun*, and later on *The Miami Herald*, where she won the Pulitzer Prize in 1986 for General News Reporting) gave her the opportunity to stretch her writing skills and established her as one of the top crime reporters in the country. A Calvin Trillin "Profile" for *The New Yorker* in the same year increased her national exposure and brought her to the attention of the publishing world.

Her true-crime books *The Corpse Had a Familiar Face* (1987) and *Never Let Them See You Cry* (1992), which were based on her crime reporting, along with her first novel, *Nobody Lives Forever*, which was nominated for an Edgar for Best First Mystery, demonstrated that she was a world-class story teller. Since then the award-winning Britt Montero series has confirmed her as one of the best of her generation of mystery and crime fiction writers.

Although she stopped writing daily journalism in 1988, Edna Buchanan continues to contribute articles, book reviews, and short stories to such publications as *USA Weekend, TV Guide, Family Circle, Mary Higgins Clark Mystery Magazine, The New York Times, Vogue, The New Yorker, Cosmopolitan,* and other leading periodicals both here and abroad.

The following interview originally appeared as "Edna Buchanan" in *Mystery Scene,* No. 62 (1999), 54–58.

Silet: Tell me about your life, your background, where you were born, grew up, went to school.

Buchanan: I was born in Paterson, New Jersey, and I came down to Miami when I was in my early twenties. The first time I saw the city, it was like coming home. It was the right place for me. I felt like I'd been a displaced person all my life. New Jersey was a black and white, gritty newsreel, and Miami is Technicolor and Cinemascope. I felt such a strong emotion the first time I saw the city, and I still feel it several times a day. Palm fronds silhouetted against the sky or the color of the water or the way the clouds sail by, it's like a magic place to me.

Silet: Where did you go to school?

Buchanan: I didn't go to school much. I learned writing mostly just by doing it. My father abandoned the family when I was seven, and my mother worked two and three jobs to support my sister and myself. I was really unhappy in school. I was gawky, awkward, nearsighted, and the tallest girl in my class. So I quit school when I was sixteen. The only bright spots when I was younger were reading and stories and my seventh-grade English teacher, who thought I could write. She asked me the question that changed my life forever. She said, "Will you promise that someday you will dedicate a book to me?" By the end of that term I was trying to sell short stories to the *Saturday Evening Post*. Since then, when I think that I am in over my head with my job, I remember that my seventh-grade teacher thought I could do it. I dedicated *The Corpse Had a Familiar Face* to her.

Silet: How did your writing develop?

Buchanan: Writing was always my real love. When I was four years old, although I couldn't even read for myself yet, I told people that I was going to grow up and write books, because stories always brought me so much joy. In my late teens I went to an evening creative writing course being offered at Montclair Teachers College by David Shaber, a struggling young writer. I felt really intimidated. Almost everyone in the class had published before. We were to write short stories and send them to him at his Greenwich Village address, and then we would talk about them the following week.

The next class session he said that something had happened to him that every teacher hopes will happen. He began to talk about a short story he had received which he said read like early Tennessee Williams. As he went on I realized he was talking about my story. Later, I saw his name listed on a movie as the screenwriter and through a mutual friend I got his phone number. I wanted to call him and tell him I was still writing and had won a Pulitzer Prize and how much his support had meant to me. So I called him and interestingly enough he didn't remember me at all. Isn't it amazing how someone can touch your life and not remember you? But I was glad I had the chance to tell him. So often in life we cross paths and affect other people's lives and we never know.

Silet: How did you get into journalism?

Buchanan: When I first came to Florida, even before I got an apartment, I signed up for another writing class because that first one had been so stimulating. In the class I mentioned to another student that I was looking for a job. He was an assistant city editor at a small newspaper, the *Miami Beach Daily Sun,* and told me they needed someone. So I thought, very naively, that I could make a living as a newspaper reporter by day and write the great American novel at night. I didn't know that the whirlwind of daily journalism leaves you no time to read a novel much less write one. The editor said to me, "Have you ever worked on a newspaper before or studied journalism?" I answered "no" to all his questions and my heart sank. But he said, "Good, you're hired. I won't have to unteach you anything." What a stroke of luck. The next day I wrote my first story, and the guy from the class shook my hand and said, "Congratulations, you're a journalist."

On a small paper you get a chance to do everything. I worked on the women's section; then I was on the city desk. I did celebrity interviews, wrote a column and obits, and covered city hall for a lot of the little municipalities in the greater Miami area. I wrote letters to the editor, under the pen name of Solomon Maxwell, because no one wrote to us. I even set hot type in the back room and the lead would splash on my shoes. I worked there for five years, and I learned it all by doing it.

During the five years I won a lot of prizes: best photograph, best feature, best deadline-story, best column, best movie review. We were up against the *Herald* and it was embarrassing for them. So I knew the people at the *Herald* were aware of me. When it looked like my paper was going to go out of business because they were selling it, I approached the *Herald* about a job. I thought because I didn't have a journalism degree that they probably wouldn't hire me, but I was desperate. So I wrote the executive editor a letter. I reminded him that I had applied before but had been told that I either needed a degree or five years' experience on a daily paper. Since I had just celebrated my fifth anniversary on the Miami Beach paper, I mentioned that in my letter and said, "How about it?" It was a shot in the dark, but within twenty-four hours they asked me to apply for a job.

Silet: What did you do at the *Herald?*

Buchanan: For the first year I was on general assignment at the city desk. So again I did all kinds of things—politics, features, and a few police stories. The first time I covered a shooting, Mike Gonzales, who is a police legend in Miami and who I wrote about in *The Corpse Had a Familiar Face*, threatened to arrest me because I stepped across the yellow rope at the crime scene. I loved the job and couldn't imagine why anyone would want to work anywhere else.

Silet: When did you win the Pulitzer Prize?

Buchanan: The second year they had me cover the criminal court, and I covered the heck out of that beat. It was a gold mine. I realized that many of the crimes on trial had never been covered initially. That meant that we were missing a lot of crime news. So I suggested to my editor that somebody ought to go to the major cop shops every day, rap with them, look at the reports, the overnight logs, go to the morgue and the jail, and make a beat out of it. He just said, "Sounds good, do it." He turned around and walked away and left me standing there flabbergasted and panicky. For the next sixteen, seventeen years I covered the police beat.

In 1986 I won the Pulitzer for work I did on ten unrelated police-beat stories. One was on the highway robbers who were throwing heavy objects onto the freeway causing accidents and then robbing the occupants of the cars. I covered a couple of big murders, a story about a former heavy-weight boxer who hanged himself in a park, and a story about a bag lady who died on the steps of a local church downtown. There was also a story about a guy walking down the street naked who was carrying his girlfriend's severed head.

Silet: Your first two books were non-fiction: *Carr: Five Years of Rape and Murder* (1979) and *The Corpse Had a Familiar Face* (1987).

Buchanan: I have always been fascinated by missing person's cases; I guess because my own father had gone missing. I was doing a Sunday magazine piece about the most intriguing missing person's cases in Dade County, and I got a tip from a cop source that they had caught a rapist who claimed that he had killed people around the country, including several from Dade County. The police didn't know whether to believe him or not. He claimed to have killed two little boys from Miami, and I said, "My God, Mark and Todd." I had their pictures on my desk for the story I was doing and I was convinced he was the real thing. The officials who traveled around the country with him to retrieve the bodies kept telling me that I had to talk to this guy. Then he began to write me from jail telling me that I wrote the only true stories about him.

When a publisher's representative called me and asked me if I was interested in writing a book on this guy, I did go talk to him. He said he wanted to tell his story. He was a really evil man, but I wound up doing the book. It was a tough experience because I didn't take any time off from the paper. I worked on it for three years. At the very beginning he told me that although he wanted his story told he would eventually turn on me, but he said to promise him that I would write the story anyway. He did turn on me, because when he didn't get the death penalty, he didn't want the information in the book to damage his chances of parole. He would write me letters that were so violent that the paper was full of holes where he had pressed hard with his pen. Just before the book came out my editor left the firm to start up his own publishing house, leaving me without a friend in house. So the book was released with little publicity and not much distribution. It is a good book and I'm very proud of it. Recently I learned that it is being used as a teaching tool by the FBI.

Then in the fall of 1985 my editor called me at home and said, "I've got some news that will change your life: Calvin Trillin wants to do a profile about you for *The New Yorker*." Since I usually did all of the interviewing, I felt a bit uncomfortable about it. The piece came out in February 1986, and it got an astonishing amount of attention. I began to get calls from publishers who wanted a non-fiction book about my experiences as a crime reporter. In the meanwhile I had gotten an agent, and I had been talking to him about writing a novel. I wanted the heroine to be a newspaper reporter. He felt that it would be better if I made it non-fiction. I did finally sign a contract with Random House. I took all of my vacation time to begin the new book, and I finished *The Corpse Had a Familiar Face* in the fall of 1986. It was published in 1987.

Silet: Tell me a little about it.

Buchanan: Its subtitle is "Covering Miami, America's Hottest Beat." It was sort of autobiographical. The first line of the book is: "It was my day off, but it was murder again." The first chapter is "It's Miami, It's Murder," which I used for a title for a novel later, and the first line of that chapter is: "The crime that inevitably intrigues me most is murder. It's so final." I wrote chapters about murder, cops, crooks, the little newspaper I used to work for, sex crimes, missing people, justice, and how to get the story. It is required reading in a lot of journalism schools now. How ironic, since I never took a journalism course.

Silet: How did you finally get to do your first fiction book, *Nobody Lives Forever?*

Buchanan: After *The Corpse Had a Familiar Face* Random House wanted me to write a sequel. But I wanted to write a novel next. The editor was really reluctant. I finally cornered him and he said that when someone is known for playing the violin they had serious reservations when he announced he wanted to play the tuba. Finally, I got a two-book contract: one for the novel and another for the book they really wanted. So I did my novel. I was excited because I was finally going to get to do what I had dreamed of doing since I was a little kid. When I first sat down at the word processor, I thought, "My God, what if I can't play this tuba?" I was afraid that my writing had become too synoptic. I remembered that Hemingway once said that anyone who writes novels should first work for a daily newspaper but never for more than eighteen months. I had overdone it by eighteen years.

Sure enough, for the first few chapters, I kept looking to my left for my notebook and it wasn't there. I was on my own. Then that wonderful thing happened that other writers talk about. In chapter four the characters sprang to life and really began doing things that were shocking. The villain was far more evil than I thought she would be. My cat Flossie would sit on my lap while I was working, and I would say, "My God, Flossie, look what she is doing now!" Then there was this middle-aged detective, who was supposed to play a minor role in the book, and he became very strong and tried to take it over. I finally promised him if he would just cool it, he could come back as a major character in a future book. And he did. He came back as Dan Flood, the dying detective, in *Miami, It's Murder*. I felt bad that I killed him off, and I just recently brought him back in a short story called "Foolproof" that was published in *Mary Higgins Clark's Mystery Magazine*.

Silet: How did *Contents Under Pressure* (1992) come about?

Buchanan: That was the book I originally wanted to write about a woman reporter. Several years before I began the novel I had been covering all of the murders in Miami, because I felt that every one of the victims deserved to have their story told. I had been going from murder scene to murder scene for about a year and was shell-shocked by all the violence. That summer I was on a murder scene on the edge of the Everglades in the hot sun, and as I was coming back to the *Herald* to write the story, I stopped for a soft drink at a store. As I was holding this cold bottle against my aching forehead, I happened to notice the label. It said: "Warning: contents under pressure." I thought, "That is the perfect title for the book I am going to write some day." That was in 1981. The book appeared twelve years later. When someone asks how long does it take to write a book, the actual sitting down at the word processor and doing the research maybe takes a year, but it really is a lot longer.

Silet: Tell me about Britt Montero.

Buchanan: Because Miami is such an international city now, I wanted her to be part of both the Latin and Anglo cultures, but of course, one of the interesting things about her is that, although she is a part of both, she doesn't really belong in either. She is agile and athletic and brave. She is a role model for me. She's all the things I would love to be.

Silet: Did you begin *Contents Under Pressure* as a series?

Buchanan: Yes, I did. I thought that if the book worked, I had all these ideas for other stories that she could tell. So I went into that novel thinking of it as a series. Of course, if nobody liked it and didn't want another, then it wouldn't be a series. Luckily, they did.

Silet: In your books you talk a lot about the city of Miami itself.

Buchanan: I don't know if it's the latitude and longitude or being at sea level, but there is something about this place. Even back when it was a sleepy resort city, before it changed to an international place like some exotic foreign capitol, the crime that happened was bizarre. Miami was the last jumping-off place, the last destination for people on the run from the law or their own personal demons. Then we had people from the south, running from poverty and wars and dictators. So you have all of these people, and they come face to face. The temperature soars, the barometric pressure drops, the full moon rises, and all hell breaks loose. It is a great place to be a writer. There is something very earthy, sexy, and dangerous about Miami. People say "Isn't it terrible how violent Miami has become. It's like paradise lost." But it's always been this way.

Silet: In most of your books you use multiple stories.

Buchanan: I like to use a lot of subplots, and some of my editors haven't liked it. They would rather have me stick to one straight story line. I don't think that it would be authentic. If you're trying to get the crazy madness of Miami, the atmosphere of the news room and the hectic pace of the reporters, you have to do it with the multiple stories. I love some of the characters who pop up in the books, and sometimes I don't even know where they come from. People ask me if I'm afraid that I'll run out of ideas and have to go back to the *Herald*. On the contrary, there are all these characters in my head clamoring to get out. In *Margin of Error*, the welfare mother, Angel, who wasn't even in the original outline, just popped up. The subplots usually tie in at the end. They help to keep the books moving.

They also provide contrast. Miami is a city of contrasts. In *Margin of Error* the movie star is living in luxury on Star Island with all the beautiful people and Angel is living on welfare. Miami is always the main character in my books, and Miami has so many faces, its own pulse beat. In the first novel, *Nobody Lives Forever*, the villain was a metaphor for Miami, beautiful yet deadly, innocent-looking yet corrupt.

Silet: You deal a lot with children at risk in your fiction.

Buchanan: That's interesting because I hadn't really thought about that. Unsolved cases bother me; they tend to haunt me. There are cases I covered as a reporter that I still think about every day, even cases that were before my time and that I went back and researched in the *Herald*'s morgue or in old police files. There was a little girl, Judith Ann Roberts, who was murdered years ago and the detective who covered the case was a friend of mine. When he was dying in the hospital, he was still talking about that case which had never been solved and never will be now since most of the principals are dead. I wrote about the case in *Miami, It's Murder.* Mary Beth Rafferty is loosely based on that earlier case, but in the novel I got the chance to solve it, to lay it to rest. I have been doing that in many of the books, loosely basing them on a real case that bothered me and was unsolved. But then Britt can solve it, which I could never do.

Silet: Most of your books deal with some central social problem.

Buchanan: Fiction should mirror real life, and it's good to be able to write about how the system mostly fails. It's great to expose these things and also to show how things could be, to show how a good cop or good politician or editor or some good reporter can often change things.

Silet: *Margin of Error* has a movie plot and several of your books have been made into movies. What was your experience with them?

Buchanan: Two movies for TV were based on *The Corpse Had a Familiar Face,* and they didn't use a single story out of the book. It beats me why these people even bother to buy a book. They asked me to come out to San Diego where they were making this Miami movie. In talking to them, I found no one had read the book. The scripts were abysmal. I loved Elizabeth Montgomery; there was something magical about her. But the scripts were bad.

Silet: What attracted you to the Lance Westfall character in *Margin of Error.*

Buchanan: All the moviemaking going on down here triggered that. In 1984 Kurt Russell came to Miami to shoot *The Mean Season*, where he played a journalist. He came over to the *Herald* and went out on the police beat with me several times to get a handle on the job. I don't see that many movies, and I don't think I would have recognized Kurt Russell on the street but everyone else did. At a scene of a murder, a sort of slaughter in suburbia with the murdered couple's baby clinging to his dead mother, all hell broke loose when the crowd recognized him. Even the TV stations turned their cameras away from the crime onto him and wanted to interview him about what he was doing there. Kurt Russell didn't think it was appropriate to be giving interviews and signing autographs at a double murder scene. We actually ended up running for my car with the crowd hot on our heels. A scene somewhat similar to that is in the book. From there on it is all fiction. Kurt Russell and I did not have an affair and nobody shot at us either.

It amazed me because I thought of my job as the real thing, the gritty, realistic, true-life drama. Yet to the public the magic of Hollywood, that twenty-four frames per second, was far more exciting and real than their slaughtered neighbors. How dazzled people are by the glamour of Hollywood stuck with me. All fiction springs from some kernel of truth and that was the springboard for that book.

Silet: Do you want talk about the book you just finished?

Buchanan: I've been calling it *Heartbeat*, which is the perfect title for it. But my editor wants to change it, so I suggested *Cardiac Arrest*, but they want to call it *In the Silent Night*, from a line in the book. It makes it sound to me like a Christmas book. So we are debating the title now. The hero, a self-made millionaire, has a heart transplant. He finds out that the person he thought was the donor isn't really dead and is now trying to kill him. Of course, no one believes him, not even his wife. She thinks he's crazy and wants to have him committed. The only help he gets is from the widow of the real donor. This is a stand-alone novel.

Silet: What about a new Britt book?

Buchanan: In the last book Britt was suffering from Post-Traumatic Stress Syndrome because of the shooting in *Act of Betrayal* and that is what causes her to do some of the reckless things she does in *Margin of Error*. In the new book there is a serial killer who's a woman. I don't want to get too much into it. I'm interested to get back to Britt and her friends to see what they've been up to since I've been gone.

Silet: Tell me about why you like to write fiction.

Buchanan: I feel really strongly about good and evil. In my books justice always triumphs, the good guys win. I was really blessed to have been a journalist, and I miss it a lot now because every day was an adventure, but in journalism there are so many stories without endings, murders that go unsolved, missing people who stay lost forever, or corpses who go unidentified. One of the beauties and joys of fiction is that you get to write the last chapter. You can solve all the perplexing mysteries, and, best of all, you can get to make the good guys win and the bad guys get what they deserve, which almost never happens in real life. Real life doesn't make sense but fiction does.

Silet: What would you like to do that you haven't?

Buchanan: I'd love to write the big, blockbuster best-seller because the whole reason we're in this business is the joy of communication. It's so wonderful to see people reading your books. I was thrilled once when I was on a plane and a woman had one of my books. I insisted that she let me sign it. I love to sign books. There are certain fans who always want their books signed the same way. There is this one fan, named Bob, who every time I'm in New York has me sign a book, "To Bob, Best Wishes, Edna Buchanan." It's so boring. I've never met him. He just has a book reserved for me to sign. So the last time I put, "To Bob, the love of my life, Best Wishes, Edna Buchanan." I hope I haven't ruined his collection.

Anna Lee, Eva Wylie, and the Contemporary Crime Novel
Liza Cody

Photo © Carlo Chinca

Now that Liza Cody's tough, resourceful London investigator, Anna Lee, is appearing on television in both Great Britain and the United States, mystery readers are getting to know her crime books better. Six of the Anna Lee series have been published since the initial novel, *Dupe*, came out in 1980 and won Britain's John Creasey Memorial Prize for a first mystery, and Liza Cody has received rave notices for her strong-minded, cantankerous fiction from the critics on both sides of the Atlantic.

Enthusiasts of crime writing have come to learn about the Brierly Security Agency located on Kensington High Street in London, and its collection of personnel: its stuffy head, "call me Commander Brierly"; the redoubtable office manager, Beryl; avuncular Bernie Schiller; and other assorted operatives, both the bumbling and the able, who make up Cody's world of British private investigation. They also have come to know Anna's housemates, the boozy Selwyn, his feisty wife, Bea, and, on occasion, Anna's on-again, off-again lover, Quex. They have also learned to appreciate the strengths of the series which include Cody's detailed depiction of London's low-rent districts and her flair for using contemporary slang.

Most recently, Liza Cody has begun writing about a second character, Eva Wylie, a huge, violent, and thoroughly unpopular woman wrestler, who lives in a trailer at a salvage dump with two junkyard dogs. Eva is undereducated, distrustful, and cheats in the ring. She has made her reputation as a wrestler by being a villain, and she relishes the animosity of the crowd. About all she shares with Anna is the honesty and directness with which they both confront the world around them. The first of her adventures is chronicled in *Bucket Nut,* which won the Crime Writers' Association Silver Dagger Award and is now available in the U.S. and Great Britain. A second novel, *Monkey Wrench* (1995), was shortlisted for the Edgar Award and the third, *Muscle Bound,* was published in 1996.

Liza Cody's crime novels provide a genuinely new voice in British mystery fiction which is quite unlike the traditional ladies who wrote the cozy books that dominated the scene for so long. There are no aristocratic Peter Whimseys or genteel Miss Marples or fatuous Albert Campions in these novels, just a world of street-smart, tough-talking females who prowl the back alleys of England's nether world. For those who prefer the world of Dickens to the world of the afternoon tea in their crime fiction, Liza Cody's novels will do very nicely indeed.

Portions of this interview were published as "Eva Wylie, Anna Lee, and the Contemporary Crime Novel," *Mystery Scene,* No. 49 (September/October 1995), 20, 59, 65–68, and "Liza: An Interview with Liza Cody," *The Armchair Detective,* 25 (Spring 1992), 190–199.

Silet: How did you get into the business of writing crime fiction?

Cody: It was by accident. I was a painter; I didn't write at all. I left school when I was about sixteen, and I was dyslexic when dyslexia wasn't recognized as anything other than stupidity. So writing was at the bottom of my agenda, the thing I tried hard to avoid. I began to tell stories quite by accident on a holiday where several families shared a villa, and I was drafted to tell the children stories in order to get them to sleep before the adults. So I told a story that lasted for three weeks.

My husband thought that I could write a book, although he had a children's book in mind, but they didn't interest me at all. However, it always has interested me to *tell* stories to children because you can see from the reaction of your audience what is required and if you get stuck you can say, "And what do you think happened next?" and those little suckers will tell you. But to sit alone the way a writer has to and try to think of things that would interest adults—no, I felt I couldn't do that.

Silet: How did you become interested in art?

Cody: When I was thirteen I was taken up by a very old, doddery Royal Academician who painted several portraits of me and paid me in pencil drawings. He drew like a dream. I got *really* interested. Then I went to art school. First at the City and Guild schools and later at the Royal Academy School of Art. Most of my work was figurative studies in oil. I mainly painted figures and landscapes. I really did not have much success in painting. I still do a little drawing now and again, but I can't walk and chew gum at the same time.

Silet: Has your training as a visual artist influenced your writing?

Cody: Yes, it has. I see things rather than think them. I have a trained visual memory and am aware of balance, how one thing will affect another. I am also very patient and dogged, and am prepared to fail at something and try again. My training in art taught me that. I am also accustomed to working alone for long periods. And I'm accustomed to being stoney broke. My art background prepared me well to live the life of a writer.

Silet: Why did you begin to write detective novels?

Cody: I'm not really sure why I chose detective books. I didn't want to write about reflection or speculation or any of those things. I just simply filled the hours writing by the fireside. It has a very mesmeric effect. Once, as you probably know, you begin a story, you *have* to finish. You, in fact, have to know how it turns out because it's not a thing that you are entirely in control of and once you create the characters, you just want to know how they're going to act.

Silet: Tell me how you came up with Anna Lee as a character.

Cody: By asking myself a few basic questions like, what sort of woman would be likely to become a private detective. I thought she would have started her career in the police force or one of the security services, and therefore she would be quite unlike me. Then, when I asked myself what she would be like, I began to think about the damage that sort of background can do to an ordinary woman. Sometimes, women working in heavily macho male worlds become control freaks. Sometimes they are uncritical of the male world: they don't try to change it—they try to succeed in it. They can become very tenacious in trying to defend their own corner, to protect themselves. They can become over-protective of people outside that world. I asked myself those kinds of questions, and the answers I came up with gave me the beginnings of Anna.

Silet: Why not an amateur sleuth of some sort?

Cody: I think I mistrust amateurs in a lot of different fields. Also, in books, you have to get through a lot of fancy footwork to give them cases. You know where you are with a professional P.I. and can get into a story without wasting too much time making it plausible.

Silet: Did you know any private eyes?

Cody: No, I didn't. As I said, the beginning was an accident. I never expected even to finish my first novel, let alone to do anything else with it. So it was a sort of experiment. The way I work is by process of extrapolation. I start from something very small, like what I know about office life, for instance, and I assume that things are similar, only different in detail, in my world of fiction.

Silet: When did you first discover that the story you'd been working on for your own amusement was potentially publishable?

Cody: Well, I finished the first novel, *Hard Case*, in long hand. I showed it to my sister who has a lot of connections with literary people. She suggested that I send it to a very good friend of hers, who was at that time an agent at Curtis Brown, just to see if I had something that would be good for rather more than lining a bottom drawer somewhere. This woman simply sold it for me.

Silet: Was it with the second novel, *Bad Company*, that you realized that you had a series?

Cody: No, not really. I'd been going from one thing to another, very much by the seat of my pants. The book I was writing had to be interesting enough for me to just simply continue; I mean, in my head it's like one long novel, except that it isn't. Each time I start I'm looking to do something quite different because there are two levels—one is the story and the other is the writing. Believe it or not, I'm very serious about craft. I always have been; it doesn't matter what I'm doing. I'm very serious about trying to do it well and to improve, and set myself problems and goals which I hope to explain to myself and to somehow get better at.

Silet: Anna is a very strong character and a very young woman. Are you making a "feminist" statement in any way?

Cody: I'm trying to write a real portrait. Feminism would have very little to do with Anna. She never makes any feminist statements. I don't know if you've noticed about women who are brought up in a man's world but quite often what they try to do is to become one of the boys. They do not fight the system. They want to succeed in it. Anna simply is trying to operate on the same level as everybody else. She would be extremely resentful if people considered that she couldn't. So she would be the kind of woman who in training would attempt to be better than everybody else without really reflecting about it, who would attempt to be quite competitive in order that she should be taken seriously. That's not what feminism is about really but if anybody asked her if she was a feminist she would probably say no or that she didn't think about it. She is trying only to be accepted.

My own point of view might well be quite different. I might even myself have political, quasi-political views of such a thing but I don't see it as my job to tell people what to think, and I'm not going to put words into anybody's mouth. What I might do is set a scene or describe an incident which people may come out of—having read it—thinking what I would like them to think, but I'm not going to tell them what to think.

There are a lot of women around who are capable and resilient and flexible. There's no need for me to say that this is where women should be going. There are enough of them around. I don't have to make a fantasy for them, do I? Anna is not a fantasy figure for me at all. She is just a perfectly ordinary woman. In my terms, heroism is not doing the dangerous thing in an adventurous situation, it's being like a postman, somebody who gets up in all weathers and slogs through.

Silet: There is a remarkable dailiness to your fiction, something often overlooked in American crime fiction which relies a bit too heavily on daring-do. Is that part of getting up in all weathers?

Cody: Yes, definitely that. But it's also because I want to—what's the opposite of raise the ante? I want to lower it. I want to put things where they belong. What I would like to do is to write about smaller incidents as if they were very big incidents because I'm writing about ordinary people. I'm not writing about heroes and heroines. What I would like to do is to make my one corpse, my small violence, as shocking as another writer's carnage. I want to inhabit a real world, not a dramatic one. I want to be able to describe ordinary people and extraordinary events in ordinary people's lives. I would like to make those smaller events as interesting as the big events. I don't want to end up with shootouts.

The idea is that if you do it right somebody's ordinary incident can be a major event in somebody else's day and if you do it right the reader will also see that as being a major event. That's why I want to lower the ante. I don't want to end up with loads of bodies and lots of violence and explosions.

Silet: I don't know if *Under Contract* raises the ante but it certainly shifts it. The rock world you portray certainly is larger than ordinary life. It's crazier than the everyday.

Cody: It's obviously the subject matter which is larger than life. Once again it's from my background—my own background—and it was an idea that started with some people I knew who made a couple of movies about jazz artists in whose background were some very dodgy contracts, and the entrepreneurs who controlled the artists were little short of villains. The hold some of these agents had over their artist's material was in some ways extortionate. So I was thinking about that and I was also thinking about musicians whose rights to their own works are quite tenuous. They have to fight quite hard to get paid for what they've done. And the stories that come out about what young people will do, what they will sign, just in order to get the first grip on the ladder. It's similar in a way to anybody beginning in the arts.

On a personal level, when I was pretty young, I was a roadie for one of the worst rock bands in London. The band was of course called "One Hand Clap"; you can make what you like of that. I was the roadie because I was the only one with a clean license. It was as bad as that. So, I knew quite a lot about the naff end of the market, the really seedy end, and how people operate and what they do, how they change their names and how they reincarnate in other bands.

Silet: Why isn't Anna more romantically involved?

Cody: Well, she is in an episodic way. She has ex-boyfriends and, in *Backhand*, the big guy Quex, from *Head Case*, turns up again wanting to be serious. Then she meets a guy in the States. It is just simply a young woman's love life. You try things out; sometimes you have a lot of expectations and other times you don't have many—it's just a way not to be alone perhaps. Love affairs in the majority don't end well, because they either break up or you get married. Neither of those is really a good solution to a love affair.

Silet: Does Anna need the freedom that a marriage or long-standing relationship would inhibit?

Cody: I would say that she herself might be quite intimidating to a lot of men in the way that very competent women sometimes are, particularly those who are competent in those things that men would consider their own province. So she might well put off a lot of people that way. But there *are* other criteria. She is claustrophobic, for instance, and she doesn't like being kissed. I would say she is probably quite bad at intimacy herself. She likes working with people but I don't think she particularly likes being too close or sharing space with them.

Silet: Does Anna need to have that space in order to maintain her position as an outsider, an observer?

Cody: If Anna is a good outsider/observer it is more probably because she is a woman in a man's world, and because, as an ex-cop, she is trained to be an outsider/observer where society is concerned. However, she does not like what she would call "emotional scenes." She thinks they effect badly her ability to control herself and her work. She would like to keep work and emotion apart and deeply resents any bleed-through. Anna's emotional peculiarities are not a device to set her apart as an observer. They are just part of the portrait—the overall picture. They have to do with the way women (men, too) cripple themselves in institutional life when they try to be solely and wholly "professional."

Silet: Does this mean that she would rather remain totally detached from other people?

Cody: No, I would say she would be a good friend to anybody, but they might get very fed up with her because she would want to be somewhat in charge of the friendship. If one is looking for the genesis of an idea, maybe a big part of my mind is involved in failed responsibilities, the idea that when you take responsibility for anything, it's a lost cause. In *Bad Company*, for instance, whatever the effort Anna makes and however competent she is, she fails. Quite simply, the kidnappers are idiots, they're half-wits. She's being manipulated, controlled by people she despises. She's totally humiliated by it. She has taken responsibility for a kid and at the end the kid doesn't want to see her again. She has failed to protect;

she has failed to deliver what taking responsibility implies. That's quite a fascinating subject to me.

Silet: Tell me a little bit about *Backhand.*

Cody: Well, I knew I wanted to write about an island on the west coast of Florida—a wonderful, sunny, everything's great island which I've been going to, on and off, for quite a long time. I've made friends there. The friends live and work there in the tourist industry. From the stories they tell and from the people they've introduced me to I got this wonderful picture of a sunny paradise with all sorts of strange things going on underneath the surface. So there's a surface world and a sub-world and each feeds off the other.

I wanted to get some of that in. I also wanted to explore the difference between the American approach to crime writing and the British one. It's an odd book in some ways because I was doing lots of things which probably don't show. It's a great culture shock when you first go to the States, and it was very nice to work with Anna's first impressions. I wanted to play with her reactions to it. Also to look at her reactions to the American reaction to violence, the American reaction to a threat of any kind.

Silet: Which is more cavalier?

Cody: In some ways it is, yes, and in some ways it's more serious. For instance, the Americans are very much more aware of the threat of violence than she is. She comes from a rather more domestic environment. She looks at their guns and she thinks, "Oh please, this isn't Cagney and Lacey." But when she's really in trouble she uses a terrific British reserve. Her reaction to panic is to say, "I've got a spot of bother here," when, in fact, someone has just blasted the life out of somebody else right in front of her. But she's working with an American private investigator, and his reaction is to say something like, "Hey, you got me out of the shower just to tell me you've got a 'spot of bother'?" In other words, "Come on woman, tell me what's *really* happening?"

Silet: What do you see as the difference between the British and the American crime novel?

Cody: It's quite apparent but very hard to talk about. One of the things I'm always aware of when I'm reading Sara Paretsky, for instance, is that she tells such big stories. They just seem more important stories and there is more tang to them. I would love to have the vocabulary to answer this question. It is something that I've thought about a lot. Any British writer, I think, will tell you that the Brits suffer from a feeling of inferiority when we compare ourselves to our American friends and colleagues.

Silet: In the crime field?

Cody: In the crime field, yes. It has something to do with social attitude. It has something to do with corruption. And guns. And plausible levels of violence.

Silet: Certainly the British really codified the crime novel.

Cody: The British only codified some of crime fiction. Those who write the cozy way are probably more immune from feelings of inferiority because they have their own tradition to back them up. But those of us who try to work in the more wide-open, American way tend to have a bit of trouble when we translocate it to the UK. British sleaze just isn't in the same class as U.S. sleaze. The same goes for violence. It's harder, in the UK, to achieve a reasonable level of tension and danger. Ours is altogether a tamer society. The danger seems to begin and end at street level. After that, there's a layer of supposedly polite society through which violence is not supposed to pass. When the Brits write tough, we write street talk. What we don't get are industrialists and politicians who are physically just as tough as villains. I'm thinking particularly of Sara Paretsky's novel, *Tunnel Vision*, where that sense of violence actually goes all the way through society.

So class in the UK plays a part. Of course, class plays a part in the States as well, but there's a raw feeling that goes right up to the top. What makes it probable and true to life may well be your history—industrialists mixed up with strike breaking, for instance—quite violent and manipulative industrial relations. And there were extraordinary things which went on in The Depression and during Prohibition which seem to have ramifications even now. People like Tom Prendergast, who more or less owned Kansas City, and had his fingers in everything from the Chamber of Commerce to a shoe-shine stand, could never have existed in the UK. All these things make a difference to a literature which was "codified" in the U.S. in the '30s and '40s.

Silet: *Backhand* has essentially two parts, there's one part set in Britain, one part set in United States. Was it designed to compare these different worlds?

Cody: Yes, it was in a way. It was also meant to open up Anna's world. It was to get her to realize that there were other ways of going about things; to help her to understand the life she was leading, the way she was being treated in her own organization. Your society is much more mobile, very much more mobile, than ours. People make decisions, go somewhere else to start again. At home, people get stuck and rot. They're scared to move out. There's nowhere to move. It's harder. But at the same time it can be simply an attitude of mind. So there's a sense that, having been to the States, Anna can then think about a new beginning.

Silet: Where is Anna going to go next or do you know?

Cody: Oh, yes, I do know. She has a cameo role in *Bucket Nut* and in fact, in my head, what I saw at the end of *Backhand* was that Anna went to the States. She probably worked there for a couple of years and then came home. She now has her own agency with Bernie Schiller in South London. I thought of this when the TV program was happening. I realized, then, that I was going to have to do something quite radical with her life. I didn't want to leave her, I didn't want to kill her off, but I wanted to pick her up again some other time. In the meantime, I want to keep her going. I know what's happening to her, but from a distance.

Silet: Let's talk about the TV series. Tell me about your experience. Just explain what's happened and what's involved.

Cody: I sold the rights to the books and to the character to an independent TV producer at home who was working in conjunction with one of the big independent broadcasters. They made the pilot which was of *Head Case.* They used a very famous TV writer, Andrew Davis, to write it. They had a wonderful actress, Imogen Stubbs, to play Anna. They had a terrific cast, absolutely wonderful. The pilot was a great success. It had an audience, in our country, of between sixteen and eighteen million which is a very good figure. The producer to whom I had sold the rights is a class act. But she was fired off the project and it was given to others not so good. And I had nothing more to do with it. So they made the first series of six episodes to appeal to 13-year-olds, and they didn't allow Imogen, who is a serious actress, to develop the character. They didn't allow her to do anything except run around in pretty clothes.

Anyway, it doesn't really matter. I try not to think about it, and Imogen has sworn never to do another one. So all that was quite troublesome. In any case, even if they'd done really good things and been fairly respectful of whatever I had in mind, I think I would have still been in trouble, because basically, in my head, Anna is not Imogen. Imogen is far too pretty. There's no way *anyone* could have been Anna as I saw her. I always knew that if I ever saw her on TV I was going to be in a bit of trouble.

Silet: You're planning to continue the Anna series but just not in the same way.

Cody: Yes, but by that time I will have changed things. She will have grown up a bit and she will be several years older. I'll pick her up again when I can see Anna, not Imogen.

Silet: Let's talk a little about Eva Wylie and your books featuring her. Let's start with *Bucket Nut.* Who is this woman, where did she come from?

Cody: She began with a poster on a wall advertising wrestling. The poster showed a picture of woman called Klondyke Kate, who is the UK heavyweight champion, not a pretty woman. When I was a kid I went to the wrestling quite a few times but I hadn't been for about twenty to thirty years, and I was very surprised to see a woman wrestling. I'm always interested in seeing what women do, so I went. Certain things occurred to me while I was watching Klondyke Kate's performance. Kate is a barrel in leotards and my very first thought was, how brave, if you are that shape, to get up in a ring under the lights and take the abuse.

The next thing that occurred to me is she's a villain, she cheats. In that very first fight she was wrestling somebody half her size who had a knee injury. And so the first thing Kate did was to go to work on the knee. And I'm thinking, well, the caring, sharing face of womanhood is not in evidence here, and what's more, Kate's playing on it. Also a wrestling audience is a real character in itself, and everybody was shouting the most incredible abuse to her. I mean unbelievable abuse. If most women got one percent of that in the street they would burst into tears and never leave home again. But there was Kate in the middle of the ring, and her job is to provoke this kind of comment. The more people hate her the better she is doing her job.

It forced me to think about my work up till then and, in a way, about women's crime fiction in general. There we are flying the flag for competent, caring women: women who try and solve other people's problems, women who think about the victim, women who people can go to in trouble. And in some ways how trapped we are by the necessary fact that a private detective must be a good deed in a naughty world. I was thinking there's a trap here and I've got to get out of it. I sat there, in awe, watching this woman being completely the opposite to everything I try to be in my personal life and the opposite to everything I try to do in my working life. And I thought, "Right, go for it."

If you're going to change, really change properly. This was an interesting idea. If you deal with a character like that you can deal with anger, you can deal with the way people are treated because of the way they look.

Silet: Where did you get the title *Bucket Nut?*

Cody: The title actually came from the same evening, that first evening. There was a little geezer, about 75, at the back with his raincoat buttoned up as if his mom had sent him out. And he was so incensed with what Klondyke Kate was doing that he came rushing down the aisle, right up to the ringside. The bouncers were all there ready to throw him out, but he was too tiny and old. And he's saying, "You, you..." because he can't think of anything bad enough to say. The spit is flying out of his mouth. All he could think of yelling at her was "bucket nut," meaning "your face is so ugly it looks like a bucket." That's all he said and then he was terribly confused when he'd done it, so he trotted back up the stairs into the background where he came from.

I was sitting thinking, this is astonishing: that is a title, if ever I heard one. All the people who go to the wrestling at home are the kind of people who you tend not to see nowadays, even in the pubs, because pubs now are so smart. You don't see the people who are missing teeth and probably have a screw loose, but they all go to the wrestling. It's sort of pantomime for people for whom life is too hard. It's like the old cowboy films, the black hat and the white hat. It's all simple drama.

Silet: Eva is angry, violent, distrustful. What does creating a character like that allow you to do as a writer?

Cody: It allows me, in a lot of ways, to be far more honest than I've been till now. Some of the things Eva says, which seem quite shocking, are actually things that I think but don't usually say. When I was writing her something rather strange happened. I began to realize that literature sees life in a certain way: books try to make something reasonable of life, whereas I don't actually believe that life is very reasonable. When you're using an unreliable narrator, which Eva is, she's not reliable at all, you can say and do all sorts of unusual things. Most narrators are intelligent, most narrators are consistent. But in real life most of us aren't so consistent.

But the thing about being middle class is that you try to make consistency of inconsistent acts and facts and thoughts. You often try to impose a structure where none exists. And part of literature is this very middle-class way of imposing structure. I noticed in the stories of Raymond Carver, that he quite frequently has his characters saying and doing quite random things and just leaving them there. It reads strangely, but it's absolutely true and admirable. He's talking about a certain set of people who are acting according to their own codes and acting on impulse. He's quite clearly trying to work with a situation where people say one thing and do another, or do one thing and say another.

When you look at it, that's unusual in literature. As it's the well-read middle classes who write books, and the well-read middle classes who read books, what we expect from novels is logic. So when you deviate and write from inside the head of someone without education and without training in logical thinking, without a training in the art of seeming reasonable, you're dealing with something which is not in a literary tradition. It's hard to explain. But as a writer, I am in character, I can't come out of character. Therefore if Eva is stupid at the beginning, or if she is revengeful or unreasonable, she's going to be that way throughout. That is *my* consistency.

But Eva is not ever going to be right at the end. She's not going to be intelligent and she's not going to be sensitive. She's still going off in the wrong direction. I can't allow myself to explain what I'm doing, to intrude with authorial superiority. Well, I could have, but I thought it would have been completely wrong and untrue. I had to stick with Eva, and try to be true to her.

Silet: Anna appears in a cameo in *Bucket Nut*. Why did you do that? It obviously ties the two series together.

Cody: I wanted a voice of reason which Eva would not believe. I also wanted to do what Michael Lewin does with his Indianapolis books, which is to keep track of old characters in new characters' books. I hate losing people and I don't like losing characters, either. I just didn't want to lose touch.

Silet: What's *Monkey Wrench* about?

Cody: *Monkey Wrench* deals with misogyny and prostitution. But it isn't simply *men's* hatred of women I wanted to explore. Eva is a bit of a misogynist too, unfortunately, and I couldn't duck out of that. Eva is in a man's world and there are certain things about women that she totally despises. There are certain things about her mother which she won't admit to, which make her extremely angry with, and contemptuous of, prostitutes. The reader will know that Eva's mother is more or less a hooker but Eva won't admit it.

Angels Flight
Michael Connelly

Photo © Beth Herzhaft

Michael Connelly's novels have won just about all the awards given in the mystery/crime field: the Edgar, the Nero Wolfe prize, and the Anthony. His books have been best sellers as well, and he has published them at a steady rate since the first, *The Black Echo*, appeared in 1992.

He moved to Los Angeles in 1987 to work for *The Los Angeles Times* as a reporter, and he has set most of his stories in the Southern California/L.A. area, a locale heavy with mystery fiction associations—in the novels of Raymond Chandler, Joseph Wambaugh, and Ross Macdonald for example—and a city that "embodies the notion that anything can happen." Although he began writing a series featuring the police detective Harry Bosch, Connelly now alternates his series with stand-alone novels, like *The Poet* (1996) and *Blood Work* (1998), in which he explores other protagonists and refreshes himself for the series books.

The sixth of his Harry Bosch novels, *Angels Flight*, was published to great acclaim in 1999. The following interview was conducted in January 1999.

Silet: Tell me a little something about your background.

Connelly: I was born in Philadelphia, but I grew up in Florida. My family moved to Ft. Lauderdale when I was eleven, and I didn't leave until I was thirty. If you want a history or biography that leans toward how I ended up writing crime novels, I can give you that.

I was a teenager in the seventies which was the time of the explosion of the cocaine-driven violence in South Florida, the cocaine-cowboys and all that sort of stuff, a big news thing that I followed and that got me interested in crime. When I psycho-analyze myself, another thing that played a part in what I ended up doing was that I was a witness to a crime when I was sixteen. I didn't really see the horrible part of the crime, what I saw was a man running. He wasn't jogging, he was dressed in regular clothes, but he was running with a sense of desperation. I saw him suddenly stop and shove something into a hedge. I was sitting at a traffic light watching this.

I was curious about it, so when the light changed I made a U-turn and I went back to that spot in the hedge, where I found a shirt wrapped around a gun. I should explain that I'm from an upper middle-class background where crime was not really some-thing that happened outside my door, so this scared me. I shoved the gun back in the hedge, got back into the protection of my car, and headed down the road looking for the man who was running. I was able to spot him and from a distance followed him until I saw him go into a bar.

Silet: That was a pretty gutsy thing to do.

Connelly: Well, I don't consider it gutsy. I was definitely at a distance from him. Plus, I knew he probably wasn't armed any-more, because he had just gotten rid of the gun. So once I saw him go into a bar, which was an unsavory biker-type bar on the beach in Fort Lauderdale, I called my dad who happened to be working late at his office which was quite close to the spot where this guy had hidden the gun. He came over and I was showing him the gun when suddenly a couple of police cars drove up and put their lights on us and asked us what we were doing. We explained what I had done and then they relayed that just down the street someone had been shot in the head during a robbery. Then I pointed out the bar to them.

Although it would be questionable as far as people's civil rights go, the cops emptied the bar, took every patron out of it down to the police station. They also took me to the police station, and they interviewed me, and I had to look at several lineups to pick out the guy. But when I had gone back to show my dad the gun, obviously the guy had left the bar, because they did not have him. But I had an intensive time with the detectives describing the guy, telling what I did, explaining why I did it. They thought I was intimidated and afraid to pick out the guy, because they thought they did have him among the twelve or so patrons they had pulled out of that bar. I was sure they didn't, but they thought I was just afraid to I.D. some guy and get involved further. That was not the case, but it bothered me that they thought that.

It was also my first exposure to detectives and detective squad rooms and the whole world of the police station. It made a real impression on me. That experience didn't suddenly make me want to become a writer, but it made me start to read crime stories in the papers, pretty much voraciously, and many of them written by Edna Buchanan from the *Miami Herald*, who now writes mysteries or crime novels. So that is one seed I'll put in there for you when I think about what led me to where I am today.

Jump forward a few years and I went to the University of Florida, where I first enrolled in a curriculum that would lead me to getting a license in building construction, because my father and his father both were developers and it was almost like a traditional family thing to go into. I did not fare well as a student of building construction and, in fact, was asked to leave school after a year and sit out a year because of my grades. During that year I was out, all my friends were still in school and I was alone and this increased my interest in crime novels and also heightened my movie-going. I remember that it was during that year that I saw *Chinatown* which remains my favorite movie.

So when I went back to school the next year, I wanted to go into journalism, to be a newspaper reporter. Also during that first year back I discovered the books of Raymond Chandler. Somehow of all the novel reading I had been doing, I had skipped Raymond Chandler, probably because I was most interested in contemporary novels. I had gone to see a movie, *The Long Goodbye*, Robert Altman's version of a Chandler book, and it made me pick up the movie tie-in paperback, but having never read a Chandler book I didn't know how different it was from the book. That was like the writer's epiphany, I guess, if I've had one, and within a week I had read everything Chandler had published and started seeing journalism as a possible means to an end. I started thinking that I wanted to write these crime novels instead of just having a hobby of reading them. I thought journalism was a way to get there, because I could become a police reporter and get into that world. That was like a secret hope. I was a journalist on papers in Daytona Beach, Fort Lauderdale, and then the last place I worked was *The Los Angeles Times*.

Silet: How did you get from Florida to California?

Connelly: I was one of three reporters who spent about a year working on a story that was basically a year-later look at a major airliner crash in Dallas. A Delta flight in 1985 flew from Fort Lauderdale to Dallas on its way to L.A., and it crashed when it landed in Dallas. What was somewhat unique about this one was that while one hundred and thirty people were killed in the crash, twenty-nine survived. This was a complete crash. There was nothing left of the plane except for the tail, nothing recognizable. Myself and two other reporters were assigned to work almost six months on contacting the survivors and spending time with the ones who would allow it and write a one-year-later story recreating the crash and what the year had been like for the survivors.

That story was one of the three finalists for the Pulitzer Prize on feature-writing the following year, and it drew attention to me from a lot of newspapers. The L.A. *Times* was obviously familiar with it, because a lot of the people on that plane were heading to Los Angeles and were from Los Angeles. So I got a call from the managing editor of the *Times* and I went out there, which was also part of my secret plan or secret hope, because the most influential writers of crime novels, to me at least, all wrote about Los Angeles or Southern California. It was like a dream come true to be able to get a chance to go out to the place they wrote about.

Silet: So did you continue to do crime reporting in L.A.?

Connelly: Yeah, I did crime reporting everywhere I was. I was a reporter about thirteen years, and I'd say nine or ten of them were directly on the police beat and the other few were covering the courts. So one way or another I was covering crime. That was all part of that hoped-for plan, because in journalism the police beat is a beginner beat. You work it for a couple of years, burn out, and move on to something "more significant." But I was interested in that world, so I turned down other opportunities or offers to move on to other beats. I just liked covering the police world, and I had this thing that none of my editors realized: I was almost looking at it as research for the time I would be ready to write fiction.

Silet: When did you first begin to write fiction?

Connelly: Before I moved to Los Angeles, I attempted to write crime novels set in Florida, twice, and I never got past probably forty thousand words in either one of them. They were basically learning processes. I started with either a really good setup or with what I thought was an interesting character, but then pretty quickly foundered and gave up. The thing I learned is that you have got to have a lot of things ready before you should start. The one thing I didn't have in either of those attempts was I did not know where the story was going. Now, I'm not a person who likes to outline, so I don't mean you have to know everything, but I did not have the goal or the horizon in sight where I was heading the story.

What I decided to do was not give up but put fiction aside for a while and not start it again until I had all of those components. I recommitted to my journalism, and that's when I worked on that plane-crash story that got me to Los Angeles. So between those first two attempts and the third attempt, which was ultimately my first published book, four or five years went by.

Silet: *The Black Echo* was the first book you published. How did it come about?

Connelly: It was a weird coalescing of ideas and interests which suddenly came together in almost an epiphany. Essentially the roots of that story go way back. When I was a kid, even before I moved to Florida, we lived in a hilly neighborhood outside of

Philadelphia, and there was a storm-water tunnel that went under the street near the front of our house. It was almost a rite of passage for the little boys in our neighborhood to crawl through this dark and muddy tunnel. It was something I knew I had to do because of peer pressure, and it scared me. So I've always had this thing about tunnels.

Then jump forward a few years. During the Vietnam war there were soldiers who went into the tunnel-networks that the Viet Cong had dug for decades in which soldiers and even communities hid. This was a specialized branch of the U.S. Army, the small wiry ones, that had to go in there to seek out the enemy. I saw a "Sixty Minutes" segment on it once and read a book called *The Tunnels of Cu Chi* which played into this prior fear I had of tunnels. It is a non-fiction book, but it is one of the scariest books I ever read, because you can just imagine being in this darkness and knowing that you are on the turf of the enemy and they know where you are but you don't know where they are. So that was another seed that was planted.

Also my father was a developer and had a man working for him who had been a tunnel rat in Vietnam, and he had had some kind of bad experience that left him scarred on his face and he wore a beard to cover the scars. I'd ask my dad about what happened to him, and my dad said he had tried to talk to him about it but he would not talk about it other than to say his job was to go into the tunnels. And that was why I bought *The Tunnels of Cu Chi*, because I knew that man had had these experiences, and it also played on something that scared me. So this is almost a hobby of mine. Then the years go by and I moved to Los Angeles.

The summer of 1987 there was a celebrated burglary of a bank in downtown Los Angeles where the perpetrators used the storm-water tunnels—there are four hundred miles of storm-water tunnels under Los Angeles and these are huge tunnels you can drive a motorcycle through. They used these to track their way beneath downtown and then drilled into the side of these concrete tunnels and then dug their own tunnel underneath and up to the bank vault. They got away, and it's still an unsolved crime. They were never caught. That was in July of 1987. I think it happened the day I came to Los Angeles to be interviewed by the *Times*, so I had not been working there yet, but I was reading their paper and it was full of stories about this. Then I was hired and started in August, and there were some continuing stories. So I personally never wrote about this crime, but I was aware of it.

Then I was put on the police beat, and I spent a couple of years getting my feet wet and learning the city and learning the cops and I was not worried about writing fiction yet. I happen to be in one of the police stations when the detectives still on this unsolved tunnel robbery or burglary—technically it's a burglary since there were no humans involved as victims, but calling it the tunnel burglary doesn't sound as cool as calling it the tunnel robbery. The detectives on that case happen to come to this police station to brief the division detectives on it, because they thought that whoever did this would do it again, and they wanted to fill them in on how it was done and some of the tell-tale signs. For example, when the robbers were digging their own tunnel, they had all of this dirt they had to get rid of, so someone up on the top on the street would open up a fire hydrant so there would be water going through the sewers and it would wash away the dirt. There were little details that were really wonderful to know and that had never been reported. I was allowed to sit in on the briefing, if I promised not to write a story about it. But I didn't promise not to write any fiction about it.

When I was sitting there listening to all this, the idea for the story just came together. I had this fascination with tunnels. I had this fascination with tunnel rats. When I found out how these guys had pulled off this burglary, it struck me that this could be what I had been looking for in terms of coming up with a fictional story to write. I could have a burglary and I could have the character be a tunnel rat and it would have some kind of resonance to him. That's when I started doping out a character that I could place in fiction.

Silet: Tell me a little bit about Harry Bosch.

Connelly: Well, he first started almost as a writing exercise. I was obviously aware of mystery series and that successful authors write several stories with the same character. That was something I was hoping to do, but when you're sitting there writing the first book with the first character, you have no idea whether you'll get a chance to write another one again. I wrote him with the hope that would be the case, that I would get a chance to write several more. So I knew from my analysis of reading my favorite mystery writers that their books were for the most part character-driven. I knew that I had to have a really interesting and well-delineated character from the very first book and really even before I sat down to write. I thought a long time about the character before I started writing the tunnel story. I had two failed efforts many years before, and I was looking at this almost as an exercise to try to get going again. I wasn't sure whether it wouldn't be another unsuccessful effort.

The other thing is that I was working full time as a newspaper reporter, so I was really looking for a counterpoint to that kind of writing which has lots of rules, lots of stress. I wanted to be able to come home at night and to write about someone totally different from me and write about whatever I wanted and really have fun doing it. When I was picking out details about Harry Bosch everything was opposite of me because I thought it would be more interesting to write about him. I come from a big family; Harry is an orphan. I have been married for a long time; he had never been married. He's a smoker; I'm a non-smoker. He came essentially from that.

He was also obviously influenced by James Ellroy, but more James Ellroy the person than James Ellroy's writing. About the time I was putting this all together Ellroy's book *The Black Dahlia* came out. I was just a couple of years in Los Angeles at that point, and although he was pretty well known here in Los Angeles, I had never heard of him until I moved out to L.A. When *The Black Dahlia* came out, he got a lot of local press attention that revealed his past, especially that his mother was murdered when he was a boy. It was pretty obvious to me, obvious to everyone, that that is what he's about. Whatever happened to his mother and so forth, he's working it out now by writing about murder. I thought that was very interesting, so I made the jump and instead of a writer working out his mother's murder by writing about it, I thought what about a detective who's solving murders and in some way that helps him deal with his own mother's murder?

Silet: Harry Bosch has a very dark past.

Connelly: It's just hinted at in most of the books, and in the details it is quite different from Ellroy's life. My thought was that I would set this up as the background to him in the first book, and if I was lucky enough to be asked to write a second book, I would have him investigate his mother's murder in the second since that is the motivating factor in his life. Things changed. The first book, *The Black Echo*, did really well, and I decided to hold off on that a little bit and it finally became the story of the fourth book.

Silet: How do you get into the second book, *The Black Ice?*

Connelly: As soon as I sold *The Black Echo*, my editor told me their plans for it and their plans weren't to publish it for twenty-two months. They were that far ahead, and it was shocking to me. But she said to me, "This is really a good time to write another book because you don't have any of the pressure of will the first book succeed and all that and you can write in a vacuum." So she advised me to start my second book as soon as I could, and if I was lucky, I would have it done before the first one came out. She also said that she saw this projected as a series. She said, "Start writing your second book and do it with this Harry Bosch guy." I told her about my idea of writing a book about how he investigates his mother's murder, and she suggested that I not do that either, not yet, because she thought that was more of a culmination of his story and to jump to that in the second book was not a smart thing to do. So I took her advice but that left me without an idea.

So my second book, *The Black Ice*, became a nod to Raymond Chandler. You'll find corollaries between the plot and *The Long Goodbye*, with the betrayal of friendship and so forth. That's what kind of inspired that story.

Silet: What is the book about? What is the "black ice" to begin with?

Connelly: Well, first of all *The Black Ice* wasn't my title. Remember, I didn't know anything about publishing and I actually turned it in before my first book even came out. So I turned it in with a very unmarketable title. The "black ice" of the title is twofold, a double entendre meaning the drug called the black ice that is the seed of the story and that starts a series of murders and that impels Harry Bosch to follow the smuggling trail of the black ice to Mexico.

The second meaning is the kind of ice that you slide on. That doesn't happen in Los Angeles but maybe once or twice a year. They'll have a black ice warning when it gets really cold. So there's that meaning which is almost a philosophical thing about life. You don't see the black ice until you're on it and you're sliding and that's what happens to Harry Bosch. In this case he's blindsided by the facts of the case when they are revealed to him. Basically, the story leads Harry Bosch down to Mexico, to Mexicali which is an interesting place on the border; on the American side it is called Calexico and on the Mexican side it is called Mexicali. They are mirrored cities which also played into the story.

I was still a reporter at this time, and I had traveled down to Mexicali with two homicide detectives on an investigation, so I was able to witness their interaction with the Federales in Mexico and the completely different type of law enforcement that takes place—or doesn't take place more likely—in Mexico. That was very interesting to me, it was something I wanted to put in the book, so I constructed this book so Harry would have to go down to Mexico as Marlowe did in *The Long Goodbye*. While Harry Bosch is in Mexico he's taken to a bull fight, and while he's in a private booth at the bull fight, the villain of the story comes in and discusses bull fighting with Bosch, the novice who doesn't know anything about it. What he's really talking about is a philosophy of surviving, and he's threatening Bosch, basically. What he calls bull fighting is the art of the cape which is a literal translation of the Mexican way of describing bull fighting. The art of the cape is surviving against the odds.

I turned that book in as *The Art of the Cape*, but the marketing people said, "If we put a bull or a matador on the cover of this book you're not going to sell very many copies." Being the novice, I agreed with them, and I don't disagree with them now, it was a smart thing to do. *The Black Ice* was the title that came up almost by committee.

Silet: Had the first two been published when you began the third, *The Concrete Blonde?*

Connelly: I had just begun writing *The Concrete Blonde* when *Black Echo* came out. The one thing I saw happening when they suggested *The Black Ice* was that they saw—I had now another editor—a series, the black this and the black that, and that was one thing, even though I was a novice writer, that I thought was too gimmicky. I told them I didn't want to do it, but I knew that I had not won that battle yet. The way I won it was with the title "The Concrete Blonde" which they just loved from the beginning and that ended any desire on their part to have this "black" series. However, I was hedging my bets, so in the book there are two or three references to the "black heart." If they had not accepted the title, I would have called it *The Black Heart.*

Silet: Where did the idea for *The Concrete Blonde* come from?

Connelly: That also came from my experience as a reporter. It came from two things. First of all it goes back to the first book. I wanted the book to be very accurate regarding police procedures and politics, and I wanted to write about Hollywood, yet I wanted my detective, Harry Bosch, to be a really good detective, and in the LAPD the best of the best get moved downtown to robbery/homicide. But I didn't want to write about robbery/homicide because as a reporter I actually had less experience with robbery/homicide detectives than I did with the divisional detectives who would be in Hollywood or any of the police stations around the city. I wanted Harry's world to be in one of the smaller police stations, and so I had to come up with a reason why one of the best of the best would be in Hollywood.

In the first book I put in this back story about how Harry made a mistake and shot an unarmed man, even though that unarmed man turned out to be a serial killer. He made a furtive move and Harry ended up shooting him. There had to be some kind of demotion and that explained why he was in Hollywood and yet was one of the better detectives in LAPD. When I was ready to write the third book, it came after a year where I had been covering a police trial, a civil-rights trial, where a group of cops were being sued for shooting a bunch of robbers as they came out of a McDonald's that they had just robbed. Three or the four of them were killed. The contention of the dead robbers' families and the survivor was that the cops strategically set up their attempted arrest so that it would end in gunfire and they would be able to kill these guys. They were called by the lawyer of the families and the survivor, a "death squad." Their practice was to set up things where they could eliminate bad people. It was a very interesting, lengthy trial that I was cut loose from the cop beat to cover full-time because the L.A. *Times* saw it as a very important case.

So I was in court every day and the nuances of the trial and the personalities were obviously stuff that doesn't get into newspaper stories. That became the thing that inspired me in the courtroom drama or the courtroom track of *The Concrete Blonde*. It is a two-track novel. Harry is being sued for killing the guy, the serial killer, and depriving him of his civil rights that is referenced in the first book, *The Black Echo*. One of the contentions of the family of the dead man is that he also wasn't the serial killer. Harry not only killed an unarmed man but he also killed the wrong man. That plays out through *The Concrete Blonde*, while at the same time Harry is conducting an investigation that is heading towards his need to prove that he did kill the right guy.

Silet: *The Last Coyote* is the book where Harry finally begins to examine the death of his mother.

Connelly: By the time I was starting to write *The Last Coyote* I probably had only one book published, but yet I had gone through lengthy stories with Harry Bosch. So I decided to write it then as the fourth book, because I thought I was going to need to take a break from Harry Bosch pretty soon. It was really intensive, and I was exhausted from working at the newspaper as a full-time job. So I quit as a reporter just as I started *The Last Coyote*. That was the first book I wrote as a full-time fiction writer, I guess you'd call it. The story seemed appropriate to wrap the series up with. I was considering ending the series at that point.

Silet: There are difficulties in maintaining a series as well as positive things trying to sustain one.

Connelly: As I said before, at that point I was thinking of actually ending the series because most series somehow get stale. Either they get permanently stale or at least some of the books get stale. The writer has to find some way of rejuvenating himself and the character and the stories. It's a dilemma that doesn't really have an answer, so my thought was I will just wrap up this series and maybe start a new one. After *The Last Coyote* I wrote *The Poet*, but in the process of writing it, I found I really missed writing about Harry Bosch.

I think that points out one of the advantages of writing a series, that if you have a character you really know and love, you'll like to continue him because you have the opportunity to really delineate a full character over the breadth of your books that even a thousand-page novel can't do. You can show him over time. My books are in chronological sequence so I've been able to develop Harry in detail at six different points in his life. There are a lot of advantages to it as long as you can keep yourself really invigorated and interested in that character. I think as soon as you're not it's going to show in the books. By my writing these non-series books I have come back to Harry Bosch refreshed, and I've done some of my best work.

Silet: In *The Poet*, you changed the central character to a reporter, Jack McEvoy. How did you come up with that character?

Connelly: Two things. I was ending the four-book run with Harry Bosch, and I wanted to write something different. I didn't really want to write about a cop. I have pretty much not wanted to write about a private eye, because I write contemporary stories and I find the private-eye novel unbelievable. It has been my experience that private eyes are not out there solving murders most of the time. I think eventually I will write one of those, but I haven't found the right inspiration to do it. Having been a reporter I wanted to write about that world or I thought I did. I have to say that of the eight books I've written, writing *The Poet* was the least favorable writing experience. Just because it was too autobiographical or something, so I didn't get the same fulfillment or fun I get from writing about Harry Bosch. When I'm writing Harry Bosch, I have to think about what this wholly-created character would do, in whatever circumstances, and I have to make sure that the continuity of character is there.

When I was writing about Jack McEvoy, I didn't have to do any of that. I was basically writing about what I would do, because I had had the same experience doing his kind of reporting. The process of doing it that way was not that much fun. That was the quickest book I ever wrote because of that as well. I wrote that book in eight months. I haven't gone back to that character, although I'd like to find a way to make him interesting, and I think maybe the further away I am from being a reporter, the more interesting that would be.

Silet: Do you have a process you go through in your writing, like a daily routine?

Connelly: Not really and it's changed a lot. I became a father for the first time two years ago, and back when I did not have a child, my process was to get up as early as I could and get as much writing in by noon as I could. That seemed to be the time I was most creative. Then I would spend the afternoons rewriting or going over what I had done that morning. The birth of my daughter changed all that. It is hard to get going in the morning because of her concerns. So now I'm lucky if I'm writing by eight-thirty or nine, whereas before I would be up at five-thirty or six.

The only really overriding process that I follow is I try to write every day, no matter what, whether I'm on a book tour or the baby's sick or whatever. I don't put any kind of quantification on it. I don't care how much I write; I just write something and in order to write something you've got to think about the story. If you write every day your head will never come out of the story. That's what I think is really important. I've had experiences where I've had to stop writing. The first time I went on a book tour I didn't write during that tour. I was in the middle of a book, and after I came back, it took me a really long time to get back into the story, to really be thinking about the story all the time.

Silet: Your books are set in and out of L.A., and you mentioned Raymond Chandler and his connection with L.A. What is the appeal of L.A. as a fictional setting?

Connelly: I think that of any of our cities it's the place that embodies the notion that anything can happen. If you're writing about a place where anything can happen at any time, you're ahead of the game because that's the flavor you want to have in a crime novel, where you don't know what is going on and that anything can happen. Additionally, I benefit from having the long history of some great crime writers or mystery writers who worked this ground. There's a negative in that it sets you up to comparison, but at the same time I think there's a big audience out there that's interested in the L.A. crime novel because of the status due to people like Raymond Chandler, Ross Macdonald, Joseph Wambaugh and others.

The other thing about writing about contemporary L.A. is that it is so many different cities. It's really many different communities all put together in a so-called melting pot that's not really melted. Therefore, whatever you want to write about, whatever subject or whatever social thing you want to tackle, you can find it here and it's believable that it is here. I think another aspect is the movie business. This area is where fantasies are made, therefore it's also the place where fantasies die hard. You really see the have and have-nots here and that is good fodder for writing crime novels.

Silet: After *The Poet* you published *Trunk Music* in 1997 and *Blood Work* last year. How do you keep up the pace?

Connelly: I think I'm a quick writer, yes, and I think that is from being a newspaper reporter, where you had to be a quick writer and that gave me the work ethic. I don't think I've ever taken a long break from writing novels, and I've often started the next one a week after finishing one. One reason is that the idea for the next one usually comes to me, and when you get an idea that you know you're going to write about, it feels really urgent and so I don't want to wait to start it. The other thing is that it's essentially a mirage.

If you look at the copyrights of my books, I've published eight books in eight years. But because they held my first book for twenty-two months, I was actually close to being done with my third book before my first came out, so it's kind of a built-in buffer. It looks like, wow, I'm writing one book a year, but they're actually taking longer, with the exception of *The Poet*. It seems to me that it takes about fifteen months to write my Harry Bosch books.

Silet: Tell me about *Trunk Music.*

Connelly: *Trunk Music* was returning to the Bosch character mindful of how do you keep this series going and fresh and so forth. If there was an agenda with *Trunk Music* it was to take Harry out of L.A. Therefore a good portion of the book takes place in Las Vegas. Again, it was pursuing things that interest me, and it was also using things from my past, crimes I had written about as a reporter. I'm not a gambler, but I'm fascinated with Las Vegas, which is almost like the ultimate fantasy world in that when people come there they lose a lot of their inhibitions. When I was a newspaper reporter, many years before, I wrote about the murder—which remains unsolved now—of a sports agent. He was found in the trunk of his Rolls Royce in a hotel parking lot in Universal City. The investigation showed that he lived a double life. He was washing money for the mob and the assumption was that he took some of that money and he got whacked. Although that case wasn't solved, the components were there for an interesting story. I used many of the details from that in constructing *Trunk Music,* although I made him a sleazy Hollywood player not a sports agent.

Silet: Tell me about *Blood Work?*

Connelly: *Blood Work* was inspired by a good friend of mine who had a heart transplant in 1993. I knew what he was going through while he was waiting for the heart and then he got the heart. I was aware from spending time with him how much his life had changed, how much he was relying on the medical machinery, and how he had to take fifty-two pills a day. All that was very interesting to me as a writer. The main thing, however, that inspired it was that after he got the new heart he started exhibiting many of the emotions that I saw years earlier when I was working on that plane-crash story and talking to the survivors.

The thing that touched me so much about those survivors, which became the theme of the magazine article which we wrote, was their survivor guilt. Their emotional upset at surviving a crash where many other people didn't and the happenstance of it. You know, like one person walks away without a scratch where the person in the seat next to them is killed. Though it's no fault of their own, it delivers a burden to them.

My friend, Terry, who had the heart transplant, had the same thing happen to him. He's prepared for it, as he's waiting for a heart they're telling him all about it, but then he gets the heart and it hits him: someone died in order for me to live. He didn't know that person and had nothing to do with, in his case, the auto crash that ended up providing him with the heart and a second chance, but it just really put the whammy on him for a while. It took him a long time to work it out and to reach a point of acceptance. Of all the things that he was going through, that touched me the most and inspired me to write a story that had someone in his situation where he felt beholden to the person who provided his heart.

Silet: Let's talk a little about *Angels Flight.*

Connelly: Again, it is a return to Harry Bosch after a non-Harry Bosch book, so it was something I was really invigorated about and looking forward to. The agenda I had for *Angels Flight* was I wanted to explore a new place in Los Angeles, take Harry out of Hollywood. I wanted the book to have as one of its themes Harry recommitting to his home, to Los Angeles, at the same time that that community was possibly coming apart at the seams, which is a hard thing to do but hopefully it works. In the book there's a murder, there's a double murder actually, on this funicular train in downtown called "angels flight." Through a device Harry's called in to investigate it even though it's not in the Hollywood Division.

So in coming to an area he knew as a kid but has not really spent a lot of time in as an adult, there's a nostalgic resonance to it. In fact, he's remembering things about the city, and it brings out that although he's probably disappointed in the history his city has taken in recent years, he still loves it and is committed to it. At one point he sees a mural in downtown that he really likes, and he has this realization that there are little pieces of grace everywhere if you look for them. That is really an underlying theme of the book, finding grace in himself and in the city and its people at the same time he is moving through a really dark underbelly of the city.

Silet: What are you working on now?

Connelly: I'm working on another stand-alone. Remember when I was writing *The Last Coyote* I wasn't sure whether I'd be writing about Harry Bosch again. It only took me a few months into *The Poet* when I realized I would definitely want to write about Harry Bosch again. I came to the realization that the serious things I want to say as a writer, I want to make outside of the entertainment of a mystery and I want to make through Harry Bosch, because I think he's a pretty noble character. I think he can almost be seen as the plight of Los Angeles. I came to the conclusion that Harry is my main man as a writer and that I would be using him again and again hopefully.

Once I came to that realization and commitment to Harry, I decided that when I write non-Harry Bosch books, I have to somehow challenge myself and have some kind of fun. Not only is there a goal of taking a year off from Harry and recharging him, but there's also the opportunity to do some other things. In *The Poet* the challenge was to write in the first person which I had never done before. Also, I actually wrote some drop-in scenes in *The Poet* that are seen through the view of the bad guy, which I had never done before, either. In *Blood Work* the challenge was to write a thriller that would be fulfilling on the necessary levels of a thriller, but at its heart was a character or a protagonist who did not really fit the bill of the thriller protagonist. This is a guy with the new heart who is really fragile, who can't really get into a fight. There is one scene in the book that has the beginning of a fight but it ends really quick because of his condition. The challenge was to have an unusual protagonist being able to carry a thriller.

Then I wrote *Angels Flight* and now I'm back to writing a non-Harry Bosch book and to me this is my biggest challenge to date, because I'm writing a story with a female protagonist and that female is also a criminal. So it has two things I haven't done before. The challenge is to make this read as though it has not been written by a man and to make this protagonist, who is a burglar, sympathetic to the reader to the point where they will want her to succeed in the end, in other words, get away. I'm really only about a third into it, so I don't know how I'm doing yet.

Silet: You mentioned that Harry Bosch has become the mouthpiece for your own social concerns. What are your main themes?

Connelly: I think that's why I write the books because I can't encapsulate my themes in a few sentences or five minutes. I want the Bosch novels to be as closely reflective of contemporary life in Los Angeles as possible. In the nineties in Los Angeles there have been many problems and chief among them have been racial tensions, and I had not really written about that before I had gotten into *Angels Flight.* This is where I find it hard to express what I'm trying to do. I'm not saying I'm offering any kind of solution. In *Angels Flight* there are differing viewpoints and there are enough differing viewpoints that the reader will be upset by what some characters say and agree with what some characters say, at different times in the book. I'm not writing a book to please everybody all the time.

I think that moving through the scenes of racial tension that the case in *Angels Flight* brings to the forefront of the city reveals this noble person, this guy Harry Bosch, who has a good heart and is trying to do a good job in very difficult circumstances. If maybe people read the book and take some kind of inspiration from him, that's really all I'm trying to do. I'm not trying to solve any kind of problem because I'm not really sure I can, but I'm trying to tell the story of one person trying to put things back together.

Drugs, Cash, and Automatic Weapons
James Crumley

Photo © Michael Gallacher

James Crumley's first book, *One to Count Cadence* (1969), was among the initial novels to confront the absurdity of the U.S. involvement in Vietnam and, although it was not a crime novel, in many ways it provides a shadowy background to the detective fiction Crumley has subsequently written. In *The Wrong Case* (1975) he introduced the first of his hapless detectives, Milo Milodragovitch, and firmly established the western locale of Montana as the setting for his mystery stories. The second Milo book, *Dancing Bear* (1983), was published eight years later.

Crumley created his second series character, C. W. Sughrue, in the *The Last Good Kiss* (1978). By the early eighties his readership was firmly established, if still relatively select, and he became something of a "cult" writer among mystery buffs. In 1993 James Crumley released a second Sughrue novel, *The Mexican Tree Duck*, to broad critical acclaim. *Bordersnakes* was published in 1996 and *The Mexican Pig Bandit* in 1998.

Portions of this interview originally appeared as "Drugs, Cash, and Automatic Weapons: An Interview with James Crumley," *The Armchair Detective*, 27:1 (Winter 1994), 9–15.

Silet: You were born in Texas. Tell me about that.

Crumley: Typical working class, oil field. My father started off in the oil fields as a roughneck and by the time he had his first series of heart attacks he had worked his way up to being the General Superintendent of a small independent oil company and my mother worked as a waitress and cashier and bookkeeper. We lived in the country. I had five thousand acres to play on but no people to play with.

Silet: Where did you go to school?

Crumley: In Mathis. The town we lived closest to was Santa Cruz, an old original Irish immigrant settlement in 1830–32, but it didn't have schools anymore. The railroad ran through that part of Texas and missed a bunch of little towns. Everybody put their houses on wagons and moved them to Mathis, where the railroad crossed. You know, it was mostly Mexican-Americans; my hometown is 65% Chicano. It's still an awfully divided place. If you get closer to the border, race is not quite such a problem, everybody speaks Spanish and there's no sense of division of the groups. It's a very diverse ethnic population. There are Bohemians, Germans, Czechs and of course the Irish, and then people like us who were from somewhere else.

My mother still lives there. She still feels like an outsider in town because we were newcomers. I felt some of it as a little kid, but I think I was ostracized as much for being smart as I was for anything else. I remember being happy the first time I ever got a C on a report card. I survived the usual bullying that goes on because, fortunately, I was always a big kid. So that if you wanted to pick on me you had to deal with me.

Silet: You really did not feel you belonged to that part of Texas?

Crumley: No, and I still don't. We lived in New Mexico during World War II, and I was in the second grade when we came back, so maybe I got used to that desert air. It was humidity that drove me insane.

Silet: How did you get out of Texas?

Crumley: I got a Navy scholarship. It was an all NTC scholarship when I got out of high school. So at seventeen I got a train in Odem, Texas and got off in Atlanta, Georgia to go to Georgia Tech. There was actually a side trip to New Orleans, but it was only important because that was the first night I ever slept in an alley.

Silet: You did not stay at the university very long?

Crumley: No, I took my cruise and discovered that the destroyer just made me continuously seasick and that the Navy Officer Corps was not to my taste. It seemed awfully Southern and stuffy, class-conscious. I ended up hanging around with the enlisted men. I trucked home and told my old man that I didn't like it out there, that my grades had dropped off and that I felt quite displaced, and he said if you don't like what you're doing, get out of it. So I joined the Army the next day and took off. Back in those days it was a reasonable thing for a young man to do when he didn't know what he wanted to do.

Silet: What did you do after the Army?

Crumley: I would work in the oil field like a roughneck for six weeks, go to college for six months. I started to leave several times but then of course there was a woman involved shortly thereafter, or maybe two women. So I got married. Then I heard about Iowa City. I had written a couple of stories and my writing teacher asked me if I would like to go Iowa, and I didn't know what Iowa was and was not sure where it was. When he told me about it I said sure it sounds great. I finally ended up majoring in History simply because that was the best department on campus and had the most interesting professors. Even then without realizing I was becoming political or had become political.

Silet: Political in what way?

Crumley: Well, political in the way that the system seemed to be very unfair, seemed to be a lie, it seemed to do none of the right things; it paid lip service to all these things and never did them. I could see how poor people and Mexicans and blacks were treated differently from anybody else. There was a small leftist group hanging around campus. We did things like march on the football stadium because they made the black players live under the stadium instead of in the dorms. Things that didn't seem to have any major importance, but sort of did to me.

I never had an assistantship at Iowa. I went there with one little story, "An Ideal Son for the Jenkins Family," an earlier version of it. Then what was later to become a novel, *Labor Pains*, which was really in bad shape. One of those stories of the troubles of young men. I left Iowa with 120 pages of that novel in hand.

Silet: How was Iowa City?

Crumley: Well, it was great. I had never been around people who read and liked it, and talked about writing all the time. In the years that I was teaching I kept trying to recreate that situation, but it was impossible. Most of the guys at Iowa were older and everybody had given up something to be there. When you tried to do that with the ordinary graduate student, it didn't necessarily work. It was great for me.

Silet: Was it just the atmosphere or did the instruction help you?

Crumley: I learned from people like R. V. Cassell and Richard Yates. It was more attitude than any specific instruction. I never experienced anything quite like this before in my life. I wrote fiction while I was in Iowa and read and talked to people and tended bar, cleaned toilets, and then just lucked into this job in Montana. Then I wrote and sold my first novel, *One to Count Cadence.*

Silet: When did you decide you wanted to become a writer?

Crumley: I don't think I ever wanted to be anything else, seriously. I just loved books even when I was a little kid. Nobody in my family on either side was much of a reader. My father never finished high school. Just something about books got hold of me. My old man used to say that I'd come home and two things would happen: a book would fly into my hand and my shoes would fly off.

Silet: Let's talk about *One to Count Cadence*. What did you learn from it?

Crumley: Learned not be a schizophrenic, I guess. It's like putting parts of myself back together, but what I had in mind was something entirely different. I guess what I learned is that books don't always behave. When they decide to misbehave, there's no reason to stop because that's sometimes where your best thoughts and language come out.

Silet: So you do not block everything out ahead of time.

Crumley: I never block everything out ahead of time. I never did that as an academic either. I'd write the paper then write the outline. I guess I always figured that unless you're completely insane, you will think in certain patterns and they will be self-evident.

Silet: The army obviously inspired your first book.

Crumley: Well, the army was the most important event in my short unhappy life at that time. Plus the war was just about to get underway and I fancied myself a student of the "real politik." I got into a gigantic argument about the war with Vernon Cassell when we were out drinking in Coralville and somehow the book began as a continuation of our argument. I had in mind some fancy confrontation with classical conservative and classical liberal. Nobody knows in this country what a conservative really is, they think they're Republicans. This is quite frankly a stupid country. Books are smarter than people, that's why you have them.

Silet: Talk to me a little bit about the Vietnam War.

Crumley: I think it ruined this country, not for the usual reasons, not from losing. The war was a lie, and not only Americans died for that lie, a tremendous number of people died for that lie. People are still dying from that lie. The government continues to lie about that war. Perhaps the government lies about everything. That's actually kind of sad. So the war really tested a lot of people. Then, most of my adult male friends were Vietnam vets, have been for twenty years. So it's never quite gone away and that's why it plays such a big part in *The Mexican Tree Duck.*

Silet: How did you get into crime fiction?

Crumley: Raymond Chandler. I was in Montana to work on my first novel for some insane reason. I didn't know what I was doing there, but I was there. I don't think I had ever read but one or two detective novels and then only ones I'd found hidden under my aunt's mattress. But I read Chandler, I thought wow, he is something. I always meant to write one, and after six years of struggling with a South Texas novel, I quit Colorado State—I was at Colorado State by then working in the writing program. I hated the academic world. It was making me hate my students and that didn't seem right.

One day I told the chairman that I was leaving at the end of the year, that was it, I had all that I could stand. They did everything they could to keep me, they bent over backwards, and they begged me and offered me money, fewer classes, but I was done. I went home and, I'd had so much trouble with this Texas novel, I thought maybe I should try something else. That's where *The Wrong Case* came from, then oddly enough, they kept coming. They gave me a kind of literary caché the first novel never did.

I don't think a lot of people read the first novel. It came out maybe at a painful time. But I got one down, the next thing I knew I got another one down, then another one. Then some ten years later, after laboring mightily in Hollywood to try to pay the child support and alimony I got stuck with, another one. I never meant to write more than one.

Silet: Where did Milo come from?

Crumley: From the top of my head I guess, I don't know. He just appeared there; I started writing about this sad guy who was a good guy. What I like to try to do all the time is write about people who manage to be decent and kind in situations where the normal, run-of-the-mill, middle-class average American doesn't expect it. This is not news to poor people or black people. It does seem to be news to the middle class. I wasn't really looking for a great action hero. I just wanted to do all these little things that have never been done, and it turns out too that I wanted to have some laughs.

As I got older and had more and more disasters in my personal life, laughter became more important than serious thinking about these things. So Milo seemed to be that kind of guy. I know in some places I echo pieces of my childhood. I know where my feeling about rich people comes from, for instance. I wanted Milo to be rich, but with no money, I know where that comes from.

Silet: He is a reluctant detective.

Crumley: He's reluctantly alive. He's not thoughtless; he's a thoughtful fellow. He's good-hearted, and he takes care of things. Where all this comes from I just don't know. That bit about buying up his father's clothes, I mean, what a wonderful notion, but where did I get it? *The Last Good Kiss* was originally my own novel, but my agent talked me into changing it for financial reasons, so I did and I picked up a character out of the Texas novel. He was the poor kid across the river who's mother was the Avon lady who was fucking the rich guy on the other side of the river.

Silet: That is Sughrue? Is he like Milo?

Crumley: Well, they're friends actually. I have a pat answer for that. It's like Milo's first impulse when there's trouble is to help and Sughrue's first impulse when there's trouble is to shoot somebody in the foot. They are distinct people in my mind. To me the voices are distinct and different, and Sughrue is almost inevitable angry about something and he's not hysterical, but he could kill people without feeling bad. It doesn't bother him I guess, judging from the way the book came out, but he's always been sure of himself, in a kind of way that Milo has not been.

Silet: Your novels are Westerns in a way. Can we talk about the West a little bit?

Crumley: I need empty spaces for myself in my own life and the West has always had empty spaces and people trying to fill them up. The West has always been an economic colony. There have always been cheap myths about the West. Take the Native Americans for example. I find it difficult to think of people who used to run buffalo off a cliff as being environmentalists.

You look at the description of the village in *Little Big Man*, in the book not the movie, the movie is a lie. In the Indian village when they started to smell their camp, they moved it into the prevailing winds. In *Dances with Wolves* the village looks like a theme park, that's a pernicious lie. I think we can treat the Native American tribes with respect without making up some sort of lie. They weren't always that crazy about each other. Anytime you find a group of people whose name for themselves means "the people," you're looking at some guys when push comes to shove, they'll eat your cousin.

No cowboys were ever born out West, they were all from Kansas or everywhere else; they had Brooklyn accents. It's things like that that the movies and cheap novels have perverted. I don't know if I have a clear picture of the West. I kind of know where it begins: Virginia Dale, Colorado, and Tucumcari, New Mexico. Every place where the road crosses the Montana border.

There's a different kind of society, maybe people need to depend on each other more because it's poor or maybe they need to depend on each other more because it's more under attack. These son of a bitches from the East Coast would come out and cut down every fucking tree west of Montana. Now they're selling the land out. They're selling it to somebody else for timber, that's completely unnecessary. You can grow a pine tree in Georgia in twenty years. In Montana it takes one hundred years. That's the other great myth, the Great Plains; that's not the Great Plains, that's the Great American Desert out there. There's no reason to raise a cow out there or plow ground. It's all part of an old railroad revenue scam, build a railroad and see if they'll come.

I think of the West as a victim. I'd support division of this country. We have more in common with Western Canada than we do with Eastern American. They grow more cows in Iowa than they grow in Montana. The western seven states grow something like eight percent of all the cattle raised in America. The country is not made for cattle but everybody wants to be a rancher in the West.

Silet: There is a lot of movement in your books, a lot of driving back and forth.

Crumley: I've been known to be restless. I've been known to drive one thousand miles to play Black Jack or drive fifteen hundred miles to see a woman and I regularly drive one thousand miles to see my children. Even in my childhood I would drive three hundred miles on a Sunday afternoon looking for girls. The Scotch-Irish part of my family moved from generation to generation. They were transplanted out of Britain after Queen Elizabeth. They started down the Appalachians and never came back. They moved every goddamn generation. I always thought that the Scotch-Irish had sort of a perverse declaration of independence. Instead of all men are created equal, it's no son of a bitch is better than me. I lived a lot of places before I lived in one place. I've grown up in company houses and that doesn't make you feel like you're rooted someplace.

Silet: Do you still teach?

Crumley: No, I haven't taught full-time since 1974, otherwise five years part-time since then.

Silet: You mentioned getting some Hollywood film work, tell me about that.

Crumley: For me it's a better way to make a living than teaching is. I never got tenure, never stayed in a place long enough. I've always liked movies. Sometimes I think Abbot and Costello had much to do with forming my literary opinion. Writing films is in some ways just a job, the major mistake I see young writers make when they go to Hollywood to adapt a first novel is that they think that the screenplay is the most important of the elements in the project, and that's simply not true.

But I'm hesitant to talk about it too much since I've never had a film produced, but I've done enough scripts and people seem to like them so that every now and then I can find work. I'm certainly not downgrading it at all; writing screenplays is hard, making a movie is hard. Until you try to do it you really don't know, but because it's out here in the public's eye and it's an easy thing to speculate about, there's a lot of bullshit about it. I have no plans to stop writing screenplays. I hope eventually some day to see something on the screen.

Silet: How are your books different from other mysteries?

Crumley: Well, I'm not interested in solving crimes, solving mysteries. I don't know quite what I'm interested in, something else, justice or telling tiny stories or meeting all of the crazy people in the world. There are these early black and white TV shows like "Dragnet" in which nothing happens, the people that Joe Friday went and talked to, they didn't have anything to do with the mystery. I think I sometimes do that, just muddle around, and I've discovered it gives me a new kind of freedom.

Silet: Let's talk a little about *The Mexican Tree Duck*. Were you trying something new here? More action? More violence?

Crumley: I didn't decide that, it just all came out. I never apologize for violence, I think what's wrong with televised violence is that it's not real. It should in some ways disgust you, so that's what sort of thing I'm after sometimes. All these guys with guns, it just seemed the natural thing to do. We've got a bunch of people together with conflicting notions and conflicting means.

Silet: And enough ammunition.

Crumley: Yeah, the trinity of American power: drugs, cash and automatic weapons. I grew up around guns but I don't have a great arsenal or anything. I did turn down a K-47 the other day, I nearly bought it, but they want so much money for it. In terms of gun control, I don't think there's anything particularly wrong with the Brady Bill and I do not think that an ordinary citizen should be allowed to own several automatic assault weapons. It's just not necessary, and it's clear that some people are inflamed by the feel and the sight of an assault weapon. I used to belong to the NRA, but they got so hysterical and crazy that I dumped my membership after some twenty years. It's clear that some restraints have to be put on guns. I wouldn't mind guns being licensed like cars and cars licensed like planes.

Silet: What about the trend toward the reformed PI who gives up booze and leads a straight life and all that?

Crumley: There have been some really good books, some really good novels about the troubles with drink of private eyes. It's so easy to slip off into whining. Milo hasn't had a drink in years but Milo doesn't talk about it until maybe this new book. I think human beings need to get outside of themselves every now and then and maybe that's what drugs and drink are for.

There's nothing wrong with drugs by themselves. If alcoholism is a disease, how come crack addiction is a crime. It's just social, it's middle class, it's nothing else but racist. I grew up in the 60s. I've been around people who routinely used recreational drugs. None of them are airline pilots. I've never seen a heart surgeon stoned the night before he goes in. But, I think this is the real world.

I don't know how many million Americans smoke dope now and then but a lot. I don't always know what to tell my children, so I don't tell them much of anything. Everything you see on TV about drugs is more than likely a lie. If one out of every five people who ever tried cocaine became addicted, we could fill up the entire middle of America with addicts. I think it's the lies that are harmful, rather than the drugs. Oddly enough it seems to be about the same number of heroin addicts in this country no matter what you do. I mean they're like a stable base.

I'm certainly not interested in apologizing for how my detectives live, but I also don't want to react against this new wave of Puritanism. That's not what the novels are about. This is just what they do as they go through their day, this is how they get things done sometimes. I don't think it's as important as people make it out.

Silet: Why at the end of *The Mexican Tree Duck* do you kill off the mother and leave the child?

Crumley: Now, I tried everything in the world I could do not to kill that wonderful kid off. Lanetta Jones, the perfect American woman. You know, I tried, I must have written that ending a dozen times trying to find a way to keep her from dying, but I couldn't find it. I think maybe that's why I had the rock chip get inside of her offstage, simply because I couldn't face it. Sometimes I get sentimental over characters and can't face their deaths, but you have to, what happens to her if you don't kill her? Nothing I tried worked.

Silet: Sughrue and Lanetta cannot get married and raise the child together?

Crumley: That's what I meant to happen when I first had the notion and the baby but I couldn't make it work. If it's a failure, it's my failure, but it wasn't a failure for lack of trying. You know, I have five kids, and five grandkids. I like kids. It gives me a chance to do something different now. Write a novel without a hand grenade in it. I realized the other day I'd never written a novel or a screenplay without a hand grenade in it. I don't think I'm going to turn to the psychological or psychodramas of Ross Macdonald, but I'd like to do something different.

Silet: You mentioned earlier that you have not really read much crime fiction, do you read much now, and who do you like—I know you mentioned K. C. Constantine.

Crumley: A real writer. When *The Wrong Case* came out that would have been an easy question to answer, but now there are so many good writers working on crime novels that I could make a short list of one hundred and still miss people who I like. My favorite is Nicholas Freeling and has been for a long time. But you know Steven Greenleaf and Carl Hiaasen, Charley Willeford, and Goddamn it, there are a lot of people who are working hard and doing well. Of course there's also a tremendous amount of trash out there. I didn't realize how much.

Silet: Do you find crime stories in any way limiting as fiction?

Crumley: Not to me.

Silet: What about the division between crime fiction and serious fiction?

Crumley: Nobody in France ever asked me this question. I mean most divisions are artificial, I thought they were artificial when I was a graduate student. I still think that they are artificial; good books are good books period. If you want as a critic or teacher you can certainly judge the ambitions of a book. I think that's fair, that's a fair place to begin judgment and sometimes the so-called crime novel (sounds like a novel that you've committed) can be too ambitious, ambition can be the death of a crime novel. But they can do so many things. I'm reading Jack O'Connell's new book. I'm constantly amazed at how he's getting away with what he's doing, and it's just wonderful.

Hard Talk and Mean Streets
Barbara D'Amato

Photo © Jerry Bauer

Barbara D'Amato is an award-winning playwright, novelist, and crime researcher. Her musical comedies, written with her husband Anthony, have been produced both in the United States and abroad. She has created three mystery series both under her own name and the pseudonym of Malacai Black. Currently, however, her most famous series features Chicago freelance investigative journalist, Cat Marsala, who has appeared in seven novels: *Hardball* (1990), *Hard Tack* (1991), *Hard Luck* (1992), *Hard Women* (1994), *Hardcase* (1995), *Hard Christmas* (1996) and *Hard Bargain* (1997). All have been published by Scribners.

Her true crime book *The Doctor, the Murder, the Mystery: The True Story of Dr. John Branion* (1992) was awarded the Anthony for the Best True Crime of 1992. Her research on the Branion case was also featured on the television program "Unsolved Mysteries," on which Ms. D'Amato appeared. She has served on the board of the Mystery Writers of America, is active in Sisters in Crime, and most recently chaired the True Crime Committee for the Edgar nominations. She also writes a regular column for the crime magazine *Mystery Scene* and occasionally teaches mystery writing to Chicago police officers.

Good Cop, Bad Cop was published in 1998.

Portions of this interview were published as "Hard Talk: An Interview with Barbara D'Amato," *Clues,* 17:2 (Fall/Winter 1996), 105–131 and "Barb D'Amato," *Mystery Scene,* No. 47 (May/June 1995), 26, 28, 60–64.

Silet: How did you get started writing crime fiction?

D'Amato: My husband and I had written a couple of musical comedies that played in Chicago and London. I adapted one of them into a children's musical that also played in Chicago and London. Theater, I think, is good training for pacing scenes and for ending with something that leads into the next scene. So that occupied some of that time in between when my kids were little and when I started writing fiction and finally sold a mystery. I had been writing short stories early on and just burned every one of them this last summer. They weren't good.

Silet: So at what point then did you say, "Hey, I'm going to write mysteries?"

D'Amato: It has never been that easy to answer that question. It's not an epiphany kind of thing. I'm sure it is for some people. I guess I had read all the Agatha Christies there were up till then; she was still living. And all the John Dickson Carrs. I was not a big reader of hard-boiled mystery fiction then, though I am now, and I got to a point where I wanted to try to produce a classical mystery. I thought of a locked-room mystery mechanism that had never been used, and wrote it.

Silet: What was the name of the first one?

D'Amato: The first one was *The Hands of Healing Murders.* It was a traditional locked-room murder. A Chicago physician had invited a number of people over to play bridge. His daughter was a physician too and also invited was my detective at that time, Dr. Gerritt DeGraaf. There were nine people in the room when the eight of them started to play bridge. The doctor who did not play bridge went over to read a book next to the fireplace. At some point one of the people who was dummy got up to walk around the room to stretch his legs and discovered that the doctor had been stabbed through the temple with a scalpel, a shiny-handled scalpel which took fingerprints well.

The police came to investigate the situation, and got the fingerprints off the knife. Dr. Cotton's staff, two people who worked in his house, were in the corridor outside talking and knew no one had gone in the door. The eight people playing bridge were between the windows and Dr. Cotton and yet the fingerprints on the knife were of no one who was in the room nor either of the two people out in the hall.

Silet: What was the second one you did?

D'Amato: The second one was set in a retirement community in the Southwest and the premise behind it was that a lot of the people who moved to that part of the world were going not only to escape the northern climate but also to have a place where they didn't really have to deal with a lot of the problems of urban or suburban living where they had come from. In other words, get away from the teenagers roaring around the neighborhood and children running across lawns and through the flower beds and all that kind of thing. But what happened over time, of course, was that owners would die and leave their property to their children, who in many cases moved down there with young children which enraged the others. They had assumed they had moved to a place where children weren't permitted.

And in fact there have been cases like that both in Arizona and New Mexico where communities with restrictive statutes had originally been designed for senior citizens with access up and down the curbs for wheelchairs and so forth and a number of other kinds of advantages for seniors. In many cases there was violence against people who moved in with small children. People would leave garbage on their lawns, scorpions in the mailbox, that sort of thing. And this is the climate of violence in which this book begins.

Silet: And what happens?

D'Amato: Dr. DeGraaf goes down to visit his grandmother, who was in one of these retirement communities, because he's concerned about the violence. While he's there one of the children from the community is murdered. And that sets the plot going.

Silet: The third book was?

D'Amato: *On My Honor.* That's a mystery suspense book. It was originally titled *Foulbrood.* Foulbrood is a disease that honey bees get and which interferes with the growth of the larvae to adults. They die as larvae in the hive and have to be removed. The story concerns a troop of boy scouts in the suburbs just north of Chicago that is raising a beehive in order to learn where honey comes from and learn more about insects as boy scouts do. At the same time in this community there'd been several mysterious deaths. A couple of them looked like accidents, but it becomes eventually clear that one or more of the boy scouts is actually involved. The publisher didn't like the title *Foulbrood* and changed it to *Scout's Honor,* which makes a lot of sense given the content of the book and I liked it.

They had on the cover of the book a boy scout holding a deadly looking knife behind his back. They told me just as they were about to ship books that their distributor objected because he was a boy scout, an overgrown boy scout, and wouldn't handle it. So they changed the title again to *On My Honor,* which sounds like a Mafia book to me, and changed the cover to a scout tent, or I suppose it could be anybody's tent, pitched at the foot of a steep snow-clad mountain. There are not a lot of those around Chicago. And that was the way the book was published.

Silet: What did you learn about writing from doing these three books?

D'Amato: I think I learned a lot about pacing. I had already had some experiences with theater which also taught me a lot about pacing. I really like the traditional puzzle mystery form, but at that time it simply didn't sell well and because I had become involved in the book about Dr. Branion, I was interested in how a person did research for investigative reporting. So I developed the character of Cat Marsala out of that. But I think a lot of the laying of clues which I consider to be important I learned from those early books.

Even if you're not doing a traditional puzzle mystery where the reader can figure it out, I think you at least have an obligation not to deceive a reader in the sense of unfairly including things that would not be consistent with the outcome. Not just red herrings and so forth but things that really are not appropriate, that are not what would have happened truly in the course of the events that led up to the killing.

Silet: Where did Cat Marsala come from?

D'Amato: I had been working through the period from about late '84 to '89 on a real-life murder case. There was a black doctor in South Chicago who was convicted in 1968 of killing his wife. His second wife came to my husband to ask him, twenty years later, if there was anything he could do to free the man. The man was in prison. When I first went into the case, there were no facts available except what had come out in the trial and the Illinois Supreme Court summary opinion. I thought it would be interesting to look at it. There was a strong time alibi among other things.

I got more and more into it and instead of being an article, eventually over the years it turned into a book. My research became the foundation of the habeas corpus brief, which failed. The man died recently. He was pardoned but was already ill and had only been free about a month when he died. The book became *The Doctor, The Murder, The Mystery: The True Story of Dr. John Branion.*

Silet: So it was the work on the Dr. Branion case that got you thinking about investigating. How did you get to Cat Marsala from that?

D'Amato: It wasn't that large a leap. What I was doing in researching for the case was a lot of the same kinds of things that she would go through in the story too. Finding people to interview, and once you find them getting them to actually talk about things which in some cases they would rather not. Doing the library research that gives you the background for the events. Finding a parking place in Chicago, that's a biggie. You don't quite realize until you get into this that you may spend an entire day just going down to the criminal courts building and asking them if they can find the witness list and then they say, "Go sit down," while they look and after two hours they still haven't found it and they say, "Go sit down," some more, and you go out for coffee and you come back and they still haven't found it and then you wait. Then you keep going more and more frequently to ask them if they found it because you hope that will hurry them and they say, "Don't keep bothering us." And then finally at the end of the day they say they can't find it. So you've spent an entire work day not finding out a fact which therefore does not appear in the book. This is the kind of frustration that Cat sometimes goes through. Of course there's the delight of actually finding what you're looking for too. In writing a true crime book you might have thirty such facts on one page and all of them have to be verified. And each page probably also represents another five facts that you didn't get or couldn't find or didn't exist or you were wrong about. So Cat has some of the persistence you need in order to do that kind of thing. She also likes truth, she wants it to come out, she thinks people can handle it, she doesn't think you have to protect people from the facts, you have to protect people from deceit. So she is very much an investigative reporter.

Silet: How did you get her into a book and then the book into a series? How did that develop?

D'Amato: I was interested in the question of whether our drug laws actually caused drug dependency and crime. Obviously they cause crime; whether they encourage drug dependency or not is a harder question. So I had Cat do the research. I think that probably is the way all of the books operate. I'm interested in finding out how something works. For instance, *Hard Case* is set in a trauma unit. I was really interested in seeing how a trauma unit works, how do they decide who takes which case as they come in and so forth. So it was also not that large a leap to get her involved. If she's looking into things that I'm interested in, I have fun with researching it.

Silet: When did you decide this was a series?

D'Amato: I think I had always thought it was. She's a character that works that way. One investigation after another. In fact, I had started out giving her two competing boyfriends, significant others, thinking that in the second book we would lose one and in the third book we would lose the other. I had that as a continuing situation. Things don't always work out the way you think they're going to. She's developed another peripheral character that I didn't realize was going to come in. She has a cameraman, now that she occasionally does a TV essay, a videographer that goes around with her when she does those things, who is a nice additional character.

Silet: What does having a series allow you to do as a writer?

D'Amato: You have a lot more scope. Cat also is a person who challenges herself. She tries to take on issues or stories involving things that challenge her, sometimes challenge her fears, in the case of *Hard Tack* for instance. She takes an assignment to go out on a luxury yacht on Lake Michigan. She can't swim and she's afraid of water but she assumes by and large people don't drown out there, and it's a boat with an owner who is careful. She goes along but of course she is terrified. They run into a storm the first night out. It is very scary being out of sight of land in a small boat in the middle of Lake Michigan. You begin to realize how small the boat really is. So over the course of the book, she faces a number of different fears of her own and I think grows as a result of it.

Silet: Are there things you can't do because you've got a series?

D'Amato: You certainly can't do things that would violate your earlier picture of her character. She has to develop in the way that most of us do which is consistent with what went before. She has her own history and you can't go off in some kind of strange direction. I think it's more expanding than constricting. You have such a large scope when you think of other books to come and maybe several other books to come. You can go almost anywhere with her and take on almost any issue that comes up.

Silet: Tell me about *Hard Women.*

D'Amato: In *Hard Women* Cat says she feels that she has read and heard too much about prostitution but in fact knows too little about it. And I think that's true with all of us. It's not only that we think we know about a subject, our whole view of the world is second-, third-, and fourth-hand. Most of what we think we know comes from the media. For instance, we have the impression, I think, that we're living in a tremendously dangerous society, in a tremendously dangerous period of time, and in fact it's not so. There was a very short, very slim slice of time, maybe the last forty or fifty years, that it has been significantly safe, as far as walking the streets in American cities. In most American cities in the late 1800s the crime rate was much higher.

Silet: Right.

D'Amato: And if you go back to the 1700s and the 1600s, people in Europe had to go out with an armed guard if they went out at night, and there were footpads everywhere. An unpoliced situation. I think this is another example where our whole view of things is distorted by the way the media reports things. We have so much media which has to report something that every crime is news and particularly noteworthy or bizarre crimes are overreported. They're repeated and repeated. Things that would have gone unnoticed 150 years ago today are a big deal. For instance, many, many infants were smothered 100 or 150 years ago in this country. It was the principle form of birth control. Our way of seeing the world is not accurate.

Silet: Cat's obviously involved in another investigation but how does it all come together?

D'Amato: I walk the city a lot, I like Chicago and I walk around to look at things. If you're alert to it at all you can't miss the fact that there are prostitutes out there. And they're absolutely ignored, they're forgotten people. The society pretends they're not there until every once in a while somebody gets into a snit about it and wants to move them along. There was a big campaign in Chicago in the early 1900s to close down all the brothels, which they did. They closed the red-light district and that put all the prostitutes out on the street.

Well, then, along about twenty to thirty years later there was a big uproar because all these prostitutes were out on the streets, so they were moved off the streets and then found other kinds of places, brothels and call-girl operations and such, to go to where they were not seen as much. It just cycles that way. The problem is not solved and people are not thinking about it in any constructive way. Personally, I think that we'd do better decriminalizing prostitution and trying to make sure that these women have medical attention and possibly testing for diseases and so forth, to make it safer for them and safer for the customers also.

Silet: How does Cat get involved in this?

D'Amato: Cat is assigned to do a story on it for television. The TV people had seen her earlier articles and thought that maybe she could put together a two or three minute TV essay on prostitution in Chicago. The television channel itself is triggered to do this because there's a flap on in the City Council to get the prostitutes off the streets and out of sight, which of course is just another round in that cycle.

Silet: What does she find out in the course of her investigation?

D'Amato: Well, in terms of her own interest in the business of prostitution, she discovers that there's a very rigid caste system. It runs all the way from the very top, by-referral-only-companion prostitute down through the expensive call girl operation. At the top the women are beautiful. They're on the gold coast. You would never know it, looking on the outside, that there was prostitution going on. There are wonderful old buildings and beautiful architecture and gorgeous women. The less expensive call girls are in brothels, and then there are the girls who work bars. Of course there are more expensive bars and less expensive bars. And finally the actual streetwalkers and the very cheap streetwalkers who are obviously in one of the most dangerous businesses in the world.

Silet: Does Cat's perspective change in the process of researching this?

D'Amato: She becomes much more sympathetic. Like all of us she starts out thinking that these people are doing something very nasty and very unpleasant and it's disgusting. She comes to have a lot of sympathy for them. It's not that she wishes that they would go on doing it. If the society were different and the women had a little longer term view of their lives they could find other ways of earning a living. One of the things that's common to prostitutes, and in the course of doing this I did talk to several, is that they have a very short horizon. They do well to see through next week. So it's not surprising that they don't realize that they're in a business where their desirable professional life is only a matter of a few years. And it's not surprising that they, because of this short horizon, are willing to take this kind of risk.

Silet: Is part of it because some of them are addicted to drugs?

D'Amato: Well, many of the white hookers are addicts, not so many of the black hookers are. I think that shows you the economic pressures that cause a lot of it. But then a lot of them have gotten hooked because of factors that also lead to their prostitution, so it's not quite clear where the cause and effect are. I'm sure that it does have something to do with their very early life.

Silet: I know you do research for your books and you mentioned talking to a couple of prostitutes, but what else did you do, other kinds of research?

D'Amato: I talked to some vice cops and also I frequently go and ride around with cop friends of mine. I was out one night with some tactical team members who knew that I was researching hookers for books. They arrested a couple in order to introduce them to me. I actually felt very guilty about that, because here were these people who really would probably not have been arrested if I hadn't been in the car. After all, the Chicago police department has more important things to do than pick up women on street corners. But it did give me an idea how they feel about things. It was an educational experience. The cops didn't tell them that I was doing an article or anything.

I was just sitting in the back seat when they picked up this hooker and they stuck her in the back seat with me. Apparently she didn't think I was a hooker because I'm too chronologically challenged, you know. I assume she would have thought I was a cop or some kind of supervisor. I said, you know it's dangerous being out here like this. Yes, she knows, but what else could she do, she had two children at home. It was also interesting to me to learn if the cops find that there are children at home unattended, they will not lock the hooker up; they will figure out some way to get a relative in the house before they do that.

Silet: It's nice to know that there's compassion in the Chicago police department.

D'Amato: Yeah, I definitely have that feeling. In fact, the two cops I was with, one of them female, riding around that night, could see that the prostitute was coming down from some kind of high. They kept asking if she'd like a little coffee or would she like to lie down. I don't think they were doing that for me because I know these people and they know that I'm not a reporter. They're not dressing it up because I'm there. It's just that they face so many extremely vicious, really violent crimes that this doesn't appear dangerous to them. And it isn't.

Silet: Let's talk about *Hard Case.*

D'Amato: That book developed because I realized that, of the level-one trauma units in Chicago, fifty percent have folded in the last five or six years. Hospitals can't afford them and with health care reform coming up this is an issue. I was particularly interested in it because a citizen who is in a catastrophic automobile accident needs a trauma unit nearby. If you are seriously injured, either in a crime or an automobile accident or airline disaster or whatever it might be, construction accident, the best place for you to be is in a level-one trauma unit where they have all the equipment. You can take a person who has been essentially reduced to hamburger and get him onto life support, stop the dying process and start putting the pieces back together in a trauma unit and really nowhere else.

So the loss of these is a loss for everyone. Anyone in Chicago can be in an accident. It's not a question of whether you're rich or poor, it's a question whether they're close enough to help you. So I wanted to see what one looked like and then I also wanted to answer the question, "What kinds of doctors go into trauma work. Of all the things a physician can do after he or she graduates from school, why would he want this particular specialty?"

You never really get to see your patients after they leave the trauma unit and either go to the funeral parlor or to recovery. You are constantly faced with life-threatening crises where you have to make a number of decisions, some of which may be wrong, and you have to make them fast, and you may have more cases coming in at times than you can really easily handle. Although patients usually go on to other places if there are too many. But in a major disaster there are only a certain number of places that can handle them, and you'll have to take them.

So I was interested in what different types of physicians go into that line of work. All of them have different reasons. They're different kinds of people, but they all do it for reasons that seem good to them.

Silet: I guess it reminded me the most perhaps of *Hard Tack* because you've got a contained environment. Tell me about what you do with a mystery set in the hospital like this?

D'Amato: Yes, it's very limited. The trauma unit in this case is a state of the art rotunda shape where the people at the central desk can keep an eye on all the patients and all the different treatment phases. The murder takes place in a staff lounge, which is accessible only to staff so that you know that it's either one of doctors, one of the nurses, or one of the other regular personnel who must have killed the trauma unit director. Dr. Grant, who was very kind to Cat at the outset, gets her into the unit and tells her what to do and what not to do and so forth, is found dead the first day that Cat's there.

Silet: Found dead in a locked-room environment with virtually no clues.

D'Amato: I had fun with leaving about five or six clues around the body, a spilled cup of coffee, a quarter, a clipboard and so forth. Each of which is readily acknowledged by whomever it belongs to and turns out to be no clue at all. It's poking a little fun at the mysteries where everything that is in the vicinity of this body has some importance. In the course of investigating the crime Cat finds each clue evaporating at the moment she asks about it.

Silet: Cat is a reporter and therefore an observer. But she's also always caught in the middle. Why is she always caught in the middle?

D'Amato: For conflict. Her position in the hospital is very much like mine when I do the research. They tell you when you go into one of those units, do not talk to the patients, don't write down the names of any patients, don't get in the way of course, and don't touch any of the equipment. So this is utterly realistic. She's pressing her back up against the wall very much as I was in some of those situations. She gets in the middle in most cases because she cares about someone who is involved. She felt she owed Dr. Grant a great deal for letting her come in the first place.

It's not all that easy to get into these places, as I know from having tried. Cat felt Grant was a valuable person who should not have been killed. And Cat also, in this particular case, feels that because she was on the inside and the police detectives were not, she is aware of some of the ways things are done, the motion of people through the unit, that the police really don't give adequate weight to.

Silet: Almost all your books deal with a particular social issue, gambling, prostitution, the medical profession. Is the crime novel a particularly good vehicle for social comment, do you think?

D'Amato: Yes, partly because controversial social issues generate violence. And I think even if you were writing something you didn't call a crime novel, if you were doing a novel dealing with something as controversial as drug policy or prostitution, you'd probably either have some violence to report on or to point up the conflict that was there. If you were writing, say, a mainstream fiction set in the same situation, you would probably generate an element of violence or murder.

Silet: What attracts you to issues?

D'Amato: Well, from Cat's point of view, the kinds of cases that she likes to do are ones that involve issues society is ambivalent about. For instance, in the first book she's investigating an organization that is interested in decriminalizing drugs and treating drug addiction as a medical problem. In the second one, she's asking questions about class and wealth. And in the third one, *Hard Luck*, she's interested in questions of the lottery, and then in the fourth one, *Hard Women*, she's investigating prostitution.

Most of us are opposed to people using illegal drugs and damaging their lives and yet we live in the most medicated society that the world has ever known. Similarly, most of us are opposed to people spending their hard-earned money on gambling. And yet most Americans now live in lottery-legal states, and you can say the same thing about prostitution, we're all opposed to it, but where are all the customers coming from? And with the second book, *Hard Tack*, most of us have a very deep ambivalence about wealth; we'd like to have it but we don't like the people who do have it. We assume that if we were rich we would be good people. But we think the ones who do have money probably either are dishonest or unusually lucky or something.

Silet: What does it say about our culture, our society?

D'Amato: I actually think that people are all much more alike than they are different and that people through the ages have been much more alike than different. From Cat's point of view as an investigator, she thinks that in areas where people are ambivalent, if she asks them a lot of questions, they will come to reveal a lot about themselves.

Silet: What is *Hard Christmas* about?

D'Amato: Cat is sent to do a piece on how Christmas trees are raised and marketed because one of the editors who uses her work is totally sick of articles leading up to Christmas on either how to wrap the perfect present or how to bake a good fruit cake and so forth. When she actually arrives at a Christmas tree farm in western Michigan, she finds there are other issues involved, including the fact that many of these family farms are being taxed out of existence and, in many cases also, once they are out of existence what results is the destruction of the farmland permanently. It's used for commercial purposes.

Silet: And how is the plot going to thicken?

D'Amato: I'm trying to figure exactly how this works. Shortly after she arrives she hears about the apparently accidental death of the grandfather of the family, a Dutch family located in the Dutch section of Western Michigan just north of Holland. It's apparently an accidental death. One of the family members suspects that it may not have been. During the night after Cat's first full day there watching them harvest the trees, one of the farm workers is discovered dead; he's been put through a Christmas tree bailer. It thickens.

Silet: Where do you see yourself going in the future with your writing?

D'Amato: I have a couple of cop novels I'm working on set in Chicago. It's a milieu I'm really interested in right now and I don't know about after that.

Silet: Do you want to talk a little bit about the police books?

D'Amato: Well, I don't know quite what to say. I like the police environment, partly because I love researching it. I love riding around with cops. I think they tell the best stories; they know things about the city you would never hear about otherwise. It's never dull. And things happen that you could never have made up, people do the most ridiculous things. If you were to make something up, you'd make up something that was a little more organized, but people will do just absolutely absurd things. So you have a background of an extremely varied city doing a wide range of things from nutty to vicious. And a group of people who are trying to deal with it. I think it's an interesting group to write about. I'm just finishing one and the other one is sort of half-drafted but cooling off right now.

Silet: Is this going to be another series do you think?

D'Amato: The books concern the same two cops. As a matter of fact they have appeared in several of my short stories. Their names are Suzanna Maria Figurora and Norm Bennis and they've also been in *Sisters in Crime IV*, the first cat crimes anthology, *Partners in Crime*, and *Deadly Allies 2*.

Silet: So now they're going to come together?

D'Amato: Yes, now they're going to have their own novel.

The Bone Collector
Jeffery Deaver

Photo © Blaise Hayward

Jeffery Deaver grew up in Suburban Chicago, the son of an advertising copywriter and an artist. After studying journalism at the University of Missouri and while serving a stint as a song-writer/folk singer, he began editing (mostly art magazines) and moved to New York. He fell in love with the city, its culture and pace, but the rents were high and the living expensive. Law school seemed a way to provide a better income, and after graduating in the top of his class with a place on the law review, he went to work for a large Manhattan firm, which doubled his income overnight. Unfortunately, as he confesses, he lacked any real talent for the practice of the law. After the one court case he handled, he felt sorry enough for the plaintiff that he actually thought about loaning the man money. Besides, the urge to write which had prompted him to study journalism and earn a living as an editor, now resurfaced as a desire to write fiction.

His first attempts were unsatisfactory, but after a period of self re-education, in short order he published three books featuring Rune, a street-wise female amateur investigator. However, in a desire to extend his career and to escape the limitations of a series, Deaver began working on longer, bigger books. And with the larger format, one-off thriller he hit pay dirt. The scope of the novels gave him more room to explore the psychology of his characters and to exploit his skills as a researcher.

By the time he published *The Lesson of Her Death* (1993) he had developed a mature style and a firm grasp of the genre, and with each succeeding novel his readership has grown. Recently, a film version of his hostage novel about a bus-load of deaf children, *The Maiden's Grave*, which starred Marlee Matlin and James Garner, was broadcast on HBO. *The Bone Collector* has been sold to the movies, and with this increased exposure Jeffery Deaver is emerging as one of today's most popular and bankable writers. *The Coffin Dancer* (1998) is his latest novel.

Portions of this interview appeared as "The Bone Collector: An Interview with Jeffery Deaver," *The Armchair Detective*, 30:2 (Spring 1997), 142–146.

Silet: When did you start writing?

Deaver: Actually I started my first thriller when I was about eleven. My parents had a very liberal censorship rule: Though there were certain movies I couldn't see, I could read anything I could get my hands on. Of course in the Midwest in the late 1950s and early 1960s, especially in conservative DuPage County, I couldn't find any of the really good stuff. I wasn't reading Henry Miller at that age. But I had a steady diet of adult thrillers—James Bond, Mickey Spillane, Cold War political thrillers, the Travis Magee books, Agatha Christie, Sherlock Holmes, the Doc Savage adventures. I also read a lot of science fiction—Edgar Rice Burroughs, H. G. Wells and Jules Verne.

Silet: Two of your early books, *Shallow Graves* and *Bloody River Blues*, you wrote under a pseudonym, William Jefferies. In writing these books did your writing finally come together?

Deaver: I'll tell you how those books happened. But I have to back up. Those aren't my first two books. My first novel was the proverbial book from hell. A novel called *Voodoo*. It was a supernatural horror story, a paperback original, published by a small company called Paperjacks. I liked the theme of *Voodoo*—ancient religion conflicting with modern science. All sorts of eerie things going on in Manhattan. Fun to research, fun to write. This, by the way, was after those two thrillers I'd written and discarded. So I felt I'd learned at least *something* about writing novels.

After that came an art-thief caper—*Always a Thief.* Then I switched to Bantam and did my first carefully constructed, plot-driven thrillers. It was a three-book series featuring a young woman amateur PI named Rune. First was *Manhattan Is My Beat,* which was an Edgar nominee. Then *Death of a Blue Movie Star. Hard News* was the third. Rune was a young, irrepressible heroine—a "Downtown diva," whom some readers loved and some didn't. But the value of the books for me was the plotting. It was there that I developed the plot twists, the multiple points of view, the characters whom we think are certain people but turn out to be entirely different. I learned how to seed clues in, to pace the books, to end scenes on high moments, to write in a very cinematic way, to add a bit of low-key humor while not sacrificing credibility.

This brings me back to the William Jefferies books —which were written at the same time as the Rune books. They are grittier but still feature the twists and turns, the surprises, the careful plotting. I wrote under a pseudonym merely as a legal technicality. Under my contract with Bantam I couldn't publish books with another company under the Deaver name. In my energetic youth back then I was writing two books a year, so I sold the Jefferies books to another company. They, by the way, feature a continuing character, John Pellam, a location scout for a film company and a private eye. *Shane*—George Stevens' classic western—was my inspiration for those stories. A stranger comes to town.

After those books, I started writing stand-alone thrillers. In the publishing business these are called "big books," though no one really seems to know exactly what a big book is. As the Supreme Court said about pornography: You know it when you see it. They featured multiple points of view, more in-depth character development, more subplots, more stylistic variations than my series books. After *Hard News* came *Mistress of Justice,* my only legal thriller. Then *The Lesson of Her Death, Praying for Sleep, A Maiden's Grave. The Bone Collector* was published in 1997. My latest is *The Coffin Dancer.*

Silet: Publishers like series. Was it hard to move on to writing something more adventuresome after you had two series going?

Deaver: It wasn't hard for me creatively; I had more freedom with the stand-alones. (And I'm sure it wasn't hard for the publishers, since sales weren't so hot!) I got the most resistance from the readers who fell in love with the characters. At Bouchercon or a signing, people'd come up and say, "I *love* Rune. When're we going to see her again?"

As it's turned out I'm bringing back my protagonist and some other characters from *The Bone Collector* in one of the books I'm writing at the moment. After I sold the book to Universal Pictures and submitted it to my publisher, my agent and I were inundated with positive responses about my character and I agreed to try another book featuring him. It's a bit of a gamble but I enjoy writing about this man and if the readers enjoy him too—well, that's what this business is all about.

Silet: In the *Lesson of Her Death* you seemed to arrive at the cluster of themes and character types that you have pursued in the books ever since. What attracted you to that book?

Deaver: *The Lesson of Her Death* is about the murder of a student in a college town. It appeared she was raped and then murdered. The sheriff, my hero, is a solid, meat-and-potatoes kind of law-enforcer. The city, the college, the state, other law enforcement agencies— and the killer himself of course—are trying to stop him from doing his job, all for reasons of their own, developed in several subplots. Now, it turns out that his only ally, though he doesn't know it till the end of the book, is his 12-year-old daughter, who suffers from severe dyslexia. Because of this condition she appears stupid and no one takes her seriously—including, at first, her father—but in fact it's this very problem that gives her the creative spark to make the connection to identify the killer. I found the psychological implications of this as fascinating to me as all the scary twists and turns in the book.

Silet: The book that has probably attracted the most attention was *A Maiden's Grave*, because it was made into an HBO movie. What was the experience like, seeing your book filmed?

Deaver: I've heard horror stories about Hollywood and I've certainly had my successes and failures with the movie business. But on the whole I've had good experiences—mostly because I don't expect anything. I've been optioning books for years now. I learned early that everyone is excited by your book, everyone has great plans for it, it's definitely going to get made and Clint Eastwood or Harrison Ford is definitely going to star in it. And nothing happens—except your option check clears. Usually.

To give you an example of how the business works, let me tell you about *Manhattan Is My Beat.* It's been optioned on and off for years and never been made. Well, a few years ago an independent producer came to me and wanted to option it and my agent and I met with him. The story's about Rune, my 19-year-old white *Melrose Place*-kind of heroine. She works in a video store. Her friend, an elderly customer, is murdered after he rents an old movie a number of times, and Rune gets it into her head that he was killed because of something in the film. Okay? Now, during this meeting the producer and his wannabe director said, Jeff, we love the book, only we're thinking of changing it. The heroine's going to be an elderly black woman living in Harlem. Her "boyfriend," an elderly black gentleman, is murdered by crack dealers while they're watching a movie on TV and she solves the crime. Fine story, I said. Only it's not *my* story. Why do you want to pay for my book? The answer: We love the title and some of your characters' lines are priceless.

Hollywood…as long as you keep a sense of humor about it, you'll do fine.

Making *A Maiden's Grave* into a film was a long process. The property went through several film companies—look at the opening credits of a film sometime; who knows *which* company is actually making the film? All those corporate names…. Then I heard HBO wanted to do it, then that Dan Petrie Jr., a very talented director, was attached. Then James Garner signed on as Arthur Potter, my hostage-negotiating hero, and Marlee Matlin as my deaf-hostage heroine. Next thing I know I get the buy-out check. Which means that they'd exercised the option.

But you have to remember that books and films are different experiences. They may pull the same strings, but they use different mechanisms to pull them. You need to keep telling yourself that what the credit line says has to be taken literally: "Based on the book by..." It's not your book; it's an interpretation of your book.

Silet: So you really didn't have much input into the film?

Deaver: No. Generally in America we don't have what the French call the *droit d'auteur*—a basic right in the property you create that gives you a cause of action if someone you've licensed the book to botches the job of adapting it. Here, unless you're one of a handful of superstar authors, you have no bargaining power and if you decide to sell your book, you take your chances. The film of *A Maiden's Grave*, for instance, was renamed *Dead Silence*. I thought it was a bad decision—for me and for the film company—but the company had an absolute right to do that.

Silet: I understand you went to Toronto to watch a bit of the shooting.

Deaver: I had a great time. I'd expected to be a bit of an untouch-able—oh-oh, writer on the set, hit the decks—but everyone, from the director and stars to caterer, was nice as could be. I've written a number of scripts and studied films for years; I know it's essentially a very meticulous, often tedious process. But it's still magic.

Oddly, the best advice I've ever heard for writers—advice I'd tried to keep in mind—was from a filmmaker. Ingmar Bergman said that he had three inviolable rules for making films: "Entertain your audience, never compromise your vision, make every movie as if it were your last."

Silet: Have you seen the film?

Deaver: Yes. I enjoyed it. I thought it was very well done. But an interesting thing happened. They used a lot of my dialog, so I'd be hearing what I wrote and have a certain expectation about where the story was going only to find that it changed direction in a very different way. It didn't bother me, but it was disorienting.

The acting was great—James Garner, Marlee Matlin, Lolita Davidovich.... Oh, and Kim Coates—he made a very scary bad guy.

The only thing I would like to have seen more of was Matlin's character's relationship with the deaf children. Much of my book is about Melanie—my schoolteacher protagonist—trying to save the children, both despite of and with the help of her deafness. But in an hour and three-quarters movie, that had to go. And, if I'd been making the film, I would have cut it too. It was too internal to translate well to the screen.

Silet: A number of the reviews of *A Maiden's Grave* mentioned the hostage situation at Waco, which the government bungled. Was that situation in the back of your mind when you wrote it?

Deaver: Well, I can't say it wasn't in the back of my mind, and I used much of the information about Waco when I researched the book. But actually I had come up with the idea for the book before Waco—though after Ruby Ridge, the Randy Weaver standoff a few years ago out West.

I like to be able to summarize the concept of a novel in one or two sentences. In *A Maiden's Grave* I wanted to write a thriller in which there were two main characters—one who communicates through the spoken word for a living: a hostage negotiator. And one who can't communicate through traditional means—Melanie, a deaf teacher. I wanted to put them together in a life-and-death situation and see how each of them worked—by themselves and together—to survive and help others survive.

With that idea in mind, I worked backward and tried to create the absolutely scariest story I could. I added deaf students as hostages, I had them kept hostage in an old slaughterhouse, I created three utterly remorseless villains. It was all very constructed.

So real-life hostage situations, while important for research, had very little to do with my story.

Silet: You introduce a technique you've used extensively since, especially in *The Bone Collector*, namely to have a lot of the communications done on the phone.

Deaver: Part of that in *A Maiden's Grave* was necessity. My negotiator was talking to the chief hostage-taker via what the cops call a throw-phone. In *The Bone Collector*, my hero's a quadriplegic and has to communicate with his assistant, a policewoman, over the radio.

But apart from the practical necessities of the story the technique lets me exploit my love of dialog. I enjoy writing dialog. It gives authors a chance to reveal a great deal about their characters without explaining about them. It lets you work in a little humor and pathos and move the story along very quickly. I love patois and dialect and local expressions.

Silet: You mentioned *Praying for Sleep* was the novel, in publishing terms, that really broke you out. Why do you think that was?

Deaver: One of the things I found most appealing about that book was its central character. I have other protagonists as well but he's the character that sets the story in motion and keeps it going. Michael Hrubek is a paranoid schizophrenic who escapes from a mental institution, where he's been incarcerated for murder, to track down the woman who was the chief witness against him at his trial. The book follows his harrowing journey to get to her house. I worked very hard to make him believable and to have him shatter everyone's expectations about him and about the crime he was arrested for—the characters' expectations in the book, as well as the readers'. And readers have responded very well to him.

Silet: Let's talk about *The Bone Collector*. I see all the hallmarks of your writing in this book: the long-distance communications, the hostage situation, a love affair between two impaired characters, a compressed time frame.

Deaver: *The Bone Collector* features a quadriplegic hero, Lincoln Rhyme, a former detective who used to head the New York Police Department's forensic division. He literally wrote the textbook on criminalistics—crime scene science. He's depressed, bored with life and awaiting a Dr. Kevorkian character to help him kill himself, when into his life comes his old partner, who needs his help. A serial kidnapper is planting clues to the whereabouts of his victims and only Rhyme, it seems, will be able to figure out what the clues mean. Rhyme happens to enlist the aid of a patrol officer,

Amelia Sachs, who is just about to quit the force. She's very disillusioned with life as a cop because of a recent personal tragedy. Rhyme has to use his forensic skills and Sachs her innate policewoman abilities together to find the victims as these hourly deadlines approach and the innocent are about to die.

I had great fun with this book—all the forensics and the clues. I even include evidence charts so readers can figure out who the bad guy is and what he's up to.

Silet: You also have lots of interesting information on old New York.

Deaver: My bad guy is someone who's modeled his activity on a fictional serial killer from the turn of the century. I loved researching that aspect of the book, and many of the clues Rhyme must decipher relate to historical New York. There's so much history in the city, good and bad.

Silet: You must have enjoyed doing the research on forensics, because there is an enormous amount of material on the subject in the book.

Deaver: I've worked with the NYPD and the FBI; both of those organizations were very helpful. I also do a lot of cruising on the forensics web sites. My desk at home is littered with crime scene manuals. I often go out to lunch or dinner and take work with me—but for *The Bone Collector* I had to think ahead. I don't think fellow diners would appreciate my studying graphic autopsy photos at Denny's.

One thing about criminalistics that impressed me is how sophisticated are the mechanisms for tracking down the bad guys in this country. Certainly at the FBI and large city police departments. But in the small towns too. Criminalistics can be magic in a way, and I've tried to present a certain sense of that magic through the eyes of my character, Lincoln Rhyme.

Silet: You obviously like to do research but you don't bog down the narrative with it. The reader gets the information but is hardly aware of it because it is so carefully integrated with the story.

Deaver: Every forensics fact in the book has a payoff. It's not gratuitous. It may be a red herring, meant to lead readers (and my characters) off the scent. But nothing's thrown in just for the sake of inclusion. Oh, I may have to spend just a few sentences describing a particular forensic procedure, but even that isn't usually necessary. Readers are real smart; they'll figure out what's going on.

Silet: At times your books are quite graphically violent. Tell me about the motif of violence.

Deaver: People have sometimes complained about the violence in my books. I have two thoughts about that: First, come on, folks, these are thrillers. They're about crime and people in extreme situations. There has to be a credible risk to someone; otherwise, where's the thrill?

But second, I'm aware that my essential job is to give readers an enjoyable, if harrowing, experience and if I start to alienate them, if I make them feel uneasy with what I'm describing, it's not my villain they're going to be angry with. It's me. And I'll have failed in my job. I'll add as much violence, as many scary situations, as possible, stopping only at the point where I think readers are going to get turned off and stop reading. I have no theoretical problem endangering anyone—in *A Maiden's Grave* eight deaf children are held hostage by a trio of killers—but I'll look at the situation carefully and try to figure out if I've stepped over the line.

I should say, too, that much of the violence in the books is off-camera. I'm a believer in letting the readers' imagination supply the graphic details. It's also very tough to write a fresh and believable passage describing a murder or gunfight.

Silet: There is a resonance in your books of social issues. Is crime fiction particularly suited to deal with such themes?

Deaver: That's a very good way of putting it, resonance. I don't want to "present" an opinion on social issues. I'm not an authority on most of them anyway. But having my characters affected by such issues (like Rhyme's deciding whether or not to kill himself,

Michael Hrubek's release from a mental hospital because of budget cut-backs) I've added another dimension to them—in a very concrete, immediate way. I hope this helps readers understand and empathize with them better than they might otherwise.

And, yes, crime fiction is particularly suited to larger themes—because it involves extremes and passions, and people often feel strongly, passionately, about certain issues; people are willing to take risks to be involved in them.

Silet: What's your next project?

Deaver: I always work on two books at once. One is a stand-alone book, which happens to be very exciting to me, but I'd rather not talk about now except to say it's a psychological thriller. And as I mentioned, I'm doing a second Lincoln Rhyme book. I've been quite surprised at how people have responded to this man. It's a bit of a challenge, given the obvious limitations of doing a series with a character who can't move.

Silet: Have you ever finished an interview, and there was something you've always wanted to be asked but never were?

Deaver: Yes. The ISBN number and ordering information for all my books.

The Bookman's Eye
John Dunning

Photo © Katie Dunning

The extraordinary success of his first Cliff Janeway novel, *Booked to Die* (1992), reintroduced mystery readers to John Dunning whose earlier paperback originals, *Looking for Ginger North* (1980) and *Deadline* (1981), were both nominated for Edgars. His second Janeway novel, *The Bookman's Wake*, simply confirmed his reputation as one of the finest writers working in the crime field.

At one time or another in his life John Dunning has been a bookdealer and owner of Old Algonquin Books, worked as a newspaper reporter on *The Denver Post*, and served as a racehorse hot-walker. An authority on old-time radio and author of one of the standard references in the field, *Tune in Yesterday*, he also hosted a Sunday afternoon radio show that played the best of the classic dramas and comedies. *On the Air*, a revised and vastly enlarged edition of his standard radio reference work was published by Oxford University Press in 1998.

Portions of this interview appeared as "The Bookman's Eye," *The Armchair Detective*, 28:2 (Spring 1995), 124–133.

Silet: Tell me something about your background, your family, your schooling, that sort of thing.

Dunning: I was born in Brooklyn in 1942, January 9th. My dad was from Charleston, South Carolina and he took us back there in 1945. I was raised in Charleston, which is steeped in history and romance. Education—not much to be made of that. I was a tenth-grade dropout. I did get a GED, which is going to be a historical document some day because it's from the state of South Carolina and it says that the holder of this is guaranteed by the State of South Carolina to be equivalent to the average *white* twelfth-grade graduate. A great admission by the state how fraudulent those old "separate-but-equal" racial policies in the South really were. I did do some college-level classes, but I found college difficult to get interested in. I bummed around and had a lot of odd jobs. I was a glass cutter in shops in South Carolina and did a little bit of that out here in Denver. I came out here in 1964 with some friends, just to get away from Charleston, because everybody has to get away from where they grew up.

Silet: What did you do in Colorado?

Dunning: I became a racetracker and followed the horses around for a couple of years. It was a great time in my life. I'm one of those writers who was really influenced by reading. When I was a kid I got into the *Black Stallion* books and nothing would do after that but I had to have a fling on the racetracks and Denver was the first town I'd settled in that had a racetrack. This was just before the race meet in 1964. At that time, you could walk in cold and get a job just like that. The job paid $50 a week and a place to sleep in the tack room. But it was wonderful because everybody slept in the tack rooms, and there was great camaraderie. I'd give a lot to find out where those guys are now.

We bunked together and chased women and all that kind of stuff. I did that for a couple of years. I went out to California to work at Santa Anita, Bay Meadows, Golden Gate Fields, and the county fair circuit. The old man I worked for had a ranch in Idaho, and we went up there to work for a while. The thrill of it just wore off after a while. We worked seven days a week at the racetrack. Those horses have to be walked, have to be fed—the stalls have to be mucked out—somebody has to be there.

Silet: How did you begin writing?

Dunning: I remember something Burl Ives once said when an interviewer asked him when he began singing. He said, "There wasn't any beginning," and that's how I've always felt about writing. Even when I was a kid I told stories and tried to write them down. I began getting published in the 1960s. I remember Christmas at Santa Anita in '65. The only way you knew it was Christmas was somebody four or five rows down was playing Christmas music on the radio. It was just like any other day at the track and after a while I thought, "What else do I want to be?" I always figured that I would write for a living some day and so I just started up the ladder from the lowest rung at a newspaper. In every town I went through I stopped at the newspaper and of course having no degree, not even a high school diploma, I did not have the greatest qualifications.

Every year I came through Denver. At *The Denver Post* I got to be known by the guy who hires and because I was persistent, he finally gave me a job in the *Post* library filing pictures. I did that for about a year and then I started writing some stuff. The hardest part of any job is getting it, and I went around and made friends with all the editors and started writing for their different departments. I wrote a few articles here and there. Then I began writing book reviews, and I did thirty or forty and got them published. I think I shamed them into hiring me; they really didn't want me. The managing editor was a hard-bitten guy named John Rogers who told me in very explicit terms how little chance I had of making it there. The filing cabinets were full of applications from prize-winning journalists from back East who had worked on papers like *The Wall Street Journal* and *The New York Times* and they all wanted to come out to Colorado to get out of the rat race. But they had a program there called the "Twenty-twenty," where you could spend twenty hours a week as an entry-level reporter and twenty hours as a copy boy. At twenty-six, I was the oldest copy boy on the paper, and I had to take a cut in pay to do that. Not that the work in the library paid much; I was only making about $65 a week anyway. The first story I did I caught a judge fixing a ticket, and they headlined that across page two of the paper.

I was very energetic and I knew I had a lot of ground to make up so I was "turned on" all the time. If somebody called me at midnight, which they did a few times, and said, "There's a hijacked plane coming into Stapleton Airport, can you get out there?" I was already half dressed. I spent much of the time that I'd set aside to work on fiction writing journalism. I'd get up at 4:00 A.M. and polish stories that I knew were going to be changed for the deadline, but it was fun. I did that for about three years, and did pretty well. I became their investigative reporter in a short time. They had a three-man investigative team they put me on. Two were what they called "seasoned reporters," and I was the third one. It was really a great honor. We didn't break any wonderful stories. In fact, most of the pieces we did do they killed because the stories tended to offend some of the people who advertised in the paper.

Silet: How did you get started in fiction?

Dunning: I quit the paper in April of 1970 to write and during the next two years I managed to turn out a novel that was probably incomprehensible. The last time I looked, it had about 300 characters, was 450 pages long, and it was going in all directions.

Silet: Was this *Denver?*

Dunning: No, this was a novel that I never finished, but it was like *Denver.* It was a big, sprawling mainstream book with lots of characters. It was based on a true incident that I would still like to resurrect someday.

Silet: When did you publish your first novel?

Dunning: My first novel was published in 1974. It was called *The Holland Suggestions*, and was one of Barbara Norville's "Black Bat Mysteries," at Bobbs-Merrill. Just about that same time I published my first old-time radio encyclopedia at Prentice Hall in 1975 or 1976 and I quit the *Post* again. My wife had been working solidly all this time, and I kept thinking that sooner or later I was going to make a living writing but that just never happened. I went through some really long dry spells. My second novel was rejected by Barbara, and it took me twenty, twenty-two publishers to sell it.

Silet: Was this *Looking for Ginger North?*

Dunning: Yes, thank God for a persistent agent. Phyllis Westberg is my agent, always has been. She kept that book going. The original title of that book was *Bloodline*, and it went around so long that Sidney Sheldon used my title. After it sold I had to change the name. They decided to call it *Looking for Ginger North*. I said, "That sounds a lot like *Looking for Mr. Goodbar*." They didn't seem to mind that, everything is derivative. But Phyllis kept that book going. It's funny because I really had given up on it at that time. I got so many rejection letters saying, "This is just such a neat little mystery, but it has no big book potential." I decided to give them one that did have big potential, so I wrote *Denver* which was large.

It had fifty characters and a big, sprawling mainstream background. The Ku Klux Klan really did take over much of the state government of Colorado and several other states too in the 1920s. I started that around and when I started getting rejected, I thought, "Jeez, it doesn't matter what you do." What I didn't seem to *know* then is that most successful fiction is bought and sold on the name value of the author, and I had none. But we did sell *Looking for Ginger North*, and it became an Edgar finalist. I lost the Edgar by one vote but I got a scroll for it. I thought, "Well, maybe it didn't matter that it was rejected twenty-two times." I still haven't reread it. It's really hard for me to reread my own stuff.

My new publisher was looking for something along similar lines, and so I wrote a novel called *Deadline*, which was the easiest thing that I ever wrote. I had just sent *Denver* to Phyllis and I was full of nervous energy and post partum blues, and so I started to outline one morning and I pulled together a cast of characters and an idea. Forty-two days later I had a book. I've never come close to repeating that before or since. I sent it off and Phyllis sold it right out of the typewriter, so I had several books there right in a row. In fact, *Looking for Ginger North* and *Denver* came out, I think, the same month—in the winter or spring of 1980—from two separate publishers. New York Times Books published *Denver* in hardback, and Gold Medal published *Ginger North* and *Deadline* in paperback. *Deadline* subsequently went to England in a hardback, but originally it was only paper in this country. I thought I was going great again, but then I sunk into another one of those times when I couldn't seem to give anything away. I went four or five years without a nibble, and it was like we were really star-crossed. It didn't look like I was ever going to sell anything again.

Silet: Were you writing all this time?

Dunning: Oh, yeah. There's a shaggy dog story I could tell you about the aftermath of *Denver*. Times Books gave me a contract on another novel, a 1200 page historical novel, which I subsequently did complete. Everything that could possibly go wrong with a book deal went wrong with that one. It's still sitting here. It's been under contract twice and another publisher was about to give me a fairly substantial contract for it, but that deal fell apart too. That's one of those publishing stories from hell. There are many of those. I read about them all the time. I spent three or four years not selling books and finally decided to get into the used and rare book business. My wife and I had been talking about doing this for several years. So we opened the Old Algonquin Bookstore on East Colfax Avenue in June of 1984. We were there ten years and I've got to tell you it's the greatest business that you could imagine. I'd still be there, if I hadn't started writing again.

Silet: How did you get back to your fiction?

Dunning: I had been in the bookstore for about six years when my writer friends started pushing me to start up again. There was a group of fifteen or twenty poor young writers here in Colorado who met regularly, and only Clive Cussler hit it big. The rest of us were picking up peanuts, but my friends would say, "When are you going to write that book? When are you going to get back?" And I'd say, "Oh, I'm really comfortable in my failure." You have no idea how pain free my life was since I'd stopped writing. But in reality it's not like that, there's kind of an empty spot in your heart. If you're a writer who's not writing, you can't ever fill that up. Warwick Downing, who is one of my mystery-writing friends, has written a number of books and he kept bugging me, "Why don't you write a book about a bookstore, write a mystery about a bookstore." Every time we'd have lunch together he'd start on that. I thought, "Well, why not, why don't I do that?" It took me about a year of digging at it before I saw what the story was and once I figured it out, it wrote itself in about four or five months. That was *Booked to Die.*

Silet: Did it sell right away?

Dunning: I sent it off to Phyllis and she started it around and it took her a year to sell it. I think three or four houses turned it down. I got really frustrated. She used to send me rejection letters, but I told her I didn't want to see any of those things because I just get too depressed. I told her, "Just tell me when they want to buy it." After a year I called her up and said, "What is going on? I can't understand why they don't buy this book. I can't write a better book than this, I just don't know how to do it." And she said, "I don't know either. It's the book stuff, that's the feedback I'm getting. They're afraid of the book stuff." Publishers kept saying, "Well, gee, we never read a bookstore mystery that has this much book stuff in it, it's really pretty heavy. We find it interesting because we're in the trade, but we're afraid that the average person won't really care about your bookstore and how you find books and scout around and this kind of thing." And I thought, that's the kind of stuff they're going to love. And I told Phyllis at the time, "You just wait, if this book ever does sell, all of my flaws will be virtues overnight. I've just got a feeling that's the stuff that's going to sell the book."

Silet: It's like the Tony Hillerman story about being asked by an editor to cut all the Indian stuff.

Dunning: Yeah, cut all the Indian stuff. Unbelievable. Then Susanne Kirk bought it at Scribners. The book was published, I think, on

January 22, 1992 and the first edition was sold out within forty-eight hours.

Silet: Where did Cliff Janeway come from, how did you come up with the policeman/bookman?

Dunning: I've known cops who collect books. I know that sounds strange, but I had cops as customers. Janeway is like Walker in *Deadline*; he's kind of an idealization of myself. What I'd like to be if I had that kind of nerve, that kind of physical stamina. But when I started *Booked to Die* I knew I was going to do a cop who collected books, quits the force and becomes a book dealer. The initial plot was entirely different. I had a whole different notion which was based on some experience I'd had at the *Post* but it just wasn't working. Janeway was distant and cold, almost aloof. It was one of those things where if you dig at it long enough, it undergoes a metamorphosis and becomes something else. I approached it two or three different times.

The way I write is I start out and I just keep rewriting the same page until something breaks and I start doing something else. Sometimes that means putting in something earlier and going back and rewriting all the way up to that point because everything changes. I don't use a word processor, I just write it on an old manual typewriter. After I'd been digging at it for a long time, with the wrong story, the wrong hero, but the right background, the real story fell into my lap. Steve Wilson, a bookseller-friend of mine who bears some resemblance to one of the characters in my book, came in one rainy day when there wasn't a single customer in the store. The two of us got to talking and he said, "My God, I just heard an incredible story. In California this old man died and he had a house full of first editions and the thing fell to some lawyers to broker. They didn't have a clue to what they were doing and they didn't know a modern first edition from Adam. To them they're just books. There was a whole run of Hemingway and Faulkner. A bunch of other firsts." You know it takes a real incompetent to mistake Hemingway, but there were a lot of writers in there that nobody ever heard of but were still worth a lot of money. I could see a lawyer missing out on *One Hundred*

Years of Solitude, which is a $700 book. Steve said, "This book
dealer got wind of it. They were going to put these things out for
fifty cents a piece, and he went charging over there and he said,
'You can't sell those for fifty cents, I'll give you a dollar for them.'
And for an outlay of about four or five thousand dollars, he
walked out of there with $150,000 worth of books." I thought,
"Boy, that's a nice motive for murder."

I took it home, and I wondered if I could work that into the
book and I started dickering around with it. There was still
something wrong with Janeway, he needed a kick in the pants.
What he needed was some fire, and once I gave him that the plot
jelled. I threw out the original idea that I'd been working with and
four months later the book was done. It's as if you have to go
through all that agony before it happens but then it happens all at
once. A writer once told me that there's a point in every book
where you see the end and you know what's going to happen so
clearly, and at that point it's just a matter of typing.

Silet: When did you think of Janeway as a series character? Did you
originally?

Dunning: I'm not sure that I did. I finished the book and started
another book, a Walker book. Walker was my character in *Deadline,*
and I wanted to bring him back, and I was a good way into that
book when this book sold. Susanne said, "I need another Janeway
book." I told her that as a matter of fact I had another book. But
she said, "I need another Janeway book." So I had to stop the
Walker book and start the second one from scratch. These are
fairly intricate books in the sense that they have a lot of real
bookscouting and bookselling and stuff. I'm not real interested in
doing a series where every other story is a hunt for a valuable book
and you just merely change the book. It becomes *The Maltese Falcon*
all over again, except it's a book instead of a bird.

Silet: I thought of that when I was reading *Bookman's Wake.*

Dunning: Yeah, but then you get to the end of it and you find out
that it's something else. It's not the search for one book, because it
breaks open and there's a tragedy there that transcends the hunt

for one book. And that's what I'm interested in. In the course of it hopefully you illuminate a facet of the book world that the average person doesn't know about. If you can do that then it's fun, and it's very difficult, but I'm not real interested in doing much less than that. Therefore, it becomes really hard for me to crank these things out. I can't come up with another Janeway idea right now. I have to let the cup fill up.

Silet: *Booked to Die* was about modern first editions and *The Bookman's Wake* is about fine printing.

Dunning: The first one was about the business of modern first editions. One of the reasons why it took off the way it did is because very few people outside the trade knew that some of these books are worth the kind of money they're worth. *Carrie* is not just another Stephen King book; it's worth $500. The paperback of *Booked to Die* is now out and bookdealers are complaining; I'm getting a good deal of the blame for the fact that they're not finding books like they used to. People aren't putting them out in garage sales anymore. The second book was about limited editions of fine press books and the printers who make them. But there's a whole lot of nuts-and-bolts bookscouting around the fringes of it. They are alike in some respects, but they are very different and I'd like to do another one sometime that's different yet. I get offered plots by people who don't know what you need dramatically.

Silet: How much were you thinking about the biblio-mystery when you began?

Dunning: Not at all. *Booked to Die* was about books because I had been in the book business and, frankly, I had never read a book like that. Most of the bookstore books that I have read, and I haven't read a whole lot of them, but most of them dealt with the book world as a fringe thing. The Lawrence Block character is supposed to be a book dealer, but you really don't see him dealing books, you see him as a burglar. A lot of the other books have little old ladies with cats in bookstores, and it's just an Agatha Christie attempt all over again. But I had not seen any books about the book world I knew, which is full of strange people. Some of them are the salt of the earth, really great guys, and others are just, my God, renegades, ex-alcoholics, ex-druggies, they're not the academics and the gentlemen that they used to be, but neither are literary agents and publishers. Neither are authors.

Silet: Let me ask some specific questions about some of the earlier crime fiction. Was *The Holland Suggestions* a crime novel?

Dunning: Yeah, it was a mystery. It's a novel about a guy who was put under hypnosis years ago. He had an hypnotic suggestion planted in his mind as to the location of this treasure, and this suggestion kicked in years later and sent him on this trip that he didn't really understand. It took him from his place in the East out to the Colorado mountains which is where it takes place. I don't know if it's a good book. I keep running into people who say it's the best book I ever wrote. I think it's pretty farfetched. If that's the best book I ever wrote then I've been over the hill for twenty years.

Silet: The second one was *Looking for Ginger North*, which was a racetrack mystery.

Dunning: That had its origins when I was walking horses at Bay Meadows, where it rained constantly. *Ginger North* is like *Bookman's Wake*, it rains throughout the whole book. I was walking horses one morning and at the end of the race meet most of the trainers were pulling out and the stables were fairly deserted, like a ghost town. I was walking horses under the shedrow because it was raining, and I looked at one of these empty stalls and I thought, "Somebody could be hiding in there and stab me, throw me under the straw and they wouldn't find me till the next spring." That thought stayed with me for years and it's the basis for *Looking for Ginger North*.

It was also nominated for the Edgar but after a while you realize that those things are really strange. Nobody knows why Edgars get nominated or awarded or to whom and for what reasons. I was a runner-up two years running and that was one of them. I've won some other awards since then but I find the whole process of awards and prizes as suspicious and questionable as the notion of what makes a book sell in the first place. A lot of it is grand theater, geared more for the committee giving it than for the author or his book. Most of it is very political, including or perhaps especially the Nobel Prize. How do they give it to Saul Bellow and Patrick White, and ignore John Fowles, who has got to be one of the great writers of our time?

Silet: What about *Denver?*

Dunning: *Denver* came about because I was frustrated and I kept getting these turn-downs that said, "This doesn't have any big book potential." There was a great editor at Putnam who was forced to turn *Ginger North* down by the editor-in-chief. She really went to the wall for that book but in the end she lost the fight. She wrote me a rejection letter I still treasure. The only thing it said was, "I hope this gets made into a movie by George Roy Hill starring Nick Nolte." That was the rejection letter. So I thought, "Well, to hell with it, I'll give you a book with big book potential."

I was looking for an idea when I saw, in *Colorado Magazine*, an article called, "When the Klan Ruled Denver." It was about the Ku Klux Klan in the 20s. By the time the peak of the Klan activity came around 1925, the governor of Colorado was a Klansman, Mayor Ben Stapleton was in the Klan, the chief of police was a Klansman and so were all the heads of licensing boards. If they didn't like your looks or your name or anything else you wouldn't get a license, you didn't practice your trade. At one point there was talk about setting up armed checkpoints at every road coming into the state so if they didn't like the way you looked or anything else about you they could turn you back.

About the same time I was watching a television talk show in which James Michener was asked, "How do you start a book?" Michener said, "I start from a sense of deep dramatic freight, I have a feeling of this dramatic power, and that's what the book grows out of." I had the same feeling about this Klan business. I thought if I can't write a book with big book potential about this subject, then I can't write. And so I spent the next year and a half doing *Denver*, while the other one was getting rejected by everybody. The manuscript of *Denver* was about 800 pages long. My agent sent it off to Harper and Row, and this time the rejection letter said, "My God, it's too big." That was a pretty grim day, but the book sold to Times Books after about only three or four submissions.

Denver was about reporters at *The Denver Post*. I seem to be unable to write without putting real stuff in my books. My reporter hero at the *Denver Post* had the same problem with management that I had when I was there. When you write something that's embarrassing to the newspaper's advertisers, it's never going to see the light of day. In my novel, the hero decides to take on the Klan. Fred Bonfils and Harry Tammen, who owned the *Post*, didn't particularly care who they insulted. They weren't at all afraid to expose the Klan except for the fact that all the department stores downtown were owned by Klansmen, and all the grand dragons and the hooded idiots were chairmen of the boards. They were all members of the Chamber of Commerce, and they were all in bed with people who advertised at the *Post*. So the story gets killed. In a way, *Denver* was my way of getting back at the *Post* for a number of the stories I investigated that had the same kind of outcome.

So Denver was an anger novel, which is the best kind of novel to write. If you write it while you're feeling pissed off at something, you can write a pretty good book. *Deadline* came right in its wake, and it was a continuation of that. Walker was a newspaper reporter who had trouble getting his stories printed. Newspaper editors will always tell you that they value good writing and that they value your integrity as a reporter and all that. Then the minute you start getting close to the truth, their idea of what strong writing is and mine become two different things. They start eating it alive. So *Deadline* came along and it just wrote itself. I still had that same hot anger, I still have it. I don't think editors ought to do things like that. So that's where those books came from.

Silet: What about *Deadline*?

Dunning: *Deadline* came out of the Patty Hearst kidnapping. It was a novel about dissident students and it came out about that time. It was also about the FBI and had a lot to do with the Ellsberg stealing of the Pentagon papers, only I fictionalized that and made it something else. It had FBI goons in it. In fact one of the FBI guys is a killer. I had a killer and a kind of a white knight, both within the FBI, playing off each other. Walker is the reporter who gets the story but can't get it into the paper. Then he has to go on the run.

Silet: You mentioned earlier that your education largely came from your reading. What did you read that had an influence on you?

Dunning: I read all of the Hardy Boys. When I was twelve I read all of Walter Farley—all of the Black Stallion books—and I read all of the Rover Boys. One of the greatest discoveries I ever made was getting into this garage of a friend of mind and finding a box full of the Rover Boys books when I was twelve years old. I thought they were absolutely wonderful. I look back on them now and, of course, they're contrived, but, God, what great stuff for a kid. I also devoured the Tom Swift books, the original books from the 20s, not the Tom Swift Jr's from the 50s. Then there came a day, I was probably thirteen, when I got away from the Hardy Boys. One day they weren't quite as good as they used to be, and I started reading all the horse and dog books.

Later I got into the sexy books that you had to read undercover, like *Peyton Place* and *East of Eden*, which I read when I was very young. I read *The Grapes of Wrath*, and I read all the rest of Steinbeck and then I read Hemingway. I think everybody who wanted to write, every young male of my age, went through a Hemingway stage where you just get caught up in the language. I remember sitting with a pencil copying "The Snows of Kilimanjaro" until I had the pace and the rhythm. You just hope you can absorb some of that, it's so wonderful. Then eventually you cast it off and go on. I tried to read Faulkner but couldn't. I remember trying to read *The Sound and the Fury*. At that time I couldn't keep it straight. About four years ago I went back and bucked up the courage to read Faulkner and found it great stuff. I went through all those modern American classics writers.

I don't understand why John O'Hara isn't better thought of, and I bet he doesn't understand it either wherever he is. He was always his own most vocal champion. Occasionally, I would read in the classics, but I was never one for Homer and the Bible and all the things that you're supposed to read. I started reading John Fowles. *The French Lieutenant's Woman, The Magus,* and *Daniel*

Martin are great books. I love books like John Gardner's *Mickelsson's Ghosts*. That's a great mystery novel. I still don't know what happened, but it doesn't matter, I just love it anyway. I'm a pretty broad kind of a junkyard reader.

Silet: It used to be that there were pretty hard and fast lines drawn between what we describe as "serious fiction" and genre fiction. It seems to be blurring at the moment.

Dunning: I'm glad that's true, aren't you? You know, one of the reasons why I think that there was that distinction in the old days is because most of the crime writing was pretty awful except for a Raymond Chandler or a Cornell Woolrich. God, Woolrich just blew out of the gate, and for my money the best of all of them was James M. Cain. I think *Mildred Pierce* and *The Postman* and *Double Indemnity* are three of the best crime novels ever. The first half of *Serenade* is just great. But a lot of the stuff that was coming out in the 50s and 60s was pretty hokey.

I think today you've got some real writers that work in the crime area, people like James Lee Burke and Michael Connelly and Mary Willis Walker, and I do think that distinction is blurred. The guys who keep saying that there is a distinction are by and large academics whose interests are served by keeping that distinction. All you have to do is read your newspaper to see that crime fiction is not really so improbable, there are worse things that happen every day in real life than I could ever dream up to write about. It's as if professors don't believe that this kind of stuff can happen in real life. There really are some honest-to-God mysteries in life and that's what makes the mystery field so interesting.

Let me just put it this way, though I'm just repeating something Chandler said years ago. It's the only literary form that has never been beaten. The perfect mystery has never been written because there comes a time in every one of them where the author has to start cheating. There's just no way around it. You get to the point where the hero has to know more than he can tell the reader and therefore you have to close that door between yourself and the readers and you don't tell them. All I can say about genre fiction is that it isn't as cheap and easy as people think. I'd like to see Mr. Updike and some of those guys try it. Not to disparage their talent, which I think is great, but don't put the mystery down to me, because I don't believe it. I know how hard it is to write a good one. It's even hard to write a bad one.

Silet: Is the mystery good for social commentary?

Dunning: I got into trouble for some things that Janeway said in *Booked to Die.* The editor at the *Drood Review* felt that I had stepped over the line by having Janeway so political, but if you read that book, Janeway is really not political at all. What he's saying is, "I don't know what my politics are." The fact is I don't know what *my* politics are. I was always a life-long Democrat, but I'm not a member of any political party. I guess I'm anti-politics now. Janeway says something like, "I came back from Vietnam a dove; I went in a hawk, came back a dove. You know, I like black people, some of them a lot. I believed in busing when it was necessary, but there's something about affirmative action that leaves me cold."

The thing that got me in trouble with the *Drood* fellow, which I guess I'll have to live with, was when Janeway says, "I hate abortion but I'd never pass a law telling a woman she couldn't have one." His objection was that I was using the mystery not for entertainment, which it is supposed to be for, but to push some political agenda. I think that's a crock. That's like saying that there are certain elements in characterization that are off-limits because they happen to offend somebody's politics. There's always going to be a critic who's going to have an opinion that's different from mine, and I'm the one with the book and he's the one with the magazine, so I write the book and he can criticize it, that's the way it goes. I think he's wrong, though.

Silet: What are you working on now?

Dunning: I'm working on an old-time radio novel that may or may not see the light of day. The working title is *Two O'clock, Eastern Wartime,* and it grew totally out of the title. I was listening to an old "Suspense" show one night, and as they were signing off, the host said be sure to come back next week and hear "Suspense," nine-thirty eastern war time. I thought that was a great title for a book: *Nine-Thirty Eastern War Time.* Then I moved it up to two o'clock in the morning, and one thing led to another and suddenly I had this spy story. It's threatening to be a good book all of a sudden. I'm also putting together some notes for a Janeway plot that is probably two years down the road. I know my publishers don't want to hear that. They would love it if I could just write a Janeway book every year. But those books depend for whatever value they have on the intricacies of the book business. It is not enough, at least it is not enough for me, to say let's have another chase after another rare book. Whatever the characters are chasing, it's got to open a doorway into some facet of the book world that I haven't explored before. I would get really annoyed with myself doing something that is obviously just a rip-off of what I've done before.

Mad Dog and Glory
James Ellroy

Photo © Marion Ettlinger

T he self-described "Mad Dog" of contemporary crime fiction, Ellroy has led a life as bizarre as one of his ill-fate characters. His mother was murdered when he was ten years old, and in his late teens he dropped out of school and went on the streets, becoming addicted to drugs and alcohol and living in abandoned houses, gorging himself on crime novels.

By 1977 he sobered up and began writing: first, a classic detective novel, *Brown's Requiem* (1981), a genre that he quickly abandoned; next, a sex-murder book, *Clandestine* (1982), which was a thinly disguised version of his own mother's case; and, finally, a short-lived series of police procedurals featuring detective Lloyd Hopkins—the "Hopkins in Jeopardy" books—*Blood on the Moon* (1984), *Because the Night* (1984), and *Suicide Hill* (1985). After a first-person serial murderer novel, *Killer on the Road* (1986), Ellroy struck it big with the first of his L.A. Quartet, *The Black Dahlia* (1987), a novel about the famous unsolved mutilation death of Elizabeth Short.

The success of this book fueled the writing of the rest of the L.A. books: *The Big Nowhere* (1988), *L.A. Confidential* (1990), and *White*

Jazz (1992). *L.A. Confidential* was made into a major Hollywood film and garnered critical praise and several Academy Award nominations.

In the Quartet Ellroy explored the underside of post-war Los Angeles with its red baiting, police corruption, racist bigotry, and sexual perversion. He developed an increasingly spare, realistic style which culminated in a telegraphic prose experiment in *White Jazz*, with its riff rhythms and improvisational narrative. In 1994 Ellroy published a collection of short fiction that included the novella "Dick Conte's Blues," based on a non-fictional, investigative piece he wrote for *G.Q.*

In 1996 Ellroy published his first non-fiction book, *My Dark Places*, the story of his mother's murder and the investigation which failed to discover her killer. He worked with a retired L.A. detective to re-investigate the case using modern police procedures. Ellroy's life-long obsession with his mother's death refuses to go away.

His latest books are *L.A. Noir* (1998) and *Crime Waves: Reportage and Fiction from the Underside of L.A.* (1999).

In the following interview Ellroy discusses his past as a petty criminal, drug addict, and crime-fiction junkie. His outspoken views on private-eye novels, serial-killer fiction, and series with likable reader-friendly characters will not likely endear him to traditional mystery fans, but they will surely stimulate serious thought about the art of crime writing.

Portions of this interview were published as "Mad Dog and Glory: A Conversation with James Ellroy," *The Armchair Detective*, 28:3 (Summer 1995), 236–244.

Silet: You have been rather widely interviewed about your checkered past, the murder of your mother when you were ten, your time on the streets, your alcoholism and drug addiction. Is there anything new about that period that you thought about recently that you'd like to discuss?

Ellroy: As a criminal I was pathetic. As a drug addict and alcoholic, I was always on the cautious side. I was never a tough guy. I broke into houses and sniffed women's undergarments, sure, but I was never a bad-ass burglar. We're talking about the late 1960s primarily, and it was quite simply a different world. People didn't have sophisticated alarm systems, people didn't have telephone answering machines. So if you called up and got no answer, chances were nobody was home. And finding a loose screen or some window access or a dog door was rather easy.

I was always frightened, but the thrill of voyeuristic entry always eclipsed my fear, and I never took anything large. I took cash, I sniffed some undergarments while I was there, I stole drugs. In the summer of 1969, right after the Tate/La Bianca killings, I started to see more and more alarm tape on windows, people were getting dogs, there were stickers for the Bel-Air Patrol and Hollywood Patrol, private companies that patrolled the swankier areas, and I simply decided that sooner or later the law of averages was going to catch up with me. I thought, "Let's not do this again," and I didn't.

Silet: The ante had gone up.

Ellroy: The ante had gone up, and I didn't want to be caught. I always had that certain level of cautiousness and circumspection going for me.

Silet: You've talked about always wanting to be a writer, but there must have been some specific point when you decided that you needed to get serious about it.

Ellroy: I quit drinking and using drugs in 1977, when I was twenty-nine and a caddie at the Bel-Air Country Club in Los Angeles. At the time I was reading some recent crime fiction and rereading some of my old favorites, and I had this sneaking suspicion that I could do better than the people I was reading. I had always wanted to be one thing—a novelist—but it wasn't until a desire to simply write novels overtook me that I was actually able to start. It was a tremendous surprise to me that the story that started developing in my mind was a crime story. Big surprise!

I should have been the first one to know, since crime fiction had been the big love of my life. I hadn't thought I had the kind of brain that could come up with complex plots—which, of course, crime fiction requires. The first story that came to me was the story of *Brown's Requiem*, a little autobiographical perhaps, but primarily based on some old L.A. crimes. That's the story that came to me, that's the book that I wrote, and damned if I didn't sell it.

Silet: Were there any false starts, or did you just begin with the idea for that book and stick with it?

Ellroy: I started outlining *Brown's Requiem* in 1978, but I stopped because I was afraid that I might write the book and not sell it; I was afraid that I might fail in general. At the time I had quit caddying for a spell, to work for an attorney service. Basically I was a process server, but I couldn't make any money at it, because it was contingency work and I wasn't very good at finding people. So I went back to the golf course, where I could make my guaranteed two hundred to two hundred and fifty dollars a week. And it wasn't until January 1979 that I said "Fuck it" and wrote the book.

Silet: So you really did just sit down and write it?

Ellroy: Yes, from a threadbare outline.

Silet: You mentioned reading some old mystery favorites, and that you graduated from the Hardy Boys and Sherlock Holmes to Mickey Spillane and Nero Wolfe and finally to Joseph Wambaugh and Ross Macdonald. And you've admitted that both Macdonald and Wambaugh were your teachers.

Ellroy: I'd say Dashiell Hammett taught me much more than Ross Macdonald, and Raymond Chandler, in the end, taught me very little. I think Chandler is essentially very overrated and not as important as he's given credit for being.

Silet: What did you learn from Hammett?

Ellroy: I think I picked up the Hammett world view. Hammett wrote the man that he was afraid that he was, whereas Chandler wrote the man he wanted to be. I think that my books have evolved more and more into what I like to call "the private nightmare of public policy." Increasingly, I have focused on the bad men of history, on the leg-breakers, and that in essence is what the Continental Op was all about.

If there is a book that stands out in my past more than any other it's *Red Harvest*, where the Continental Op is called upon to restore order to a lawless mining town. He plays off all the factions against each other. He is in the pay of the big money of the mining company. He succeeds in restoring order at a great cost. In the end marshal law is imposed, the little guy gets fucked, and the mining company takes over stronger than ever. It's a dark view.

Silet: Did your reading effect you stylistically? Were you aware of how they were saying what they were saying?

Ellroy: No, not at all. I read inchoately, I read emotionally. I read for a story, I read for milieu. I read because reading crime novels gave me both a tidy sense of resolution and a sense that the ramifications of violent events would go on forever. Of course, I think that this love of crime fiction derives from my mother's murder. It's a very simple cause and effect to chart. On one level or another I write crime novels because I'm deeply curious, and the only way that I can sate my curiosity on all matters pertaining to crime and psychosexual behavior is by writing the books that nobody could write.

Silet: Did your reading also provide a sense of closure for the fears caused by your mother's death?

Ellroy: No. The only closure is that there is no closure.

Silet: What triggered you to write *Brown's Requiem*?

Ellroy: I tried to write the story that was talking to me at the moment. I tried to apply some of my own past: my alcoholism and the fact that I was recently sober, my love of classical music, the fact that I was caddying at the time. All that hokey autobiographical stuff that mainstream writers dwell on ad infinitum I got rid of in my first two books.

Silet: I was going to say *Clandestine* also has a lot of autobiographical material in it.

Ellroy: Yeah, it's a heavily fictionalized, chronologically altered account of my mother's murder.

Silet: In writing those two books did you discover anything about what you wanted to do next?

Ellroy: I wrote *Brown's Requiem*, and I had a tremendous revelation when I finished it. I realized that all modern private eye novels are bullshit, and that I would never write another one.

Silet: The next three books that you wrote were a short-lived series, the Hopkins novels. Where did the character of Hopkins come from in *Blood on the Moon*?

Ellroy: I wanted to write the ugliest and most explicit cop/psycho-killer book of all time. In the first draft the cop, Hopkins, and the killer, Teddy Verplanck, kill each other and L.A. burns to the ground.

Silet: In the original version?

Ellroy: In the original. It was Nat Sobel, my agent, and Otto Penzler, who was thinking about publishing me for Mysterious Press, who got me to do an extensive rewrite on *Blood on the Moon.* I look back now and think, "Holy shit, is this moribund." And while we're on the topic of what's dead and what's not, serial killer novels are just as dead as private-eye novels.

Silet: Yet *Killer on the Road* is a serial-killer book.

Ellroy: Yeah, but at least it's strictly from the serial-killer's viewpoint and not a *roman policier* on any level.

Silet: You started your career writing novels with different central characters, but with *Blood on the Moon* you began a series. Why did you continue with Hopkins in *Because the Night*?

Ellroy: I liked him, and I wanted to do a limited series with him, chart his psychology over a set period of time, and then abandon him on some sort of ambiguous note. There's a liberalism that I despise in crime fiction, and I wanted to create a realistic Los Angeles cop of the time, with a full component of prejudices, and place him in various violent contexts. A quote that keeps coming back to me is Raymond Chandler said that "Dashiell Hammett gave murder back to the people who really committed it." My L.A. Quartet and *American Tabloid* are designed to give crime fiction and violent intrigue back to the men who would really have perpetrated it—and they are *men* and they are *white men.*

I see hard-boiled crime fiction as heavily ritualized transit horseshit and largely spun off of Raymond Chandler. Chandler is a very easy writer to imitate, which is why so many people have been able to adapt his formula with such success, but I hate that formula, and I hate its sensibility. I wanted to give crime fiction back to the leg breakers of history, to soldiers of fortune, to bad white men, to racist shit-birds and the corrupt cops, and I think the chief risk I've taken is to ignore the old warning of crime fiction editors worldwide: namely, that you've got to create sympathetic characters that your readers can identify with.

Silet: Do your readers identify with any of your characters? There are very few who are conventionally sympathetic.

Ellroy: I identify with all of them. And I want my readers to have an ambiguous responses to my characters. I want my readers to identify with my characters on the level of their hidden sexual agendas. I want my readers to say, "Man, what a blast it would be to go back to 1952 and beat up faggots." Then I want them to realize, "*Oh,* am I *really* thinking that?" In *American Tabloid,* I wanted people to think, "Yeah, what a fuckin' blast, let's whack out John F. Kennedy."

Silet: Is that being on the edge in ways that most readers simply never experience?

Ellroy: Yes. I think crime fiction at its best is touching the fire and getting your hand burned.

Silet: You said a minute ago that you had basically planned the Hopkins series as a limited series. So you started out thinking that you would do three books and stop?

Ellroy: Three, four, or five. When I wrote *The Black Dahlia*, Otto Penzler wanted me to write a forth Hopkins' book. I wanted to build on *The Black Dahlia*, create a quartet of interlocking novels, and chart L.A. from 1947 to 1959.

Silet: Why the fascination with the past?

Ellroy: I'm from Los Angeles. If I were born in Dog Dick, Delaware or Moose Fart, Montana, I would write dark crime novels about those places. Luckily for me, my parents hatched me in a place that had a rich criminal history.

Silet: Why not write about contemporary crime? What is it about the past that fascinates you?

Ellroy: I like it because everything that's happening today was happening then, only statistically there was a whole lot less of it. I like to call it the "contained apocalypse." As a kid, I sensed that there was a secret world coexisting with the outwardly more placid world. I began to consciously rediscover that world as I started writing the L.A. Quartet. Those books dealt with hepcat jazz musicians, desperate homosexual informants, corrupt D.A.s, perverts, panty sniffers, pederasts, punks, people like that. And it's a closed world. There's a symbiotic frenzy going on among these people at all times. It's very rare that this inward world spills out into the outwardly more placid world. But it does occasionally as in *White Jazz*, and the results are hellish.

Silet: Why was that world of particular use to you? What was it that fascinated you about it?

Ellroy: On June 22nd 1958, I went back to the place where I was living with my mother. The fuzz were all over the place, and a man said, "Son, your mother has been killed." My mother had been shitty to me in the weeks preceding her death. My greatest dream during that time was to go live with my father. All of a sudden my mother is dead, all of a sudden my wish has been granted. I experienced a very ambiguous bereavement. I was frightened of my mother; I was frightened of the hold that she had over me. I felt that I should have loved her more.

But some part of me seized upon my own mother's death as an opportunity. At the time of her death I was heading toward puberty and was sexually obsessed with her. The next thing I know she's dead, and it's a terrible sex crime, and I'm living with my old man and gobbling up all the fucking crime books I can get my meathooks on—because I wanted to know why and that curiosity has never left me.

Silet: Don't you think your style shifts with *The Black Dahlia*, with your growing assurance as a writer?

Ellroy: I'd been waiting to write that book for a long time. I first learned of the Black Dahlia murder case about eight months after my mother's death. My father got two books for my eleventh birthday in March, 1959. One was *The Complete Sherlock Holmes*; the other was *The Badge* by Jack Webb, which contained a haunting ten-page summary of the Black Dahlia murder case. The two cases merged in my mind, and in many ways Elizabeth Short, the Dahlia, was the stand-in for my mother. I felt the horror of her death. It was a completely uncompromised horror. I used to have nightmares; I used to be afraid to go to sleep because I knew I would dream about Elizabeth Short. I used to have daytime flashes where I'd see her being tortured.

And in 1977, just as I was getting sober and was about to change my life, I read John Gregory Dunne's wonderful, if fanciful novel, *True Confessions*, which is *his* heavily fictionalized account of the Black Dahlia murder case. *The Black Dahlia* probably would have been my first novel, but I thought that the success of Dunne's novel precluded anyone else ever writing about the Black Dahlia. I didn't realize at the time that, *au contraire*, if you have a big, hit book like that, it spawns a great many imitators. And so I wrote my first six books, learned *how* to write in the process and embraced the writing of *The Black Dahlia* with a certain degree of conscious-ness. And I made every effort to differentiate *The Black Dahlia* from *True Confessions*. It was my first hit book, and I realized that I had to make every book from that point on more meaningful than *The Black Dahlia*, this book that I'd waited so many years to write.

So I conceived *The Big Nowhere* as a much larger story—a story with a broader societal base. In every way, I think, it's a better book. It's not as accessible as *The Black Dahlia*. The characters are harder to like, and there's no happy-ending payoff. From *The Big Nowhere* on I formed a new covenant with myself—a covenant of consciousness. The covenant goes something like this: every book has to be conceived as bigger, better, stronger, and more stylisti-cally evolved than the book that preceded it, or I am fucking up big time and should be considered a second-class citizen.

Silet: Certainly *L.A. Confidential* and *The Big Nowhere* are much bigger books, especially in terms of plot, but *White Jazz* is quite different. Among other things, it's a stylistic experiment. Some of the critics had a little trouble with it.

Ellroy: The style evolved this way. My preceding novel, *L.A. Confiden-tial* came in too long in manuscript. I cut sentences, trimmed the book down and saw that I had developed a unique semi-telegraphic style. I started writing *White Jazz,* in a normally discursive, first-person style, but the book felt flabby to me, so I started cutting words. I realized that I had developed a paranoid tone, a stream-of-consciousness style that made the book read like a fever dream. That style was uniquely suited to Dave Kline, the narrator—a terrible man whose life is burning down. And so I wrote the book in that style, and a lot of people found it difficult. I think it's a groovy, seamless work of art, and I'm thrilled to death with it. And that style was suitable for that one book—and I'll never go back to it again.

Silet: You talk about not wanting to entertain your readers but to confront them. What is this confrontation? What is your relation-ship with your readers?

Ellroy: I want to thrill, I want to horrify, I want to titillate. I want to shock. I'm getting more obsessive as I get older, and I'm getting more controlled and more contained in my obsessiveness. I want to jolt my readers out of their everyday lives and share my obsessions with them. I want them to obsessively read my books.

Silet: How would you respond if somebody said, "You're just exploiting people's sickness?"

Ellroy: I'd say, "Fuck you!"

Silet: Critics often describe your writing as neo-noir. What are you doing that's different from traditional noir?

Ellroy: I think I've shaped noir far into social history. Nobody's written noir books as big as mine, with their scope and with their heavily detailed societal backgrounds.

Silet: Most noir novels tend to be short and very personal, very limited.

Ellroy: I like big books. I don't like anything small.

Silet: You've said that the cop has replaced the private eye as the center of the hard-boiled novel. Why do you think that's true?

Ellroy: Because, to paraphrase Evan Hunter, "The last time a private eye investigated a murder was never!" Because Joseph Wambaugh ascended and became the most important writer of realistic intrigue since Dashiell Hammett.

Silet: What is it you learned from Wambaugh, specifically?

Ellroy: He has a unique vision. I think he's a right-wing absurdist and how many right-wing absurdists have you run into in your career as a critic? I used to get hassled by the L.A. cops as a young misanthrope about town. And I never hated them, even when they were hassling me a bit more roughly than they should have been. I admired them and I sensed their inner drama—and Wambaugh made that inner drama real for me.

Silet: You talk about having an affection for things as they are and not really trying to push for social change or betterment in your books. Can you expand on that idea at all?

Ellroy: I'm a white, Anglo-Saxon, Protestant heterosexual born in America, and I've never shared the counterculture ethos revered by so many people of my generation. I get ragged occasionally for being fascist, racist, anti-Semitic, and homophobic—because my characters are, I think. Some people hate my characters because their fascism, racism, homophobia, and anti-Semitism are in no way defining characteristics—they're just casual attributes.

These characters, who are meant to be empathized with, say "nigger," "fag," and "kike," and people don't know how to respond to that. I love these characters of mine. It's as if I lived their lives long ago. Thus I try not to condescend to them, and I show their heroism, co-existing in them with their dubious attitudes out of another time.

Silet: Let's talk about *American Tabloid.* Tell me about the Kennedy assassination and the FBI, and America in the 1960s.

Ellroy: I had read Don DeLillo's novel *Libra,* and it blew my mind, fucked my soul, and scorched my sexuality. I felt that, holy shit, now I'm tremendously interested in the Kennedy assassination, but now I can never write about it—because the book is just that seminal. Then I began to see that I could write a novel where the assassination would be but one crime in a long series of crimes, I wouldn't even have to use Lee Harvey Oswald, who DeLillo portrayed so brilliantly. I began to see that all the harbingers of the assassination started to percolate in the late 1950s, and that I could write an epic-length novel about government/criminal collusion with a huge cast of characters.

I knew the historical elements I wanted to co-opt: the CIA and their war against Castro's Cuba; the Bay of Pigs invasion; the Kennedy assassination; Jimmy Hoffa and the Teamsters; Bobby Kennedy's war on organized crime; J. Edgar Hoover; Howard Hughes. I realized that these people were all in bed with each other, and that more than anyone else, it was Joe Kennedy who got his son killed—because it was Bobby Kennedy's oedipal drama that resulted in Jack's murder. Bobby had a strong moral sense, and he understood that the gangsters he was chasing were his father once removed.

As I started writing the book I realized that this isn't just one novel. This is a trilogy about America between the years 1958 and 1973. I want this trilogy to fuck crime fiction in the ass. Fuck mysteries, fuck mystery readers, fuck all the strictures of genre fiction. I'm going to write an epic trilogy that nobody else would have the stones or the patience to write.

Silet: Let's talk a little bit about your first work of nonfiction, *My Dark Places*, which came out in the fall of 1996. What was your experience writing that and resurrecting all of the trauma surrounding your mother's murder?

Ellroy: In January of 1994, my friend Frank Girardot, a reporter for the *San Gabriel Valley Tribune* in California, called up and said, "I'm doing a piece about the L.A. County Sheriff's Unsolved Unit, and I'm going to spotlight five unsolved San Gabriel Valley homicides." Frank told me he was going to see my mother's murder file, so that he could review the case in his piece. I said, "Oh, holy shit, I want to see the file, too." I called up my editor at *G.Q.*, Paul Scanlon, and said, "I want to go to L.A. and write a five thousand-word piece for *G.Q.* about the experience of seeing my mother's homicide file thirty-six years after the fact." Paul said, "Go, Daddy-O."

Girardot had told me that he was dealing with two cops about to retire from the Sheriff's homicide bureau: Bill McComas and Bill Stoner. I called up Stoner and talked to him. He said, "Yeah, you can see the file," and made arrangements for me to come out and look at it. In April of 1994, I went out and saw my mother's homicide file. I saw her nude on the morgue slab. I saw her dead on the road where she had been left after she was raped and strangled, and as I read through the file, it completely blew all my preconceptions about the case apart. And it was just as shocking an experience as you'd think it would be. I realized *this isn't over.*

Bill Stoner impressed me, too. I had never met a cop quite as intelligent, quite as humane, quite as perceptive as this man. He seemed to be a very evolved human being. I went back home to Connecticut, and wrote the piece for *G.Q.* It was a wrenching experience, and it left me wanting more. I realized what I had to do. I called up Nat Sobel, my agent, and told him that I wanted to turn the *G.Q.* article into a full-length book. I mentioned it to Sonny Mehta, the boss and my editor at Alfred A. Knopf, and he said that he heard about the *G.Q.* piece and was hoping I would want to expand it. He read the article and said, "Yes, let's do the book."

I saw the book thusly: It would be my autobiography, my mother's biography, Bill Stoner's biography, and it would have two basic dramatic thrusts. One, I would go back and recreate the original 1958–59 investigation from official records and surviving witness testimony. Two, if he were willing to help me for a cut of the proceeds, I would enlist Bill Stoner and we would re-investigate my mother's murder in the present. Stoner's retired from the Sheriff's Department now, and we've become very close friends.

More than anything else, it was exhilarating, and there were times though when I felt my mother's presence very strongly. I stayed in an apartment in Newport Beach, because Stoner lived in a neighboring community and we traveled a lot together. I put up corkboards with pictures of my mother, and mugshots of various perverts who were brought in for questioning and later exonerated, maps of the area where her body was found, and lists of the witnesses that we needed to find.

I could feel her, and I could smell her after thirty-seven years. I could smell the perfume she used to wear, and her breath, suffused with Early Times bourbon and L & M cigarettes. She came into focus in ways that I had trouble assessing, and Stoner underwent the same thing. I started to feel the killer, too, and I started to feel the lower middle-class, middle-aged alcoholic desperation that resulted in her death.

Silet: What do you do better than anybody else in your writing?

Ellroy: I think I sustain concentration better than anybody I know. I've brought a rich curiosity and a rich emotional need to the craft, and I have a strong will to surmount and get better. The older I get, the more self-referential I become, and I don't compare myself at all to other writers. And the older I get, the hungrier I get—which makes me believe I'm going to write a lot of great fucking books.

Nottingham Noir
John Harvey

Photo © Barbara Hall

John Harvey is a poet, a scriptwriter for television and radio drama, a publisher of Slow Dancer Press (and until 1993 *Slow Dancer* magazine), a writer of paperback fiction for both adults and children, and the author of the Charlie Resnick crime novels.

Born in 1939, Harvey is a native Londoner who attended Goldsmiths' College, University of London and Hatfield Polytechnic. He has a masters degree in American Studies from the University of Nottingham, where he also taught courses in Film and Literature. For twelve years he was a secondary school teacher of Drama and English, until 1975 when he became a full-time writer.

John Harvey is the author of over ninety books, including some fifty westerns, novelizations of movies, poetry, juvenile fiction, and several thrillers. He is currently writing a series of short stories featuring Charlie Resnick, and putting the finishing touches on his second collection of poetry, *Bluer Than This*. A jazz buff, in 1995 Harvey made a recording of his poetry, *Ghosts of a Chance*, with the Second Nature jazz group, one of two bands with which he performs regularly. In 1996, he published *Easy Meat* and *Men in Black*.

Portions of this interview appeared as "Nottingham Noir: An Interview with John Harvey," *The Armchair Detective*, 29:3 (Summer 1996), 272–279.

Silet: How did you begin writing professionally?

Harvey: It's a longish story but not a bad one. I'd been teaching for twelve years and had enjoyed it but had got to the point where I wanted to do something else, but I didn't really know what I could do. I edited literary magazines and newspapers at school, and Goldsmiths' College, University of London, but I'd never written a book or even a short story. I *had* written some bad poetry.

I had a friend, Lawrence James, who had been the paperback editor at New English Library that had published a lot of successful pulp fiction paperbacks: westerns, thrillers, teenage books, biker novels. He had become a writer, and he kept urging me to do the same. The New English Library wanted another biker novel, from Lawrence, but he didn't have time to write it. So he said to me: "Why don't you do this book." I didn't know how to go about it, so he gave me to read the ones he'd written, and he said, "I'll help you write an outline and a sample chapter, and you send it off to the editor with a covering letter from me." So I did, and they commissioned me to write the book. It sounds like fairy story stuff but that's what happened. Not only did they publish it, they asked me for a second one. I thought, "Fine, I'm a writer," so I handed in my notice at my teaching job, and as they say in the best stories, I never looked back.

Once you've sold one novel it's easier to sell a second one, and so for the first four or five years of my writing life I wrote twelve, thirteen books a year, most of them westerns, all of them directly into paperbacks, some of them, I swear, untouched by editorial hands.

Silet: What did you learn about writing from your early experiences?

Harvey: I learned certain basic skills. If you write that much you either get better or, hopefully, you give up. I learned to write dialogue. My early dialogue was awful. In the first books my

characters never spoke, and the editors would send the manuscripts back. They wanted lots of white space on the page. I learned
to write a story so that people wanted to turn the page. The more
confidence I got, the more I felt able to fool around a little, what in
fancy terms would be called subverting the genre.

Silet: How did you begin writing crime fiction?

Harvey: I wrote four paperback detective novels quite early on.
When I wrote them I thought, "OK, I'm going be the first guy to
really crack the problem about writing an American-style crime
novel with a setting in London." Fortunately, very soon I realized
the error of my ways, and that they weren't good. An American
private-eye novel with a London setting doesn't work. Later, I
wrote crime-suspense novels, one called *Frame*, one called *Blind*,
and then a kind of sub-John le Carré spy novel called *End Game*.
But in the main, I'd been writing other things, and with almost a
similar ease to the ease with which I wrote a first book, I had a first
play performed on television, *Just Another Little Blues Song*, which
was a story about an ex-saxophone player who'd got into gambling
debts and had his hand smashed by some heavies in a Soho night
club. Then I did adaptations of classics, Arnold Bennett and so on.
I moved from writing westerns and pulp fiction, via *Just Another
Little Blues Song*, into doing upscale television, and then I slowly
worked my way back to wanting to write good crime fiction.

Silet: Was the first Charlie Resnick novel another attempt to write
a British crime novel in an American style?

Harvey: That's absolutely what I wanted to do. I've never read a lot
of British crime fiction, but what I had read seemed to be set in
unreal places with unreal people. I was living in Nottingham at the
time, which is a medium-sized, fading, industrial city with an
interesting racial and class mix, but I wasn't seeing *that* world
reproduced in crime writing in England. I wanted to write about
Nottingham and what living in a city in post-Thatcher Britain was
like. I admired the writing of American authors who did have a real
sense of place, and I didn't want to be wordy in the way a lot of
British crime fiction was. I wanted fiction to be driven by dialogue

and character and to be able to move between humor and serious incident in the way writers like Elmore Leonard and George Higgins do. I also wanted to use multiple story lines.

Silet: Tell me about living in post-Thatcher Britain.

Harvey: During the years that Margaret Thatcher was running the country, the culture changed from a basically compassionate one to one that was not. She made this famous comment: there is no such thing as society. I think that sums it up. It was also when unemployment rose and when a lot of heavy industries, such as the coal mines around Nottingham for instance, started to close down. I wanted to show something of what living for a cross-section of people was like in those days, because I believe that most crime is socio-economically based, committed through a mixture of need and ignorance.

Silet: Why did you decide to make this a police series?

Harvey: Because after my embarrassing experience with the four private-eye novels, I could only believe in a hero who was a policeman, and I knew I wanted multiple story lines and with private-detective fiction that is more difficult to do. Although I ended up with Resnick, a very strong central character, the series is nevertheless in a police procedural setting. I wrote a television series called "Hard Cases," which was set and filmed in Nottingham, about the probation service and their clients, and that series was a kind of blueprint for the Resnick books. It had six probation officers, and there was something about their private lives, and a lot of stuff about their clients. Also it used multiple story lines, was set in the city, and used the city in the same way that the Resnick books do. That was one of my keys into the series if you like.

Silet: Did you research the local police force?

Harvey: A little. I contacted the Public Relations Department of Nottinghamshire Constabulary. I visited the police station I wanted to set the story in, which is a station just a little way out of the city center. They sent me out there and arranged a meeting with an officer, and I spent half a day with the guy. I wanted to know the basic routine. I met the officer who was actually doing the job that is Resnick's job in the novels, the detective inspector in charge of the Criminal Investigation Division unit, and I spent another half day with him and that was all I did initially, two half-days. Since then I've made a couple of contacts with serving officers, and from time to time, I ring them and check out stuff. I wanted to get the basic routine right so that the way the police go about doing their job in the books would be basically sound.

Silet: Tell me about Charlie Resnick.

Harvey: Let me talk a bit about the way Resnick came about. I was going to write this book; at the time, only this one book. I knew I wanted a police character, and I had a physical sense of him. I saw him walking down the hill from a police station toward the center of the city. He was big and bulky, and he was wearing this shabby raincoat, a bit like a Jim Rockford who went to Colombo's tailor. I never saw his face. I wanted him to be believable as an ordinary policeman, but I also wanted to be able to give him some interesting characteristics. That was when I hit on the Polish idea. With a Polish background he would have been brought up in two cultures, speaking English at school and Polish at home. I could lay all his oddities at the door of his Polishness. Buying the stuff at the Polish deli, making all of the sandwiches, the romanticism and the jazz, the way those things go together, has something to do with his Polishness.

His compassion is part of his upbringing as well. The key was when I hit on the name. The name Resnick was good for an English reader, because you know the English are very bad with foreign names, but anybody in England can pronounce Resnick. Then I hit on Charlie, and Charlie sounds so matter of fact, down to earth. Charlie is the Nottingham/English side of him, and Resnick is the slightly foreign/European, slightly different sense of him. Then slowly I began to find out more about him, and still I'm finding things out about him.

Silet: Let's talk about *Lonely Hearts,* the first novel.

Harvey: I was dating a social worker at the time, so that's why the heroine in that book is a social worker. It also fitted in with the story. When I write I don't have a kind of beginning-to-end outline. What happened in *Lonely Hearts* was that I managed to get the sub-plot about Resnick's childlessness, the secondary plot about the child-abuse case with the social worker, and the main plot of the professor who's been attacking women all to come together. At the end the killer kills himself—when you might think he will attack the social worker—in the room which has been the nursery which Resnick was hoping to use for a child.

The title *Lonely Hearts* had reverberations then through all of the characters in the book and had several layers of meaning. Always one of the exciting things about writing is, if you're lucky, four-fifths of the way through you suddenly see how you can bring all of the elements together. I never necessarily know what is going to happen in the end. The only exception to that is *Cold Light* where I knew the last sentence before I wrote the book, before I even knew the story. I had to write that book in order to write that last sentence.

Silet: In *Lonely Hearts* you were not planning a series.

Harvey: No, I didn't have a series in mind, but as soon as the editor at Viking read it and liked it, then he started talking about a series and the possibility of television, so from that point on I thought I was writing a series. Even though I knew I was writing a series, I didn't want to write the same kind of book every time. So the second one, *Rough Treatment,* was a conscious effort to write a different kind of Resnick novel, closer to Elmore Leonard in tone. The comic burglars are more the central characters than Resnick.

I also wanted to write a nice book about middle-aged sex, which tends to be disregarded in fiction. What usually happens to sex in crime fiction, when it is written by men, is that the men are in middle age and the women are in their middle twenties and beautiful. They wish! *Rough Treatment* was more like taking a step to the side. It was only really with the third novel, *Cutting Edge,* that I felt that I hit a line I was happy to move along through the series, a mixture of crime stories which are anchored in the community and in people's lives and which involve aspects of Resnick's life with feelings for the things that concern him.

Silet: What has writing a series allowed you to do?

Harvey: I think maybe by the forth book, *Off Minor*, I knew that what I was going to do was write a sequence and not a series, knew I wanted to write ten books, but not more, about Resnick in Nottingham, and that's what I'm going to do. Thinking of the books as a sequence gave me the luxury of developing characters and themes very slowly so that what happens to Divine in *Easy Meat* is a kind of, if you like, divine retribution for all the things he's been able to get away with in the last seven books.

There are other things, like Patel's murderer from *Off Minor* has never yet been caught, and the whole, slowly-developing thing between Resnick and Lynn Kellogg has to find some kind of resolution. Knowing that I'm going to write ten books has allowed me to feel my way through all those situations, so that, if someone ever reads the whole ten books, they will see a kind of patterning of relationships unfolding throughout as well as the individual crimes in each one.

Silet: Do you plan out your books around the major criminal?

Harvey: Well, I do to a degree. I plan to the point where I think there are going to be these possible suspects, but I don't necessarily know who did it. I do a circular plan which begins with the key event at the center and then I work out which people might be involved. Up to a certain point I can change my mind. Raymond, the kid in *Off Minor* who works in the slaughterhouse, could have been the killer. But then I decided that I didn't want that to be the case, but by this time I had this character with all of this hate and anger within him and I knew that there had to be some payoff. I couldn't just let it drift, and because he is an example of this all-too-prevalent—unfortunately—white working-class racism, I knew that what was going to happen was that he was going to kill Patel.

There is a scene in about the middle of the book where he and his girlfriend are in a pizza place and Patel comes in with a woman he's started seeing, who is white, and at the end of the chapter Raymond says something like, "I hate that," and he looks across the restaurant at Patel and his girl. I knew then that he was going to kill him. For me, that was the only logical end for that part of the story even though I didn't plan it that way from the beginning.

Silet: In *Wasted Years* we learn a lot about Charlie's past through a flashback technique which you had not used before.

Harvey: I think two things are happening in that book. I wanted Resnick to have to confront his past and his broken marriage, in ways he had not done in any of the other early books, so that then he could move on and be ready for a proper relationship. Also as a way of keeping myself alert, I often set myself a little technical task in the books. In *Wasted Years* it was to do a long—almost one-third of the book—flashback, that didn't occur until almost halfway through the book, to see if I could take the readers back into it and then bring them out the other side without losing them.

But the flashback keeps being put off because Resnick keeps not wanting to think about that time. One of his officers says to him, at one point, "Don't these burglaries remind you of those others ten years ago?" and Resnick brushes him off because he doesn't want to think about them. He remembers that ten years ago a guy went crazy with a shotgun because he found out his wife was being unfaithful, which reminds Resnick that *his* wife was also unfaithful and that broke up their marriage. Finally, he realizes he can't not think about it anymore, and that's when you go into the big flashback.

Silet: Often in your books one of the subsidiary characters has a traumatic experience. Lynn Kellogg is kidnapped, for example, in *Cold Light.*

Harvey: In *Cold Light* I was fascinated by the relationship that has grown up between Resnick and Kellogg, who's obviously the best of his officers. I was interested in the idea that is suggested in the last line of that novel: "…the daughter he had never had the lover she would never be." There is often an attraction for men of his age towards women who may be a generation younger. It can be partly sexual but also partly paternal. Because of their jobs, Resnick has a paternalistic relationship to her. But in jobs where people work closely together, especially under stressful situations, they can become emotionally and sexually attracted to one another. What gets Lynn into trouble in *Cold Light* is the attraction she feels to the man who kidnaps her.

She behaves stupidly in this book in a way that she doesn't elsewhere for two reasons: firstly, because she allows herself to become attracted to the wrong person, and, secondly, because she is distracted by her father's illness. There is some kind of correlation, which I haven't totally got clear in my mind, between her feelings for her father and for Resnick. There is a scene in *Easy Meat* where, because she has been seeing a therapist, she actually confronts Resnick. That story is going to play out further in the next two books.

Silet: *Living Proof* is about mystery writing and the whole media, book business, conference kind of world. What compelled you to write about that?

Harvey: First, let me say that I don't think *Living Proof* works as well as it should. I think it is the weakest of the books, despite the fact that I did a lot of rewriting on it. To be honest I was being opportunistic. I knew that Bouchercon was going to be in Nottingham, and there is this festival called Shots in the Dark every year which I'd been involved in. Since I was writing a book set in this city which has an annual crime and mystery film festival, I thought why don't I write it the year that Bouchercon is going to be there? The book will be published at the same time, and we will get a lot of additional publicity. Which happened. I got a lot of publicity.

But it didn't work as well as the other books for two reasons: a) I had to try so hard to make sure that the woman crime novelist didn't resemble any of the American women crime novelists I know, and b) I had to make sure that the character of the man who runs Shots in the Dark wasn't anything like the man who actually runs the festival, because I wanted to say things about his relationship to his wife that would be crucial to the plot.

I spent so much time making them not like real people that they didn't quite become real characters. In *Living Proof* I also wanted to write a lighter book, since I had written a lot of quite depressing books, one right after the other. *Cold Light* took it out of me a little.

Living Proof became a lighter book that didn't deal with social issues in the same way the other books do. With *Easy Meat* I'm back in the swing.

Silet: Let's discuss *Easy Meat.*

Harvey: *Easy Meat* is a book about what it is like to be a young, working-class, white male in England. It's about being unemployed; it's about having little hope; it's about ideas of masculinity; it's about how that all gets mixed up with racism and incipient fascism. Just after I moved back to London several years ago, there had been several incidents of male rape on the underground, and although all rape is punitive, these seemed particularly punishing. They seemed like extreme versions of gay bashing. Nobody that I knew had written about that in crime fiction in Britain.

It seemed to me that would fit with what I wanted to say about ideas of maleness and how really impossibly difficult it would be if you were one of these young, working-class males and you were gay. My God, how would you tell the people you hung out with, whose idea of a good Saturday night was going out and getting drunk and beating the shit out of people, that you were gay? I don't think you would.

Also the newspapers were full of the disturbing increases in young offenders on remand taking their lives. I wanted to use all of that; it all seemed to come together. Then I thought I can bring Divine into the story here, because in a way he suffers from the same things that those people suffer from. He wears his heterosexuality on his sleeve a little too much. He is a racist; he is sexist. He is a kind of version of those people, but he happens to be in a uniform. I also wanted to try to write about a single mother trying to bring up kids on her own, and what the problems can be even if you try as hard as you damn well can.

I wanted to create a believable character in the mother and have all of these things about working-class maleness moving around in this story. And because I didn't think *Living Proof* had worked very well, I wanted this to be an absolutely great book.

Silet: You also have Charlie, the reluctant lover, besieged by women in *Easy Meat.*

Harvey: Resnick having a relationship with Hannah is the payoff for what happened in *Wasted Years*, and he has a false start in *Cold Light*. I knew that this was not, on the whole, going to be a pleasant book, so I wanted to find a way of letting small pleasures into it. As a relationship it runs counter to most of the other relationships in the book, which are in one way or another not working. The function there is to a) move Resnick's character along and b) to give a counterbalance within the texture of the book.

Silet: You are also a poet, run Slow Dancer Press, and write for television and radio. How does all this work together with the crime fiction?

Harvey: Well, with some difficulty. One way of looking at it is they're different kinds of writing activity which call on different skills. They also allow me to spend some time writing on my own and some time working with other people. I really like that immediate response you get from working in very pressurized situations with others. The nice thing about writing for television is that you are working with other people, where, if I'm spending four months doing the first drafts of a novel, then I'm not. The other thing that happens is that the novels bring together the other skills.

The dialogue writing from television and the movement of narrative you get in a script comes into the novels. I hope the poetry influences the language. When the prose is working well, there is a rhythm to it which the fact that I also write, publish, and read poetry helps. Thank God, I don't think it is poetic prose in the way that term is often used, i.e. flowery and ornately descriptive. They are all forms I am interested in, and apart from the poetry, they are all ways of earning a living.

I'm a professional writer, and like all writers I have certain talents and I sell them. You are always looking for a way of writing about things you want to write about within what other people want you to do. There's that tradeoff all the time in commercial writing. With the Resnick books I've found a perfect combination.

Silet: How does the jazz work in the books?

Harvey: One of the things I wanted to do when I began the series was to find a way to write about the experience of listening to jazz, to have it be one of the things that suggests some of Resnick's characteristics, especially an appreciation of what is artistic, and a way of suggesting that the kind of music he listens to says something about his inner feelings. There are moments when what he has intuitively grasped from the experience of listening to music helps him to deal with the kind of life he has to deal with on the streets. There is a kind of emotional correlation there. The other thing that it does is to provide still moments in the narrative where he's at home and he's listening to music which allows the reader to do the same thing. It's a little quiet moment before the shit starts hitting the fan again.

Silet: Why the cats?

Harvey: You know, I almost regret the cats. I had to put a section in one of the books explaining where all the cats came from because people used to ask me all the time, especially in America. It's another way of showing the needs Resnick has in his life, of showing his compassion and his warmth. But I think not in a sentimental way. The cats are just there, and they're a part of his life, but he's not silly about them. In one of the books he says that he knows that a cat is a cat and a person is a person. He doesn't make the mistake of confusing the two which some crime readers do.

Silet: I understand that you are writing some short fiction about Resnick.

Harvey: I've just finished doing the fifth Resnick short story. Over the last year or so I've suddenly got this love of writing Resnick short stories, because it enables me to write about some of the other characters in the books who I have not had enough of. Or else, sometimes, I use it to introduce characters, try them out, who later turn up in the novels. It's kind of like doing footnotes to the novels.

Silet: What is the next-to-last of the Resnick novels about?

Harvey: Since I've dealt with male attitudes towards homosexuality, one of the things *Still Water* is going to deal with is power and sexuality in heterosexual relationships. Nottingham is also setting up a Serious Crime Squad, and the novel will deal with that and Resnick's move up to being a Chief Detective Inspector in that squad, which is going to set up the final novel to be called *Last Rites.*

Beekeepers, Fools, and Sherlock Holmes' Wife
Laurie R. King

Photo © Jerry Bauer

Laurie King is a third-generation Californian. Her mother and grandmother were both native San Franciscans, and she was born across the bay in Sausalito. She attended school in the Bay area and went to the University of California at Santa Cruz, where she did a B.A. in Religious Studies at Kresge College. Then she did a Masters at Berkeley in the General Theological Union, a consortium of various religious denominations. It was a setting she later would use in her second Kate Martinelli novel, *To Play the Fool.* Her thesis on "Feminine Aspects of Yahweh" explored the mythology of the Cannanites, and its influence on the Hebrew concepts of Yahweh.

She pursued this idea by tracing the feminine myths as they were later incorporated into the Hebrew views of god. As she notes, she pursued the development of threads of thought that had different beginnings: "It was very good training for writing fiction." Her theological interests now play a part in the life of the central character of the Mary Russell books.

King's first Kate Martinelli book, *A Grave Talent,* won an Edgar from the Mystery Writers of America for the Best First Novel and launched her career in crime fiction. However, rather than follow up her initial success with another in the series featuring the S.F.P.D. homicide detective, Laurie King promptly began a second: an historical series featuring Sherlock Holmes and Mary Russell, an energetic young American woman who becomes an apprentice—and later wife—to the retired detective. As King adamantly claims, "This is not a Sherlock Holmes book!" Ms. King has now published three books in both series and has two more Mary Russell books and another Kate Martinelli in the works. She enjoys writing series fiction because it is like constructing one long novel in parts, each with its own set of individual characters, with an on-going story of the central characters.

King prefers mysteries for their internal form: novels with a definite beginning, middle, and end. Also she sees them as twentieth-century morality plays in which traditional issues such as right and wrong, good and evil, and life and death can play out in the fictional story. In short, they are books about things that count.

Laurie King is married to a retired Anglo-Indian professor of Religious Studies, Noel Quinton King, who studied religion and history at Oxford, and has traveled all over the world with him. Currently she lives in a vintage farmhouse in Watsonville, California with her children, Zoe and Nathan, her husband, and assorted cats.

Her most recent Sherlock Holmes/Mary Russell book, *The Moor,* was published in 1998, and her latest, an Anne Waverley novel, *A Darker Place,* came out in 1999.

Portions of this interview appeared as "An Interview with Laurie King," *The Armchair Detective,* 30:1 (Winter 1997), 77–99.

Silet: How did you get started writing?

King: When you're a student you're always writing, aren't you? I finished my M.A. in 1984, the year after my son was born, and I started playing with the idea of writing fiction almost immediately. I wrote a futuristic novel which taught me a lot about how not to write, but then I put it away, and it wasn't until 1987 that I sat down and wrote *The Beekeeper's Apprentice.*

Silet: What attracted you to writing crime fiction?

King: I like the structure of the mystery, and I like the fact that it gives you a place to go while you're looking at what's going on in the sidelines. I always find the sidelines much more interesting than the story itself, which could mean that I'm just lousy at plotting so I'm making a virtue out of a weakness. Let us pretend that it is a deliberate thing. I don't know what it was that came together to make *The Beekeeper's Apprentice.* I am not a deliberate writer; I do not outline; I don't plan things out. They grow in the back of my head until they are ready to emerge. At any rate, I sat down and wrote the central 280 pages of that book in twenty-eight days. I don't normally write that quickly, but I had a fair head of steam worked up and that's how it came out.

Silet: So the initial attraction of crime fiction was its structure? Do you remember which crime writers you had been reading?

King: I wish I could remember. I'm now keeping diaries about the writing because it is interesting to look back to see how a book develops. When I reread Dorothy Sayers I was astonished because I remembered reading one of hers some years before and thinking how mediocre it was. Hard to believe. Now I reread her every couple of years. I read a lot of English crime fiction. Josephine Tey fills me with joy, and I'd give my left hand to write like Peter Dickinson. I also read a lot of the new writers even when I'm not on the Edgar committee for the first novel.

Silet: When you started the first book featuring Mary Russell and Sherlock Holmes, did you think of it as a series?

King: I think so. In fact I wrote *Beekeeper* in the fall, and the following spring I wrote *A Letter of Mary.* As a book, *The Beekeeper's Apprentice* is incomplete, it is not a finished development of the characters. So I had to write the second one to see what happened after they were together, and then I wrote the third to see what happened in the middle, and the fourth to see what happened before the middle. Doesn't that make sense?

Silet: Most writers start with *a* series, and if they develop a second one, it begins some years later. How did it come about that you started with two series?

King: It's a little deceptive, because I went five years between beginning to write and actually selling a book. The first two were Mary Russell books. The third one that I wrote started with an idea about a woman painter set in the Mary Russell period. Now, as every new writer does, I had begun sending out my work to various houses and receiving the manuscripts back completely unread with a xeroxed note attached saying this does not meet our needs thank you very much. Having that happen half a dozen or more times was becoming depressing, and I thought that perhaps I would have better luck if I were to change my setting.

So I transplanted the idea about the painter to this end of the century and set it in San Francisco, a town large enough to justify a number of fairly complex homicides. I wanted it in an area that I knew something about but that could also keep my interest. I also wanted the investigators to be realistic. The Mary Russell character is a sort of romance in the old style, dressing up in costumes and going off to Wales or Palestine. It's great fun, but the whole basis of the thing is fantasy. When I moved into this part of the century, I wasn't as comfortable writing fantasy. I also needed a central character who would have a reason to investigate homicides, and therefore she would have to be a professional. Hence Kate Martinelli. Once I had that format, all kinds of things started growing as they do when you plant the seed of a book.

For example, any homicide department is going to be dominated by men. Kate comes in as an outsider which is further complicated by the fact that she is a lesbian but not an "out" lesbian. Her detective partner in the real police world would be almost inevitably a male. There are all kinds of interesting modern things, more real and nitty-gritty things, going on in that series than I can deal with in the Mary Russell books.

Silet: Let's talk about the three Kate Martinelli books. What did you want to do with *A Grave Talent*?

King: My daughter is in high school, taking English classes and analyzing stories, and every time she says, "I hate analyzing stories," I have to agree with her. I hate analyzing stories, especially if they're my own. I don't know that I can say I was trying to do anything if you mean was I making conscious decisions about effects and statements. At the most, I suppose you could say that I was attempting to write a book whose central character doesn't really *do* anything until the very end. I had this character who is possessed by her artistic ability—she's really a force of nature—and is accused of these truly gruesome crimes. How she got in that position and how good people can get her out is what the book is about.

At the same time I had the main character, Kate, who is a very tight, self-controlled, well-hidden individual for a number of reasons, not just because of her sexual orientation. In this case she is forced to come out of herself to a certain degree, not only "coming out," but allowing herself to risk.

Silet: You start the book with her relationship with Lee and her growing relationship with Al. How do those work for you in the ongoing story in the series?

King: To my mind that is the whole purpose of a series. A series allows you to write a mega-novel. You start out with a blank slate and you then watch your characters develop over a period of three hundred pages until they're at a certain point, and then you close it and open the second three hundred pages and develop perhaps a slightly different side of them. It's the pleasure both of writing and reading a series, that these are people you know, you come to care about, and want to know what comes next in their lives. Of course, in the Martinelli series I seem to have made the best of both worlds, although it wasn't until I was working on the third one that I realized what I was doing.

In each of those, and in the one I'm beginning to work on, there is a central character who is not a part of the ongoing series. There's one book about Vaun Adams, one about Brother Erasmus,

With Child is about Jules Cameron, and each of those characters is more or less used up in that book (although Jules is spread out a bit more). At the same time I am free to take a more leisurely and intimate approach towards the series characters, because they will be with me for one hopes some time. I get to explore one character fully and use him or her up while at the same time I'm working on the on-going lives of the characters of previous books.

Silet: Let's talk about the second in the series, *To Play the Fool.*

King: That one started as deliberately as I ever get with my writing. It was an effort to see if I could make a twentieth-century fool. The holy fool as a person is not native to this century, we are all too foolish to need any holy fools in our midst. The fool is a product of a much more tightly structured society, such as the feudal monarchy or the orthodox church in Russia in past times. His role was to challenge the concrete structure of whatever piece of society he was confronted by, religious or royal. In that sense, the fool doesn't belong here.

However, in another sense we are also a very tightly structured society, each within our different compartments. What Erasmus does is to wander in and out of separate compartments, such as the theological seminary and the tourist attractions on Fisherman's Wharf, becoming slightly different in each setting. Each individual place is as tightly structured as any society a holy fool would have encountered years ago. What I was aiming for was to make a fool who would be both realistic in the history of what a holy fool was and a real character in the twentieth-century world.

Silet: Children keep working their way through your books. In *With Child* you focus on them more.

King: Originally *With Child* started out as Lee's book, but to my surprise she walked off into the islands in Puget Sound and I didn't quite know what to do when she left. It became a book about families and adult responsibilities and how we raise our children. Even in a loving, supportive background it is not easy, and in a background with people who never grew up and never took responsibility for their own lives, let alone their children, you end up producing kids who may be intelligent and full of good will, but don't have a chance to be what their natures would have them be. They're either destroyed or twisted. That's what that book turned into, a look at relationships between adults and children.

Silet: What does having your central character a lesbian allow you to do as a writer?

King: It's one of those things that comes from not writing deliberately. I'm always astonished when I do panel discussions or group signings with people who say that they normally write hundred-page outlines for three-hundred page books. I am always aghast at the idea of writing any kind of outline. I hate outlines. I do know the end of the book; otherwise I don't have a point to pull myself toward, but how I get there is a mystery to me. It's the most amazing process. I'm going through it for the ninth time now and each time I think, this is never going to come together, this is just nonsense, and somehow all these little bits and pieces that I put in not quite knowing why begin to fall together. All of a sudden I see that something I put in chapter two ties in very nicely with something in chapter eighteen.

It's a magical process, it really is. So why is Kate a lesbian? I think looking back—although again it was not a deliberate decision—what it allowed me to do was to let her have a friendship with a man, her partner Al, that didn't have any erotic overtones. There are so many books where one investigator falls in love with another or where the witness falls in love with the policeman, that I think my subconscious was saying, "Right, we'll have none of this." So I made it impossible for them to have a sexual relationship.

Silet: You start to develop something with Kate and Lee and then have Lee move away. Do you know where that is going to go?

King: Oh, I think toward the end of *With Child* their equilibrium is more or less restored. What's happening in *With Child* is a recognition that the life-changing effects of Lee's injury have to be worked out somehow. Lee needs some space, some time to redefine who she is outside of the relationship with Kate.

The whole business of how a person in a relationship relates to the stronger one without becoming utterly dependent, and in Lee's case not only on her lover but on her care-giver, interests me. As Lee begins to get control of the physical aspects of what has happened to her, she needs to wrestle with the emotional and spiritual component. She has to get away into a retreat and meditate about who she is, as a person, as her own person, not just in a relationship. To my mind there was never the possibility of a complete breakup, although obviously Kate fears that. Lee just needs to regain her psychic space.

Silet: Your central character seems to get injured quite often. Is that a mechanism you developed to help her discover herself?

King: I try not to have one of these poor characters who are forever getting beaten and shot, I really do try. I admit Kate gets her back cut in *A Grave Doubt,* and in *With Child* she gets whacked in the head, but I promise not to do that anymore. However, yes, to a certain extent it is a part of the plot mechanism in a book involving action. You have to come to a climax in order for the plot to be shunted onto another track, which is what happens in both those books. In *With Child,* the whole first section is about one character, and something dramatic has to happen in order to shift the viewpoint sideways to focus on Jules.

Silet: Let's talk about the Mary Russell books. Where did she come from?

King: God knows. Mary Russell is a case of things working themselves out in the back of my head, so that I don't know exactly where they come from. One of the pleasures—I won't say one of the deliberate things, because that makes me sound much more competent that I am—but one of the pleasures of Mary Russell is that she is a modern young woman confronting the epitome of the Victorian male world. She and Holmes are very similar people underneath but they do not mix, any more than oil and water mix, although stirring them together may make for some interesting visual effects. I have to admit that I occasionally feel as if I'm channeling these characters, that Mary Russell sat down and wrote that first sentence: "I was fifteen when I met Sherlock Holmes...."

Silet: When you picked Sherlock Holmes for your series, you picked a character with an enormous amount of previous background. Why did you pick him?

King: You will insist that I make these decisions deliberately, won't you? What other character in the history of crime fiction—of any fiction—could you find who would create the sparks with a young woman like that? What other turning point could you think of when the old and new meet too dramatically, and the male and female face off? Beyond that, though, Holmes has grown on me. He is a perfect example of a character bigger than his creator, and I have found it both a challenge and a pleasure to free him from Conan Doyle's preconceptions.

Silet: Did the period attract you?

King: I have come to find it fascinating, but I did not choose it; it came with the territory. I couldn't begin the books any earlier because the latest Holmes story is set in 1914; in order to have him free of the whole canon I had to start after "The Last Bow." Conan Doyle can have him before then, all the people writing Baker Street pastiches can have him before then, but after Mary Russell meets him in 1915, he is no longer involved in adventures of Conan Doyle. After 1914, Holmes is mine.

Silet: *The Beekeeper's Apprentice* is really a series of short stories.

King: It is. I couldn't really get away from the fact that it was episodic because in the story of an apprenticeship you have to have small experiences building up to bigger adventures. This is one of the reasons it took so long to sell, I think, and over the two or three years I was rewriting it I gradually brought together some of the adventures. The whole Wales section, for example, was added to tie in the episodes of her apprenticeship with the big case that makes up the end. In a sense, *The Beekeeper's Apprentice* is not really a novel. But all the more fun for that, perhaps.

Silet: Religion plays a central part in the Mary Russell books. Why did you give her this theological interest?

King: Well, assuming that I give anyone anything, I think for any number of reasons. She is too complex a character just to be a detective; too, religion is one of the things Holmes feels very ambivalent about. There are bits and pieces in the stories that suggest his awareness of some sort of higher power, but for the most part Holmes is very skeptical. So to have an apprentice who is actively interested in theological things, and yet otherwise competent, is a challenge to him.

Silet: What does this interest allow you to do with her as a character?

King: It gives her the opportunity to look at issues from a different perspective. In *A Monstrous Regiment of Women*, for example, her excitement at finding the possibility of a real, live mystic is something that enriches the whole book. It is not just a question of good guys and bad guys but it is a question of eternity as well. In *A Letter of Mary* a papyrus appears which could either be threatening to the structure of Christianity or enlightening to Christianity and liberating, and Mary, a Jew, is in the middle with the papyrus, not knowing quite what to do with it but knowing that she has to hang onto it somehow. Theology gives me a whole new dimension to play with in writing the books.

Silet: In *The Monstrous Regiment of Women* you deal with a quasi-religious group of women who do good works, with feminism in the early years of the century, with class questions, with social questions of poverty and so on.

King: In that book Mary Russell is looking for her own identity. She is torn between, as I believe she says somewhere, the appeal of a women's community and everything that Holmes represents. There are a lot of things that are pulling in different directions. There's the women's side, there's the personal religion, which is an emotional thing as opposed to the intellectual side that is Holmes, yet at the same time you have the emotional pull of Holmes on her.

It's not as simple as men/mind and cool emotions, women/ warm emotions and God. Carl Jung says something to the effect that consciousness is found in the tension between two unreconcilable opposites. It is the point of tension that brings us closer to enlightenment, and that is what she's doing in that book: she's being torn in a lot of different directions, and she has to find who she is somewhere in the middle.

Silet: There is a dance between Holmes and Russell which began in the first book which intensifies in that book. Are you going to push this farther in the coming books?

King: In *A Letter of Mary* Russell's relationship with Holmes is similar to the one in *The Beekeeper's Apprentice*, except that they are married. It is very matter-of-fact—although I do have a really hot sex scene where the two of them are sitting in a chair and he rubs his fingers over her knuckles. Steamy. In *The Beekeeper's Apprentice* there is a lot of very real but unrecognized sexual tension on both sides; in *Monstrous Regiment* it is much more open but nobody quite knows where it is going. By the time you get into *A Letter of Mary*, that particular source of tension is resolved and they can get on with what they are doing. Which isn't to say that all is sweetness and light. God forbid.

Silet: Tell me about *A Letter of Mary*.

King: It's about a woman archeologist Holmes and Russell met in Palestine—she is mentioned briefly in *The Beekeeper's Apprentice*— who brings a box containing a papyrus apparently written by Mary Magdalene, in which the author refers to herself as an apostle. Now, to many liberal Christians, having a woman apostle would not be a problem, but to others the idea of a woman following Christ and being in a position of some authority would not be easy to accept. And among the people the archeologist comes into contact with are those who are bothered. When this woman is killed, the question of course comes up, is it because of the papyrus or for some other reason? So Holmes and Russell go off in different directions in search of the answer.

Silet: Is there a difference between mainstream and crime fiction?

King: I think so. Mainstream fiction quite often has no direction. It can be about anything and can go anywhere. One of the reasons crime writing is so popular is that the structure holds the book together; it is traditional story-telling in a nontraditional age. Once you've got the structure, though, you can write books that go anywhere, do anything, even books that have very little relationship to crime. Josephine Tey is a superb example of that; in one of her books she has no body, in another the bodies are several hundred years old. So you can do whatever you want within the basic structure if you have a beginning, you have some sort of question, and you have some sort of conclusion.

Silet: Your novels often deal with social issues. Do you think that the crime novel is basically a social novel?

King: Crime novels have to deal with something real. The best crime novels develop an emotional attachment felt by the writer, whether that is about industrial pollution or child abuse or whatever. I hesitate to call what I write "social novels" because that sounds as if I deliberately chose a topic that is in need of reform and wrote the book to provide a soapbox. In some countries, it is true, the crime novel ss a very active means of social criticism. I'm very wary of it myself because it diminishes the integrity of the story. As soon as you climb on that soapbox you risk losing the story.

Silet: What are the pros and cons of writing a series?

King: Pro is that you get to involve yourself and the reader in the long-term growth of the main characters in the series. It's like having another family. On the other hand, as a writer you run the danger of being trapped into writing about the same people doing the same things, over and over again. If you run out of interesting people and your editor nonetheless wants you to keep writing, you would die. I would not like to plan a finite series, but I don't know that I want to write about Kate Martinelli for the rest of my life.

Mary Russell probably has "longer legs"—I imagine that I can go on for quite a while before I get tired of her.

One of the advantages of having published first *A Grave Talent* and then *The Beekeeper's Apprentice* is that by the time *To Play the Fool* appeared nobody knew what the hell I was doing, I had already gotten the reputation for being unclassifiable. If I had published *The Beekeeper's Apprentice* first I would have been known as that woman who writes Holmes pastiches. Having published my books the other way round, especially since *A Grave Talent* won the Edgar, it established me as a different kind of writer, with considerably more freedom.

Riding the Rap
Elmore Leonard

Photo © Linda Solomon

Elmore Leonard is one of the most critically respected and popular authors of crime fiction writing today. His books have also proved irresistible to Hollywood, and they are highly sought after as sources for contemporary movies. Such films as *The Tall T* (1957), *3:10 to Yuma* (1957), *Hombre* (1967), *The Big Bounce* (1969), *The Moonshine War* (1970), *Mr. Majestyk* (1974), and *Stick* (1985) were all made from his novels. Most recently, Leonard's fame expanded greatly with the release of three big-production, and highly acclaimed, films: *Get Shorty* (1995), *Jackie Brown* (1997), and *Out of Sight* (1998).

In spite of the fame and the money he has received for these movies, and although Leonard has written widely for the movies himself, he no longer does so, preferring to spend his time on his novels and leaving the scripting of his books to other hands. However, in his latest project, *Be Cool*, he does envision John Travolta playing the lead part in this reprise of his character Chili Palmer from *Get Shorty*.

The principal effect of his movie fame, aside from the money he has received for the screen rights, has been the increasing recognition he has received for the importance of his novels, each of which now routinely appears on the bestseller lists of *The New York Times*.

A portion of this interview, "Elmore Leonard on the Movies," appeared in 1999 on-line at Mysterynet.com.

Silet: Let's begin by talking a bit about your background. Where you were born, grew up, went to school.

Leonard: I was born in New Orleans in 1925 and lived in Oklahoma City, Dallas, and Memphis before coming to Detroit in 1934. I will jump right into why I think that living in the South was an important period in my life. I have a picture of myself taken in Memphis when I was nine years old, standing with my mother and my sister next to our car. I have my foot on the running board, and I'm pointing a cap pistol at the camera. And I have a cap on. The cap wasn't a prop though; it was something I wore.

This picture was taken only a few months after Bonnie and Clyde were gunned down in Louisiana and that famous picture of her, with a foot on the front bumper of a car, holding a revolver and a cigar, must have appeared in every paper in the United States, perhaps the world, at that time. Well, that was in May and the picture of my mother, my sister, and me was taken only a few months later, just before we came to Detroit.

So what was going on at that time, the notoriety given famous bank robbers, like Pretty Boy Floyd and Machine Gun Kelley, Dillinger, Ma Barker and her guys, all that made an impression on me, during this very impressionable period of my life between five and ten years old. I think it inspired the kind of characters I write about today.

Silet: So it was a sign for things to come?

Leonard: I believe so. I just picked up on desperadoes who at the that time were seen as heroes, robbing banks that had foreclosed on poor farmers.

Silet: So you got to Detroit and finally settled down and you remained for the rest of your younger years and went to grade school and high school in Detroit.

Leonard: I've been here since, with no desire or reason to leave. I attended the University of Detroit High School, run by Jesuits. After that I went into the navy in 1943, and came out in 1946 and went to the University of Detroit.

Silet: Had you been doing any writing up to this point?

Leonard: No, none, but I was reading. A lot.

Silet: You got a degree in English and philosophy from the university. Was getting the degree helpful to your writing later?

Leonard: Not really, because who we read in English were mainly just a lot of historically significant writers. We didn't get into any modern fiction. But I was reading the latest novels. My mother had joined the Book-of-the-Month Club when I was a freshman, so I began to read those books. In many of the popular novels of the time, I felt the authors were belaboring their prose, using far too many words. I had that feeling even then, but it wasn't until later, in fact, not until I was out of the service and at the U of D that I first read Hemingway and was inspired by that lean prose and the way he made it look easy.

Silet: After graduation you went to work in advertising.

Leonard: I went to work at an ad agency, Campbell-Ewald. This was a big agency and Chevrolet was their main account. In fact I went to work there before I finished college. I completed my courses in night school and I was married by then. I was doing traffic production at Campbell-Ewald but left after a couple of years and went to a small agency. I wanted to learn what advertising was all about, how it worked. I got a job as a writer and then came back to Campbell-Ewald as a writer on the Chevrolet account. And skipped a few years in pay raises.

I decided I would learn how to write westerns, because there was such a marvelous market for the genre at that time. You could aim for *The Saturday Evening Post* and *Colliers* and then down into the men's magazines, *Argosy, Blue Book, Adventure,* then down into the pulps, the dozen or more pulps that were still being published, the better ones paying two cents a word. I wrote a couple of westerns and sent them to pulp magazines and they were both rejected, so I decided I had better research and do it right. I researched the Southwest in the 1880s, Arizona in particular, and I subscribed to *Arizona Highways* magazine for the look of the land. Then read what I could about cowboys, what they wore and what kind of coffee they drank, the kind of guns they used, and I also did in-depth research on Apaches, because Apaches were very big in the 1950s.

Silet: Had you been reading any western writers?

Leonard: Not much. I liked western movies, and I think that was the main reason that I chose westerns. I wanted to learn to write and to sell to the movies. And since I liked westerns and since they were very popular on the screen at that time, I thought: write westerns. Then I started reading the westerns that were in the *Post* and *Colliers* and paperbacks. At that time Ernest Haycock, Luke Short and James Warner Bellah were the big names in western fiction.

Silet: You were writing short fiction and finally longer stories. Your first novel, *The Bounty Hunters,* came out in 1954.

Leonard: That was the first book. I had sold the first story, which was a fifteen-thousand word novelette, to *Argosy.* They paid a thousand dollars for it and I couldn't believe it! Then an agent in New York, Marguerite Harper, contacted me, and she represented me through the fifties and into the sixties. In sixty-six I wrote my first non-western. But by then Marguerite was ill, went into the hospital, and sent the manuscript to H. N. Swanson, the Hollywood agent who had sold the film rights of two of my stories and a book to studios.

Silet: The market for westerns disappeared about this time.

Leonard: Yeah, at the end of the fifties there was no market unless you wanted to write for television. But I didn't care for any of the television shows; I thought they were phony. Almost all ended the same way, with the fast-draw shoot-out in the street, which probably never ever happened in the West. I never did have that scene in a book or short story.

Silet: What motivated you then to go into crime fiction?

Leonard: The market was there. It's funny though, when you start out you have trouble deciding what to write about. Now ideas present themselves all the time, if not for the plot of a novel, at least for a scene in the book, or to serve as the backstory for one of the characters.

Silet: With *52 Pickup*, you began to set your books in Detroit. Why the shift to an urban-based crime fiction?

Leonard: Well, *The Big Bounce* took place up in the thumb area of Michigan. Now I was finally going to do Detroit, using the city because I live here. That was the only reason. *52 Pickup* was the first time I had pause when I realized I'm going to be describing places now where people have been, streets they've crossed themselves. I wasn't sure of my ability to describe locations in an interesting way. But by this time I had developed the style of writing always from a character's point of view; so what's described is how he sees the scene, with whatever attitude he brings to bear.

The fact that I use a lot of dialogue to move the story along is the reason so many of my books have been picked up for the movies. They look like movie scripts. But then when you bring the 350-page manuscript down to a 120-page shooting script much of the good stuff's gone and you're left with the plot, which is not what my writing is about. From that standpoint I'm surprised I've been able to sell so many books to Hollywood, where plot and theme are all-important.

Silet: The direction a lot of crime writers go is to start a series. Why didn't you go that route?

Leonard: I almost did. In 1980 I went with Don Fine's Arbor House. Don had been an editor of mine twenty-five years earlier at Dell, when I was doing westerns. The first one I did for him was *City Primeval,* which he wanted to call "High Noon in Detroit." I said, "You can't call it 'High Noon in Detroit,' this is fiction and you can't use a fiction title based on another fiction title." But he insisted. My original title was "Hang Tough." He didn't like that at all.

So I had to come up with "City Primeval," which I still didn't care for, and then he tacked on "High Noon in Detroit" as kind of a subtitle. After that book did pretty well—for that time in my career—Don Fine said, "Do a continuing character, that may be the way to sell you." Don was the reason I went to Arbor House, because he said he would sell me, something no other publishing house seemed that interested in doing.

Even Delacorte, when I was there, in the mid-1970s, labeled me, as a lot of reviewers did, a second coming of Raymond Chandler. There is no similarity at all in the way we write. I didn't come out of that Hammett/Chandler school. I wasn't influenced by them at all. I never cared that much for Hammett and although I enjoyed Chandler, I didn't learn anything from him.

Anyway, Don Fine said, "Let's do a series character, maybe that's the way to sell you." So in the next one, *Split Images,* I used a homicide cop, Raymond Cruz, from *City Primeval,* as the main character. When my agent, Swanie, got the manuscript he said, "You've got to change his name." This was because he had sold *City Primeval* to United Artists and the studio owned the character. I said, "But Don Fine wants a continuing character." He said, "I'll talk to Don. Change his name." So I went through the manuscript and changed his name every place I saw it to Bryan Hurd, but I missed one place. The name Raymond shows up on one page and is still there in the paperbacks, which have been reissued a number of times. I've left Raymond in there and every once in a while I hear from someone asking, "Who's Raymond?"

So I didn't go with a continuing character, and I'm so glad I didn't because I would have gotten just too bored with the same guy doing the same thing. I would have been doing police procedurals over and over. At about that time I was talking to John

D. MacDonald and he was on his, I think, twenty-eighth Travis Magee. He said, "Oh, my God, I don't know if I can do another one."

Silet: Had you been reading John D. MacDonald or any other crime fiction writers?

Leonard: No, I didn't read much at all. I've never liked mysteries, that is the classic type. I liked some of the private-eye stories, and I was reading them in the 1950s. MacDonald was writing the kind of stories I would read in *Cosmopolitan*, and I remember at the time thinking that this is what I should be doing, because they were a lot more fun than the westerns. I didn't realize when I started out that I could have fun writing. Now, that's what keeps me going.

Silet: When did you discover that?

Leonard: I discovered it certainly by the late 1970s in those books I did for Delacorte, *Unknown Man No. 89* and *Swag* and *52 Pickup*. Then what I did for Don Fine getting into *Glitz* and *LaBrava*.

Silet: What was fun about writing those books?

Leonard: Playing with the characters. The bad guys are always the most fun. Since I don't know what the book is about when I begin, or until I'm one hundred pages or so into it, I would introduce characters and audition them in early scenes. I have to make sure my people can talk, because if they can't, they have no business being in the book. And they have to have the right name or they won't talk. It might take weeks to come up with the name "Bob" for a character, after trying other names and the guy remains practically mute.

Almost always there is an unexpected character, one that I didn't count on who plays a very minor role, who will insist on being in the plot and pushes his way in. He might not even have a name when you first meet him. The next time he appears, he has a name, says something kind of interesting and before I know it he's become a turning point in the plot.

Silet: I read somewhere that you didn't do much plotting before you begin to write a book.

Leonard: No, never.

Silet: How do you get started with a new book?

Leonard: I think of a scene. For example, in the one that is coming out, *Be Cool*, I'm going to put Chili Palmer, my central character, in the music business. I want him to get into the business accidentally. And, in an early scene, I want to describe what he's doing, what's happened to him since *Get Shorty*. I wondered if I would be able to imagine John Travolta in the part, and I was happy that it worked out OK. Because when I wrote *Get Shorty*, I had no one clearly in mind, the character is a type more than anything else.

So in the first chapter he is telling a guy that he used to know from his mob days that he's made two pictures, *Get Leo* and *Get Lost*. *Get Leo* was a hit; *Get Lost* bombed. The guy he's having lunch with now runs a record company, and he wants Chili to make a movie about him: he came up from the street, a life of crime, to where he is now, a success in the record business. Chili doesn't think too much of the idea. They're sitting at a sidewalk cafe in L.A., and Chili goes inside to go to the men's room. As he comes out, a car pulls up, a guy gets out of the car and shoots the guy he's having lunch with. Chili thinks, well, maybe a movie about the music business isn't a bad idea after all.

That was the way it started. I had no idea who shot him or why, but would have enough time to figure it out in the next ninety thousand words. That's the way I work.

Silet: Do you come up with a voice or a name first?

Leonard: The voice of the character and then I've got to give him a name. I've tried Frank. Frank used to always be a bad guy in westerns, so I've tried Frank as a good guy and it's never worked. In *Bandits* when it opens up the main character is working for his brother-in-law in a funeral home in New Orleans. I was going to call him Frank, but he acted too old and he was somber. I don't know why but I couldn't wake the guy up. He was Frank Matisse. I thought Matisse was a good New Orleans-sounding name. So I changed his name to Jack Delaney and I had the guy. It's obvious once you name a guy Jack Delaney that, for some reason, he's going to be a talker.

Silet: Although you've set a number of books in Detroit, you also move around in locale. What attracts you to a locale?

Leonard: It's what's going on. *Be Cool* is in Los Angeles because so much of the music business is there. I used Atlantic City when I wanted to do a gambling casino, that background. Actually, *Glitz*— which was the first one of mine that was on *The New York Times* list, in 1985—I wrote because Walter Mirisch and Sidney Poitier wanted to do a sequel to *In the Heat of the Night*. It was Poitier's idea to set the story in Philadelphia, his character's area, and then bring the Southern police officer up with a problem. Kind of reversing the original story. So they said why don't you research Philadelphia, south Philly, and Atlantic City.

I sent my researcher—and this is the first time that he had gone out of town for me—who had done library and newspaper file work for me, and he came back with the 1983 Pennsylvania Crime Commission report, all kinds of photographs, and his tapes of talks with people who worked in casinos. I thought, "God, I'd like to do my own story rather than get Mr. Tibbs involved in it." Just about that time Walter Mirisch called and said, "The studio doesn't want to do a sequel, not that way. You're on your own." And I was very happy to hear that.

Silet: You mentioned research. Do you do much research? How do you use research in your books?

Leonard: I need an awful lot, and I have a researcher, Gregg Sutter, who does all the hard work. For example, in *Rum Punch*, that became *Jackie Brown*, I said, "I want to do a bail bondsman." A bail bondsman in books and movies is always seedy, really disreputable-looking; you don't know if he's a good guy or a bad guy. I told Gregg, "I want to do a bail bondsman, as a lead character,

someone who's good at it, and is working in Palm Beach county."
Where we know a lot of people in law enforcement.

So Gregg talked to several bondsmen until he found one who
knew what he was talking about, who read, and who even had
taught school in Ohio prior to this. Gregg found out what a bail
bondsman does, what his typical day is like, taped it all and sent it
to me. So then I read it, and I went down and talked to the bail
bondsman, got to know him. I'm not looking for a character, but
only what the character does in his business.

When I got into the book, I could call him up any time. I could
say here's a guy who's been stopped for drunk driving and the
police find a pistol in his car and they look him up on the
computer and find out that he has a prior conviction, selling
machine guns. What would be the bond? And the guy says ten
thousand bucks. He doesn't even have to look it up. I called him
quite a number of times while I was writing *Rum Punch*.

Silet: Do you use such contacts in your other books?

Leonard: Oh yeah, in all of them. In *Maximum Bob*, a judge friend
of mine in Florida was the reason that I thought, let's do a judge,
but a very hard-sentencing one. The main character will be a
probation officer, a woman, and the judge has his eyes on her and
she's got other problems. Gregg found a probation officer and
then I met her and talked with her, got to know what her job
entailed. We also did that for *Out of Sight*, this time with a deputy
U.S. Marshal, a woman, found out what she does and then put my
character in the part.

Silet: You have done several books now set in Florida. What is it
that's attractive about Florida?

Leonard: I've been going to Florida every year since about 1950. I
bought a place for my mother in Pompano Beach at one point in
the late 1960s, so I was always visiting her. A lot was going on in
South Florida, especially following the Cuban boat lift in 1979 or
1980. When I first saw South Beach I decided I had to set a story
there. I used a little bit of South Beach in *Stick*, the book, and then
in *LaBrava*, which is entirely set there, but this was before it

became the trendy place to go. Then it was all old Jewish ladies sitting in a row on the porches with their sunglasses and their hats on, and their nose shields, while down the street the boat-lifters were shooting one another.

Silet: Now Florida is a hot place as a setting for crime fiction.

Leonard: I've used South Beach since and I've used other areas in *Pronto* and in *Riding the Rap* most recently. The next one is going to be in L.A. again. I like L.A.

Silet: Do you have a title for the next one?

Leonard: Not really, no. I'm going to bring a priest out of Rwanda, a guy who shouldn't have been a priest. He's got a drinking problem. He was there during the genocide in 1994 and he sees evidence of it happening again, in the present. While he didn't protest or do anything to aid victims of the massacres that took place, he does now and gets away with an heroic act. He takes his collar off and moves to L.A., where his brother is a personal-injury lawyer working with a woman who manufactures insurance fraud situations. I think I'm going to open with the woman who was in prison in Florida.

Last month Gregg Sutter and I visited a woman's prison, Broward Correctional, and I talked to women there about what's funny in prison. My judge friend called the superintendent and asked if it would be OK. The superintendent said sure and he arranged it. He asked who would like to talk to me about humor in prison, and I got fifteen ladies who showed up in this conference room and we sat down and talked and Gregg recorded the whole thing. We have twenty-two pages of pretty good stuff. What I think is funny about their experiences, they didn't think was funny at all. They thought it was awful.

The woman in the book, who stages fraud situations—slip and fall or auto accidents—is in there on another charge, assault with a deadly weapon, and she comes out wanting to do stand-up comedy. It opens with her doing her stand-up act. The priest is going to fall into her clutches, and she sees ways to make a lot of money using this guy who she imagines as an heroic missionary priest who now is here to raise money for all the poor orphans back in Rwanda.

Silet: A lot of your male characters fall into the clutches of some woman who has a scam. At what point did you bring your female characters from just being background figures more to the foreground?

Leonard: I don't know when exactly. I think right from the start that the women in my fiction were important and strong and could be funny. In the westerns the woman usually stood around wringing her hands. But in *Valdez Is Coming* I developed a very strong woman, and in *Hombre* also. I've worked hard on my women. There was a review of one book from the *Detroit News* where the reviewer said that my opinion of women seemed to be on a par with Mickey Spillane's.

I resented that, but I thought if she feels that way then maybe I'd better work on it. So I did. Or a woman would complain at a book-signing, "God, all these women in *Stick*, they're just bimbos." I said, "Who do you think these women would be attracted to? The guys are their counterparts." But still the female lead in *Stick* is by far smarter than any of the other characters. She's a financial consultant.

Silet: In your novels you often find humor in places perhaps that others would not find it. How does humor work in your novels?

Leonard: I guess it all comes from my attitude, that I tend to see more humor in everyday situations perhaps than most people. And I tend to feel a little sorry for the bad guys, because they're not very bright and tend to get themselves into impossible situations. I don't try to make my books funny, since I don't write comedy. I said that to Barry Sonnefeld, who directed *Get Shorty*. "This movie is being advertised as a comedy and I don't write comedies." And he said, "No, but it's a funny book."

Silet: The latest books are basically dialogue driven. When did you decide to make them more dialogue rather than plot driven?

Leonard: I'd say from the beginning and that was the Hemingway influence. I'd read a Hemingway short story and see all that white space on the page, and I liked that. You read it fast. But then you say, "Hey, wait a minute," and you go back and read it more slowly and see how much more there is than you originally thought. I was influenced greatly by Hemingway, until I realized that I didn't share his attitude about life. I certainly don't take myself as seriously as he did. Then I had to find other people and there was one in particular that I loved, Richard Bissell.

Richard Bissell in the 1950s wrote *Seven and a Half Cents* which became *The Pajama Game*, the musical. And then he wrote *Say Darling*, which was about the making of *The Pajama Game*. Many of his stories were set on the Mississippi River, where Bissell was a pilot, the first literary pilot since Mark Twain. In books like *High Water*, and another one, *A Stretch on the River*, you'd be on the tow-boat and hear the crew members talking. I loved it. They were real. And they were funny without trying to be funny.

When I wrote *Killshot* I had scenes in Cape Girardeau, Missouri, and the male lead takes a job on a towboat. I read a little bit of Bissell again to refresh my memory, to get me into the mood, and I was amazed to see how much he had influenced me.

Silet: One of the hallmarks of your prose is your ability to capture voices. Is this something you have consciously cultivated?

Leonard: No, not consciously at all. I do listen when someone's talking to me. I know that. Especially since I quit drinking and that was twenty-two years ago.

Silet: And just by listening you pick up the rhythms and speech patterns?

Leonard: That's the main thing, the rhythms of speech. I can hear a black guy or a Hispanic person talk and I can hear the rhythm or lilt of their speech. Almost all black women speak with a certain lilt, at least the younger ones, that I think is fascinating. So I try to get it into my writing, whether it is recognized or not I don't know. When I was going to do *Bandits*, set in New Orleans, I thought, well, I can do a New Orleans accent because I can hear my cousins talking, but I thought, no, I'm going to get into dialect because I'll start writing phonetically. I didn't want to do that. So I just hint at the sound and hope that the reader picks up on it.

Silet: You've had a dozen or more of your stories and novels turned into films. What has your experience been with the movie world?

Leonard: I found out soon enough I didn't like writing screenplays. My goal was to become associated with a director I respected and he and I would see the story exactly the same way and the studio would go along with our view and we'd make a good movie. For the most part the studios would concentrate on plot, on action, on making the central character more heroic and less a recognizable person. All I was doing was rewriting. Of course that's all any screenwriter does. You keep rewriting, incorporating ideas that people in meetings have off the tops of their heads.

They'd say, "Well, what about this? Why don't we do this? You know that scene really worked in..." And they'd mention another movie. "Yeah, that should work right here. Why don't you just slip that scene in?" Then they'd take off from a Friday meeting, and over the weekend you'd sit in a hotel room writing, staring at the wall about two feet away. If you want the money, you write it, and by the next Monday meeting they would've forgotten all about those ideas but there they are, in the script.

It's not writing; it's just taking in writing. It's tailoring; it's shortening the pants. Where's the writing? There is some in the dialogue, but certainly in a scene description you don't have to write. You say: "Interior bedroom, day." For some screenwriters, of course, that's where they do their writing, to show that they know how to write. You know, overwrite that scene description. So I just got tired of it. Finally I got to the point where I was making enough money with the books that I didn't have to rely on sales to Hollywood or screenwriting.

Silet: Did you ever have an experience where you felt that you and the director were working in the same direction, had the same thing in mind?

Leonard: Yeah, as a matter of fact, I felt that with Burt Reynolds, of all people, for *Stick*. I thought that he certainly could play it, but then I realized that it would have required a good strong director to keep him in character and not let him become Burt Reynolds.

Silet: The last few years with *Get Shorty, Out of Sight, Jackie Brown* the movies made from your fiction have become very successful. Has that altered in any way your experience with the movie world or the way you write your books?

Leonard: No, it has not changed my approach to writing. I'm not going to design my books to be more adaptable. I'm still going to write them the way I want. Although *Be Cool* is so obviously, so shamelessly, made for the movies that it's OK. Making a movie of what's going on is the whole idea of the book. I write in scenes so that if I want to tell a scene, because I don't want to do it live, then I have the character Chili Palmer telling Elaine Levin, the studio executive in charge of production, the scene. In a scene, for example, at a record company, Chili is talking to an executive about how the money works, what the advance is and so on. He tells this to Elaine and she says, "Well, is that a scene in the movie?" And he says, "I don't know. Let's leave it up to the screenwriter." Because this is what you're doing anyway.

Silet: You mentioned with *Be Cool* having John Travolta in the back of your mind. Have you done that with any of your other books?

Leonard: He was in the front of my mind. He's got to do it. But usually not, no. For example, in *Hombre* I pictured Richard Boone in the part that he played, and I couldn't believe it that he actually played it, that they cast him without any suggestion of mine. He was in *The Tall T,* and he recited his lines exactly the way I heard them while I was writing the story. I didn't write the screenplay, but they picked up a lot from the original.

Silet: What do you think about awards? What do they do for a writer's career?

Leonard: I've received a couple of awards from the Mystery Writers of America, also achievement awards sponsored by groups dedicated to supporting and encouraging activities in the arts. But I've never looked at awards as an inspiration or a goal. Usually they came as a surprise.

Silet: What about critics? Do you think you've been well treated by the critics?

Leonard: You have to keep in mind that reviewers also consider themselves writers and giving your book a bad rap is an opportunity to sound authoritative, like they know what they're talking about. Most reviewers, though, see that the purpose of my books is to entertain and they like them. I read the reviews. Some writers say they don't; I don't believe them.

Silet: Do you ever learn anything from the reviews?

Leonard: Well, I do as a matter of fact. Yeah, sure if they're intelligent and make sense and they say he was weak in a certain area and I can agree with them I'll try to do it better. I've spent forty-seven years at this and I'm still trying to do it better.

Silet: A lot of crime fiction deals with social problems. Is the genre inherently a social form?

Leonard: I don't think of it that way. I see characters involved in some kind of hustle, usually in over their heads. As I get to know each one I seem to develop an affection for them that brings them to life. Their attitudes, then, guide the plot, give it direction.

Silet: Often you don't make much distinction between the good and the bad characters.

Leonard: That's because I think of my antagonists as normal people when they aren't committing crimes. After I left the women's prison I went to the South Florida Reception Center, and I talked to five guys who were lifers, who had been in thirty years or so. They were up for parole and taking part in a program on how to behave in the civilized world once they were released. Talking to these guys I had the feeling we could have met in a bar and started talking and I would never know they were criminals—other than the prison stories they told.

I remember one time watching a news story on television, the police were closing in on a bank robber. They had a hunch about what bank he would hit next and they were right, they got him. You see him walking along the sidewalk toward the camera, in a long shot, talking to a woman police officer and she's laughing. I wondered what he was telling her. Probably how he screwed up. He thinks it's funny, because he sees whatever he did now as a dumb move. That's the kind of guy I use. I've talked to people you would never know were bad guys. I don't care for the one who's completely corrupt or vicious. He's no fun. They have to have some recognizable spark of humanity about them.

Silet: Is there any distinction between crime and regular or mainstream fiction?

Leonard: You know that if you're writing a crime story you're most likely going to draw conclusions that satisfy the reader's sense of right and wrong. Unless you don't care to make judgments, as I do, and leave that up to the reader. But something is going to happen. There's going to be some tension, there's going to be suspense to keep the plot moving. As opposed to say in a literary novel where you may wonder what's going on, what it's about, why is the author telling us so much. The analysis of characters and their motivations may be stunningly written, but it can also be boring to many readers.

Silet: So crime fiction is just a better way to tell a story?

Leonard: It isn't a better way, it's a way in itself to present a dramatic conflict in which you offer the reader usually a clear resolution.

Silet: What do you think you do best as a writer?

Leonard: What I have the most fun doing, developing characters, bringing them to life, getting them to talk. It's the most satisfying thing that I do writing a book. Even though I can make problems for myself and have to rewrite a paragraph a dozen times; but that's part of it. Writing is rewriting. I don't go through a draft and then start over and rewrite. I rewrite as I go along. As the pages pile up I continue to go back through them. Sometimes, once I get to a part in the book where something is going to happen and I have to have established it, then I go back and insert what's needed. So I'm always conscious of making the thing work.

Silet: What would you like to be remembered for as a writer?

Leonard: Simply what I'm doing. I don't aspire to do anything else, like write a serious novel. Mine are all serious to me. But I know what I can do and what I can't do. I learned that early on. I can't write from the omniscient author point of view who knows everything and uses his language to tell the story, because I don't have that language. So I rely on my characters and their language.

Silet: Is there anything you'd like to do that you haven't done?

Leonard: No, because I never know what I'm going to do next. That's part of the fun.

Sergeant Cribb, the Prince of Wales, and Peter Diamond
Peter Lovesey

Photo © Valerie Cooper

Peter Lovesey has said that when his writing is successful it can be subversive, suggest ironies, spring surprises, and now and then, chill the blood. Lovesey first achieved recognition as a writer with the creation of a series of Victorian crime novels featuring Detective Sergeant Cribb and his associate Constable Thackery. Beginning in 1970 with *Wobble To Death* and almost each year thereafter for the next eight years Lovesey wrote mystery novels around various Victorian sporting and recreational activities. In the early 1980s Granada brought Cribb and Thackery to the television audience, dramatizing many of the novels and running half a dozen new adventures written for television by Lovesey and his wife Jacqueline. The series played successfully in both Great Britain and in the United States on PBS's highly popular show, "Mystery."

At the end of the television series Lovesey found that he had exhausted his plot ideas for Cribb and Thackery and he began to explore other crime venues. He next wrote two crime books set in the inter-war years, one on a transatlantic ship crossing, *The False*

Inspector Dew (1982), and the other in Hollywood during the period of the silent film, *Keystone* (1983). Lovesey followed these books with two set during the Second World War. Both *Rough Cider* (1987) and *On the Edge* (1987) draw on Lovesey's memories of his experience during the war, and they moved him out of the historical genre and brought his fiction more or less into modern times.

The lure of the nineteenth century remains with him however, and in 1987 he launched a second series of Victorian mysteries, this time starring as the central investigator, Edward, the Prince of Wales. *Bertie and the Tinman: From the Detective Memories of King Edward VII* was followed by *Bertie and the Seven Bodies* (1990) and *Bertie and the Crime of Passion* (1995). Now, Peter Lovesey would like to alternate between fictions in contemporary and historical settings.

In addition, he is at work on a contemporary crime series with ex-Detective Superintendent Peter Diamond. The first Diamond novel was *The Last Detective* (1991), the next *Diamond Solitaire* (1993) and the third, *The Summons* (1995). *Do Not Exceed the Stated Dose* and *Upon a Dark Night* both were published in 1998.

Portions of this interview appeared as "An Interview with Peter Lovesey," *Mean Streets*, Issue 6 (May 1992), 24–30, and "The Mystery Scene Interview with Peter Lovesey," *Mystery Scene*, No. 49 (September/October 1995), 22, 24–26.

Silet: How did you get started writing?

Lovesey: I saw a small advertisement in *The Times* offering a thousand pounds for a first crime novel. Macmillan, the publishers in England, wanted to start a new crime list. Initially, I hadn't read much crime. I'd been through the Sherlock Holmes stories when I was young and enjoyed those and I'd read about one Agatha Christie, but my wife, Jax, devoured crime fiction and was very enthusiastic for me to try. By this time I had become a teacher making about nine hundred pounds a year, so a thousand was a lot of money. A lot of people are inspired by higher things; Peter Lovesey wasn't. Jax said maybe she could help with the plot if I could think of something. Why don't I use the sports background?

I thought about it for a day or two. For my first book, *The Kings of Distance*, I'd done a lot of research in old newspapers. And in these papers, I had come across accounts of six-day races that took place indoors in London at the Agricultural Hall, Islington, and in New York at Madison Square Garden. It was big business.

Silet: I didn't realize they were in America as well.

Lovesey: Oh, yes. There were several stars—I don't know whether you can call them athletes really—but they were walkers or runners who were professionals, often impoverished men exploited by managers who were making much more money than they. But they would go round and round this track six days on end trying to beat each other. They could take rests in little tents by the side of the track. The events were officially known as "go as you please" contests because they could run or walk or just take a rest and ultimately it was the one who'd covered the most laps who would be the winner.

They did about six hundred miles in the course of the six days. It had to be done between two Sundays because nobody did anything on a Sunday in Victorian times. Well, I thought maybe this is a possible background. It's got a lot of the elements of the old-fashioned Agatha Christie mystery. You've got the characters confined in this hall, over six days, and you've got a race to be decided which adds a certain amount of interest as well.

Silet: It had a built-in plot structure.

Lovesey: Yes, right. So, I talked about it with Jax, wrote the book and then we had to decide what the title would be. We thought of *Go As You Please Murders* and that didn't seem quite right. She said: what did the press call these races? I said: they call them "Wobbles," so we called the book *Wobble to Death*. Not a bad title.

Silet: Not a bad idea either.

Lovesey: Yes, well it was different and it won the prize, so that was my beginning. After that, it was a matter of following it up. The publishers wanted a second one. If you invest in someone who has won a prize, you want him to carry on. So I did and I wrote altogether eight Victorian mysteries starring the same detectives. I hadn't thought *Wobble to Death* would become a series; I just thought of it as a "one-off" book for the competition.

Silet: Did you consciously think about Cribb and Thackery as being like Holmes and Watson?

Lovesey: I wanted them to be real, credible policemen rather than the kind of omniscient character Holmes was. I didn't want Cribb to be a Superman character. I wanted him to be a believable policeman—a human sort of character who might have aspired to higher things but was stuck in his rank of sergeant and would probably never progress because he had this man Jowett over him who was going to keep him at that level forever. That was about as far as my thinking went at that early stage and then I began to develop the character more as I went through the series.

Each novel started with some kind of Victorian entertainment as a background—in the first book, the race; in the second, it was prize-fighting; and then I turned to the music hall, which I suppose was the American equivalent of vaudeville. And I did one on spiritualism. I wrote about those things that Victorians would get excited about and would provide me with a colorful plot.

Silet: Did you consciously craft each one of these novels to cover a different type of crime fiction?

Lovesey: For my own sanity I looked to do different things. I was working on this series for eight years. I don't like to work to a formula plot. I thought it would be interesting to try a book from Thackery's point of view; that was the book that was called *Invitation to a Dynamite Party*. In another I excluded Thackery altogether and had a more serious story—a book called *Waxwork* which was very much more from Cribb's point of view. So, yes, I was trying different things out.

Silet: But you stopped writing the books about Cribb and Thackery.

Lovesey: Yes, what happened was that to my great good fortune a television series came along. I'd written all eight novels when an English television producer, June Wyndham-Davies, saw a review of

Waxwork and thought it would be good as a "one-off" television play, which they made. Then they discovered that I'd written seven others: the magic number for a series. They asked me to do another six stories—to go into a second series—which weren't based on books, just straight television plays. They wanted them in a remarkable short time, six or seven months. Panic! I had to dragoon Jax into dividing the work with me.

Happily for me, she said okay she would write three and I would do three and then we'd compare notes and knock them into shape. And that was how we wrote those six just for television. But I found that at the end of that time I'd used up my entire stock of ideas, all the things that I had faintly in mind to do. And the other thing was that when I began to think about Sergeant Cribb as a character, wondering if maybe I could dream up some other plot about him, the television image was so powerful and Alan Dobie's performance so strong that I couldn't get back to the original concept of Cribb, I could only think of Dobie.

Silet: Now, however, you have come back to the Victorian period with the Bertie series. Why did you come back? Can't you stay away from the Victorians?

Lovesey: I thought I'd like to go back and do something Victorian but without featuring a policeman. I adopted my original method which was to plan the background and I thought, what fun to do something in Victorian times on horse racing, not quite what Dick Francis is doing on modern racing but with a racing background. So I read up what I could about the turf. I came across this story about Fred Archer who was the supreme jockey—flat racing jockey—of his time and more successful than anybody else, who one day picked up a gun and killed himself.

There were various explanations given which didn't seem very satisfactory and his last words had been, "Are they coming?" which I thought rather tantalizing. That began to suggest all sorts of things. So having got that, I had to think who my detective was going to be. I didn't want a policeman and Bertie was the supreme patron of the turf, really fascinated by it all and passionately interested in it, and he knew Archer because Archer rode for him. They had even exchanged photographs. There were obvious links.

The more I began to think about it, the more Bertie suggested himself as a detective. He was given little responsibility by the Queen and at this time he's in his forties. He's got certain interests, he's got the ladies, so it seemed fairly obvious that he might want to know what the explanation was for Archer's death. I'm not saying that he would be a good detective, because he isn't, he just bumbles his way through. Things get solved almost in spite of him. But, I rather like the idea of a detective who is not too competent.

Silet: It's an endearing quality about him. He is earnest but he's not very good.

Lovesey: And there's a certain appeal in writing a book in the first person. I enjoy writing as if I were Bertie and letting the reader read between the lines and have some fun at the expense of the Prince of Wales. It's got appeal for me at the moment and I hope I can sustain that enthusiasm and carry on for some more books because I'd like this one to be a series, too.

Silet: *Bertie and the Seven Bodies* is the second in the series. Tell me about that book.

Lovesey: Well, I got to thinking if Dick Francis has influenced one book, how about an Agatha Christie influenced one? Why not see if I could work out a plot in which a number of murders take place, one each day of the week with a rhyme to connect them in the Christie tradition. I thought it might be a challenge. So using the voice I had found for *Bertie and the Tinman*, with a Christie plot, *Bertie and the Seven Bodies* arose.

Silet: Now you've written a third one.

Lovesey: Yes, that's called *Bertie and the Crime of Passion* and again I'm trying to work within the convention of his real life. I've tried to stick pretty closely to biographical details. He did frequently go to Paris to escape the pressures of being a public figure in England.

Silet: And to escape his mother as well?

Lovesey: Right, right. He often went down to the south of France, but he called at Paris for a while before doing that and his wife, Queen Alexandra, didn't always go with him. I began to look at the number of mistresses or alleged mistresses he had in England and France, Paris particularly. I found the names of at least a dozen women who were supposed to have enjoyed his favors and one of them was Sarah Bernhardt. She, again, is a fascinating character, and there's a lot of material on her. I began to think about a story in which she would act as his sidekick but be far more astute and alert than Bertie was.

Silet: *Crime of Passion* is set in Paris.

Lovesey: Yes, in the 1890s and the murder takes place at the Moulin Rouge, and we move through one or two settings which seemed fairly obvious ones to somebody who was looking at Paris at that period.

Silet: Let's move on from the Victorian period because you've written about other periods. You seem to be working your way through time with *The False Inspector Dew* and *Keystone Murders* in the 1920s and now the World War II novels, *Rough Cider* and *On the Edge*. Both of the novels are much more violent, gruesome than your earlier ones.

Lovesey: Yes, I suppose there wasn't quite the element of fun that I discovered in the other books. But for a boy growing up, World War II was a period of great fun and excitement. You didn't experience the fears that your parents were feeling at that time. All that I was interested in was getting my collection of shrapnel, fragments of bomb that you collected as you went round the streets and round the bomb sites. Competing with all the other boys to see who could get a piece of bomb that was actually recognizable. Exciting times.

Our house was bombed in the war and my two brothers had a very lucky escape. They were inside the house under an iron table and my parents survived as well, so we were very fortunate, whereas the people next door were killed. It made a strong impression. I can remember the 1940s more vividly than the 1950s.

When we were bombed we obviously had to move to somewhere new and we went not to the area I've described in *Rough Cider* but to Cornwall, which is further west. As a child that seemed quite a sinister place to me because it was unfamiliar territory and because these people spoke differently from Londoners.

Silet: You do quite a bit with the difference in the dialogue.

Lovesey: Yes, while I didn't have the experience of the boy in the book, I could well imagine how that could happen. To get background I read as much as I could about evacuees' experiences. Fortunately, there are all kinds of anniversaries going on about the war, and there's a spate of books. People my age are writing about how they felt about suddenly being shifted out to the country for safety reasons and hating it. That really fed my imagination.

Silet: Where did you get the idea for the head in the cider?

Lovesey: I came across a book on methods of making wine. It had an historical treatment of it. I found these accounts of what they called mutton-fed cider, which was made on farms. It was very powerful stuff. Cider is a strong drink in England; I think in America it is more of a soft drink, but at home it's a really intoxicating, heady drink. To assist the fermentation and to make it brew even stronger, they would hang a joint of meat inside the keg. Any cider maker will tell you that was the custom. The meat would be picked clean—you just take the bone out at the end because there would be no meat left at all. You can see how a crime-writer's imagination got to work on that.

Silet: Your next novel, *On the Edge,* is set in a very different kind of place.

Lovesey: I enjoyed writing *Rough Cider* and I wanted to get something in about that immediate postwar feeling and about the position women found themselves in at the end of the war. In the war they had been active and useful and had a glamorous time on the fighter stations, as these two characters in the novel had, as plotters in the control room.

Silet: Is it also a novel about class?

Lovesey: I don't think I was so conscious of that. There is a big class element in English society, still is and always has been, but I was more interested in women and the fact that suddenly after the war they were expected to go back to a humdrum existence as housewives. It was exceptional then for women to carry on working. The men too had to go back; they were no longer the gallant fighter pilots winning the Battle of Britain. The character Barry becomes an embittered man who takes it out on his wife. I was in the Air Force sometime later and I saw people like that who talked constantly about the glamorous times in the war and how dull and boring it was now. They became embittered men.

The character Rose, in *On the Edge,* is married to such a man. So I sought to show how two women who had gone their different ways and who suddenly come together again discover a spark between them. The idea of getting back to something more exciting, a murder and possibilities of freedom, release, more glamour, suddenly suggests itself to them.

Silet: I think the postwar world of austerity adds to the novel's feeling.

Lovesey: Yes, it is a blacker story, I suppose. So many of my books have been written from the point of view of the detective, whether it's a police detective or whether it's Bertie as a kind of incompetent amateur detective, but it intrigues me from time to time to look into the mind of the killer and see how that develops.

Silet: It's fascinating how Antonia who appears quite willing to murder her friend and/or her husband seems totally without remorse, guilt.

Lovesey: Obviously, Antonia is the evil one at the beginning. You rather think that poor little Rose is being drawn into something that she doesn't understand. Rose has far more reason to kill her husband than Antonia does. That intrigued me—how one person might persuade another who the reader will identify with. I hope that the reader is persuaded to think, "Oh, if I were in Rose's position, what would I do now?" And at each step, is this the moment when I would draw back and say, "No, I'm going no further with you"? The plot develops in such a way that it's very difficult for Rose at any point to turn back and stop.

Silet: It puts the reader in an unusually compromising position.

Lovesey: Numbers of people have said to me, "I think she should get away with it. I think the ending should be different." I thought she shouldn't; I never intended her to get away with it entirely. But I left it just a little open at the end.

Silet: *The False Inspector Dew* is the story of a woman who falls in love with dentist and suddenly is helping to plot the murder of his wife.

Lovesey: It explores my interest in the ambivalence between the killer and the policeman, and the notion that at times the policeman identifies closely with the killer. It was suggested by a book about the famous murderer, Dr. Crippen. The writer was Inspector Dew, who finally arrested him. Dew was so sympathetic to Crippen and put himself so much into his position that he describes him in the book as the "little fellow," an endearing term. They used to talk about Chaplin as the "little fellow" and I rather like the idea of Chaplin coming into the story in the early scenes and that there are sections of the book based on Chaplin's films.

That idea about the detective who is fascinated by or sympathetic with the murderer is a very interesting one. He has to get into the mind of the murderer to understand what he's about, and maybe even think of himself carrying out the murder. Immediately after the trial Dew—the real Dew—resigned; he never took on another case. He retired from the force at the age of forty-seven and went off to grow roses somewhere on the south coast. The whole story built from that suggestion.

Silet: You mentioned reading the book about Inspector Dew and Crippen. Have you read much other crime fiction?

Lovesey: Not much. I've tended to catch up on people I met and obviously you join organizations. I've joined the Crime Writers' Association and the Detection Club in England and you meet other writers that way and that makes you want to find out what they've written. Yes, I've caught up gradually—I've probably read as much as most without being a real enthusiast. I tend to read the ones who have a psychological approach to crime and who investigate the minds of killers. So it's writers like Patricia Highsmith and Ruth Rendell who interest me greatly.

Silet: A lot of critics still try to differentiate between "serious" literature and genre or popular literature, and certainly crime fiction fits into that latter category. Is there a distinction, do you think?

Lovesey: I suppose the pat answer is that it's a pity there are these divisions and that we have these labels. I think there's a certain amount of material that gets published because it has the label mystery or science fiction or romance that may not get published otherwise, but at the better end of the scale I think there are writers, two I've mentioned, Rendell and Highsmith, who must be regarded as major novelists irrespective of the fact that they are crime writers.

I think there was a time in the 1920s and 1930s when mysteries were just written as entertainment and there was little treatment of character, but these days more ambitious things are being done in the mystery novel. And with more real innovation than most of the stylistic experiments in what's called mainstream fiction writing.

Silet: Where did your new crime figure, Peter Diamond, come from? He seems to be a total departure from your earlier work.

Lovesey: That was something I wished to do after writing mysteries for approximately twenty years. I had done quite a number of short stories where one could experiment and try different things without the big risk of commercial disaster. So I've written contemporary stories, but I've been cautious about attempting to write a contemporary novel, when I was better known as a writer of the historical mystery or the period mystery. But the time came when I suppose the interest in those short stories gave me the confidence to attempt one totally modern novel.

I placed the setting in Bath, where I live, so I'd be able to go along and visit the scenes and make it as realistic as I possibly could. The only problem really was that I still wasn't sure whether I was fully up-to-date with modern forensic and police methods. You see one of the great advantages of the historical mystery is that you don't worry too much about keeping up-to-date with the latest theories on genetic fingerprinting, for example, which I don't know a great deal about, but one has to face that coming to a contemporary book.

My way of coping was to have this character, Peter Diamond, the kind of a man who feels himself a little at odds with the scientists and the men in the white coats. In his mind he harks back to the detectives of the 1940s and 1950s, guys in trilby hats and raincoats. He buys books covering that period and the memoirs of detectives, Cherrill of the Yard and Fabian of the Yard. He idolizes those people and sees himself like that. But for me it's a way of having Diamond despise the modern methods. Along with the genuine detective work going on in the course of the story, he's able to use his interviewing skills to bring out the truth.

Silet: In *The Last Detective* he was a member of the police force, but he was relieved of his duties.

Lovesey: That developed. I usually control my books quite rigidly by working out a plot and keeping to the synopsis pretty faithfully. But towards the end of that book I had him have an interview with the Assistant Chief Constable. And as I was writing it I began to think, "Well, if there's any integrity about this man he's not going to take the dressing down from the Assistant Chief Constable." He's going to hand in his badge; he's going to walk out. And then I thought, "Well, is it possible with him outside the police to bring the book to a conclusion and solve the mystery?" I had to work out a way in which he could, so I allowed him simply to resign rather than be demoted or whatever.

In that particular book, *The Last Detective*, it seemed to work. It sold well and, critically, is probably my most successful book. It had some pleasing reviews and won an award. So I was encouraged to follow up. And then I had a real problem: what do you do when your policeman is no longer a policeman and you want to write another book about him?

So I was left having to devise a situation in which events drew the character I'd made into the story. In this sequel he begins out of work and has taken on a number of unsatisfactory part-time jobs such as a security man. But then suddenly something happens which pulls him into a mystery plot. A small girl is lost in Harrods and sets off the security alarm. Finding a way of involving one's character in a plot is a challenge some writers face all the time. But it was a new situation for me. Normally, I've had somebody who is handed assignments as a professional detective or, like Bertie, an amateur who can indulge his own whims. But this was a new situation and *Diamond Solitaire* was the result. It's more of an action thriller, I would say, than a conventional detective story.

Silet: Are you going to continue the series?

Lovesey: Yes, hopefully, for many more years to come.

Beyond the 87th Precinct
Ed McBain

Photo © Dragica Dimitrijevic

Ed McBain, aka Evan Hunter, is one of the most prolific and celebrated writers of contemporary crime fiction. His 87th Precinct novels, now numbering close to fifty, stretch back into the mid-1950s and represent one of the longest running, most sustained mystery series on record. The Matthew Hope books, a second series now entering its third decade, have extended McBain's talent and range.

Writing under his real name, Evan Hunter has been a critically important, best-selling novelist since his early work, *The Blackboard Jungle* (1954), received acclaim both as a novel and as a hit movie. Through the years many of Mr. Hunter's other novels have been made into successful Hollywood films. He has also written for the screen, adapting his own fiction as well as the work of other writers. His most notable film project was as scriptwriter for Alfred Hitchcock's classic film *The Birds* (1963).

Mr. McBain's output continues to be prodigious. His latest Matthew Hope novel, *Last Best Hope*, was published in 1998. His current 87th Precinct series book, *The Big Bad City,* appeared in

1999. Ed McBain/Evan Hunter books have sold in the millions worldwide. In the process he has gathered just about all the awards available to writers of crime fiction.

Portions of this interview appeared as "The 87th Precinct and Beyond: An Interview with Ed McBain," *The Armchair Detective*, 27:4 (Fall 1994), 392–399.

Silet: One of the jobs you had after you got out of college was at a literary angency. Did that job help you in your writing?

McBain: Absolutely, I was handling some pretty good writers—P. G. Wodehouse, Arthur C. Clarke, Mickey Spillane. I read their stories as they came in, commented on them, sometimes asked them to make revisions. Here was this twerp straight out of college asking P. G. Wodehouse to add a chapter. I was also talking to editors every day of the week, having lunch with editors, learning what their needs were, and I was writing stuff and submitting it under various pseudonyms and selling it. I eventually made more money selling fiction than I was earning at the agency, which is why I left.

Silet: What did you learn form writing your early novels like *The Evil Sleep*, *The Big Fix*, and *Don't Crowd Me*?

McBain: The earlier novels were largely premised on plot. They weren't too heavy on character; they were plot and action like the stories. The stories I was writing in the beginning were for the pulp magazines which didn't go in for deep thinkers. I didn't recognize until much later on that character can emerge from plot, that a good plot can develop a good character. *The Evil Sleep* was about a drug addict who wakes up with a dead woman in bed with him. He's on the run from the cops who are seeking him for her murder, and he also has to get a fix because he's a heroin addict. It was an interesting plot, I thought.

I used to try in every story I wrote to learn a little more about the craft because if you're writing for the pulp magazines you're not writing great literature. I was just writing to get that half a cent a word. I would try dialogue tricks, I would try narrative tricks. In each of the stories try a new technique so that it moved it beyond—for me—just selling the story to the pulps.

Don't Crowd Me is pretty similar in structure to *The Evil Sleep. The Big Fix* was just *The Evil Sleep* with a new title. *Don't Crowd Me* was very similar in plot. An advertising man escapes New York City to go to Lake George for a weekend and he gets back to his cabin that night and there is a dead body in it and he's accused by the local police and he has to find the killer. I think *The Evil Sleep* was better than *Don't Crowd Me*, actually.

Silet: Could you see yourself developing as a writer in these early books?

McBain: No, not really. In writing you stay on a certain level until there's a leap forward. I was writing a lot of science fiction in those days. Most of it very bad. I read a book called *The Demolished Man* by Alfred Bester and it was a wonderful book, I thought. It inspired me to write the one good science fiction thing I ever wrote, which was called "Malice in Wonderland," and later on I expanded it into a novel called *Tomorrow and Tomorrow*, alternately called *Tomorrow's World*. It was really inspired by the work Bester had done and caused me to leap up to the next plateau.

The same thing happened when I began *The Blackboard Jungle*. I had read *From Here to Eternity* and I consciously tried to mimic James Jones' style. So instead of an army it was a troubled high school, but I was really trying to imitate his style. When I started the 87th Precinct books that was a jump up from the mystery stuff I had been writing, a real quantum leap up. And that fed off *The Blackboard Jungle* because it really had a similar style. Instead of teachers there were cops, instead of a teacher's lunch room it was a squad room, instead of a classroom there were people to be interrogated. But the level of writing was much higher than the level of writing I had been doing before. So the 87th Precinct novels were another leap for me in terms of moving the mystery novel forward.

I think because I was writing under a pseudonym I was able to take great risks with the mystery. I just didn't give a damn. I knew all of the rules of mystery writing by then because I'd written a lot of mysteries, short stories and novels. I knew all the rules, and I felt

I'm going to break them. I wanted to break some new ground with the new series. I didn't care what the critics said or what fellow mystery writers said.

Silet: Why did you decide to begin the 87th Precinct novels?

McBain: Pocket Books approached me. There was a novel kicking around called *Cut Me In*, a mystery novel set in a literary agency, which we were showing around—under a pseudonym—after *The Blackboard Jungle* had come out. My agent sent it to Pocket Books which had done so well with *The Blackboard Jungle*.

We sat down at lunch and the gist of the matter was that Earle Stanley Gardner was getting old and he was the mainstay of Pocket Books Inc. They kept bringing out his books with new covers on them every six months. They wanted to know if I had any ideas for a series character. As I said, by that time I had written every type of mystery possible, and I had also written some short police stories. It seemed to me that the only valid people to be investigating crimes were cops. I had done the private eye and the woman in jeopardy and man on the run.

I proposed to them that I should do a realistic police series set in New York, at the time—the fictitious city evolved later. It would deal with policemen, not only as professionals investigating crimes, but also as human beings with wives and lovers and children and mothers and fathers. They said good, we will give you a contract for three books and let's see where it will go. That was the start of it.

Silet: How did you evolve the mythical city of Isola?

McBain: Well, it started to become troublesome. While I was writing the first book I was calling the cops every ten minutes, because I had done my research with New York City policemen, and I would call to check things while I was writing it. You do your research, but you don't always get all your facts straight the first time around, and this was going to be a realistic series about cops in New York. I found that I was calling them a lot, and they were getting a little impatient—I didn't have all that many contacts in the department anyway—and also I found that things changed. "Oh yeah, we used to do it that way three weeks ago but a new directive came down and the way we do it now is this way." I thought my God this is going to be an impossible task keeping up with these guys.

I realized too that policemen ask a lot of questions in their work and some of the questions they ask are what's your address and what's your phone number. If I was going to use a real city, I was going to get in trouble with addresses and phone numbers, and if I described a building on West 12th Street, I would have to go to West 12th Street and look at the building. I didn't want to do that because this was just a sideline, I wasn't getting a lot of money for these books. I had determined that I was going to write them as well as I knew how and that I was gong to make them real, but I didn't want to make a career of it. I had a career already. I was Evan Hunter.

So I decide after I was maybe fifty pages into it to change the setting to a mythical city, and in the beginning it was just loosely disguised New York, New York just slightly tilted a little to the right. Over the years it has emerged as a truly mythical city. I invented geographical locations and historical backgrounds that never really existed.

In the first one it was a deliberate decision, this is not going to be New York, this is going to be a mythical city with five sections like New York, Isola, Riverhead, Calm's Point, etc., but it's not going to be New York and it's not going to be the New York City Police Department. It was going to be my police, and if I was uncertain about a rule, here's my rule, my regulation, and this is what it's going to be in the book. I set the rules.

Silet: You mentioned that the city changed through the years. How so?

McBain: The immigrant background is entirely different now. The people who were the new arrivals are now well-established, third-generation Americans and New Yorkers. You rarely see a Puerto Rican who speaks with a Spanish accent anymore, rarely. The Hispanic groups that have Spanish accents are coming from other places. A lot of the Oriental population has changed completely. The cab drivers used to be Jews or Italians, now they're all Sikhs and Pakistanis. It's very strange. It's a different city, a whole different city.

Drugs in the early books were almost nonexistent. When I began the early books marijuana was smoked mainly by musicians, and then it began filtering into the ghetto, the black ghetto usually, and then it started filtering into Puerto Rican Harlem. Hard drugs were almost unheard of. But then they became popular and now most of the crime in the city is drug-related. If you wanted to write realistic murder novels, you would be writing about drug-related crimes all the time. It would be boring. You have to struggle not to use drugs as motives for crimes because they're so prevalent.

The weaponry in the first book was a teenage gang using a zip gun. Now AK 47s, 9-millimeters, Glocks are on the street. The street gangs used to be into rumbling with each other; now, they're into dealing drugs. Rumbling, that's kid's stuff. What are we going to fool around with that for. The whole scene has changed, and I think the whole motivation of the city has changed too. There was still the sense that the city would become one great tribe. All these various nationalities and ethnic groups and racial groups would get together and be America.

In a city like New York now—and I see it in other cities when I'm on book tour—there is a lot of anger and the anger seems ready to erupt all the time. Strangers seem ready to take offense for no perceptible reason except that you may look at them crookedly. It's strange. It's a much more violent world that I write about nowadays than back then.

Silet: How much have you used the actual police procedures through the years?

McBain: I've used those a lot. In an investigation sooner or later the cops always end up with Sam Grossman at the police lab finding out something about the crime. I use it for a different reason. I feel that if anything rings false in the novels then the whole thing is going to fall apart, the whole structure will fall apart. So I try to make everything absolutely believable.

If I'm talking about chicken feathers, I'd better know what there is to know about chicken feathers, and I'd better put it on paper, and if I'm wrong then some chicken farmer will write to tell me about it, but in the meantime the average reader will say, "Yeah, hey, that's how they found out about it." I try to let the reader in on the documents, court orders, on everything so the reader feels privileged to be in there and feels that he has all the information the cops have. I think it makes for fun in the book. I'm sure it is part of my art training to use actual documents in the book, but I don't know where it came from and I don't care but it's in there.

I think the 87th Precinct in many respects offered something that hadn't been done before. One was this sense of clinical verity. This is the way the cops work. The other was that the writing was good. Before I came along there were very few good mystery writers. You could name them on one hand. Even some of the very well-known ones were writing terribly. The plots were good, and the mysteries were tight, but they were very badly written. Worse nobody expected them to be written well. I told other mystery writers, you can write well and it's OK. People will read them anyway even if they are well-written.

Silet: The 87th Precinct series has been running for forty years, making it one of the longest in crime fiction history. How do you keep it fresh?

McBain: I find out new things about the characters each time, or I'll highlight one of the characters, because of the very format of the books. Robert Parker once said, talking about me to some other journalists, he's hit on a great formula because he's got all these guys, and he can put them in any combination he wants to. There are so many combinations and permutations that he can use endlessly. Pair Carella with Kling or pair Carella with Meyer or pair Meyer with Willis, use any of these guys in any combination or multiples of combinations. It becomes endless.

At the same time it gives me the opportunity to put into the spotlight in one book a detective who hasn't been in the spotlight before and find out things about him, use him as the lead character where Carella is sidekick. It enables me, because I know the characters so well now, to delve into new situations. I didn't know when I was writing *Widows*, before I began the book, that I was going to have Carella's father killed in a holdup of his bakery shop. So when that happened it forced me to investigate how Carella felt about his father. Was there anything about the relationship between Carella and his father that caused Carella to become a cop in the first place? What influence did Carella's father have on his life and what effect does the death of Carella's father have on his life now?

Another thing that keeps it fresh is that the cops are ageless, they don't age. Whereas the city and the society does around them. If you read the books from the first until now you will see the changes in crime in the city, and you'll see a pretty good portrait of urban America.

Silet: You were the first to use the ensemble story, does it bother you that it's been widely imitated?

McBain: Well, I consider it sort of an homage, except when they steal stupidly. In police work, for example, the twenty-four hours preceding a murder and the twenty-four hours after it are considered the most important. The twenty-four preceding because you want to know everything the victim did, in order to get to the criminal, and the twenty-four hours following because the gap is widening between the time of the murder and catching the murderer. But I labeled this the "24/24" and a guy in one of his books went into this whole business about the twenty-four hours preceding and the twenty-four hours after and he said, "In police jargon, this is known as the 24/24." Well, I *invented* that! It doesn't *exist* in police work! So I found that very funny. I do not find the remarkable similarities between "Hill Street Blues" and the 87th Precinct books quite so funny.

Silet: Tell me about the bad guys in the books, especially the "Deaf Man."

McBain: He's sort of my Moriarity or really more than Moriarity because I didn't grow up reading mystery novels or stories about Sherlock Holmes. I grew up reading comic books. He's more the Joker or the Riddler, or maybe a combination of both, in the Batman stories than he is Moriarity. I made him deaf because I thought it would be interesting if the person who is the bane of Steve Carella's existence is deaf, whereas the love of his life is deaf as well. That nice kind of irony there. If he is indeed deaf. We don't know if he is deaf or just pretending to be deaf.

Everybody likes him, and it's fun to bring him back. It's amazing because he kills so many people and always gets away in the end of the book and they love that. They keep waiting for him to come back. When is he coming back, they always ask me? When is the deaf man coming back? He comes back infrequently because it's hard to think of plots for him. He has to be very brilliant and concoct these massive schemes that would work if only some little thing didn't go wrong. It has nothing to do with the cops; they never solve what's going on until it's too late. It's hard to work a thing like that out.

Silet: Your policemen are flawed and some of the crimes never get solved. A lot of mysteries don't do that.

McBain: I can have my characters make mistakes, which is nice because people make mistakes. In *Poison*, for example, Carella is paired with Hal Willis, and Willis really has the spotlight because he falls in love with this woman Carella thinks is the killer. But Carella is wrong as it turns out, and he's giving bad advice. His perceptions are dimming their prospects of finding the real murderer. I like it that these guys are flawed and that they do make mistakes and some of the mistakes can be fatal.

Early on in the series, in *Like Love* I think it was, a woman is on a ledge and is about to jump and Carella is trying to talk her in off the ledge. Finally he says as a psychological ploy, "Oh, go on jump, who cares." And she jumps, and she gets killed because he made a misjudgment. That bugs him for the rest of the book, until one of the cops calls him aside and talks with him. That wasn't the main plot, that was the personal story in the book.

Silet: How do you decide to introduce new characters?

McBain: Most of the new characters are criminals, and some of them are worth keeping around. I always regretted killing Brother Anthony; I thought he was a wonderful character. The guy dressed like a monk with combat boots and his girlfriend was the fat lady and she'll be back because she is still alive but Brother Anthony is gone. Often if I like somebody and I kill them off, I can bring them back in another guise. It is really easy for the fat lady, Emma Forbes, to say, "She thought at first that she was looking at Brother Anthony. He looked exactly like him. True, he wasn't wearing the monk's habit but aside from that...." So I bring him back as Brother Ralph. I killed a cop once early in the series, Roger Haviland, who was a bad apple, and I realized that he was sorely missed in the squad room. There has to be the bad apple, and I brought him back as Andy Parker.

Silet: Each novel in the 87th Precinct series seems to set up a different kind of writer's problem and then solve it.

McBain: I don't know if I consciously set writers' problems for myself, maybe *challenges*, you know. The way to keep a series fresh—for me, anyway—is to find new things about the characters and to find new ways of approaching them. I certainly should know how to describe a character by now; if I don't, I should really hang up my jock. But the fun is to find new ways of doing it. Now I must have written the scene 10,000 times, where they break the news to someone whose relative has been killed, correct?

But in *Lullaby* a teenage girl, a baby-sitter, is killed on New Year's Eve. So I did a riff—instead of it being New Year's Eve and that forevermore for the parents of this girl this was no longer going to be New Year's Eve, it was going to be the anniversary of their daughter's death—I did the whole riff *before* they come in the door. It's 3:00 in the morning and the parents open the door and it's the police and they're looking at them and Carella says, "May we come in, please?" and that's the end of the scene. I didn't have to play the scene, you see? I look for different ways of doing things that keep the series alive for me and I'm hopeful this keeps it alive and fresh for the reader as well. Otherwise it just gets to be hack work.

Silet: Do you decide ahead of time which characters you will feature in each novel?

McBain: In each of the books there is always a personal situation that is open-ended. Kling meets a black cop and falls in love with her and what's going to happen with them? Carella's brother-in-law is a junkie—is anything going to develop from that? There are always these open-ended things in many of the books, and I can pick on any one of those personal stories. The personal stories keep going from book to book, whereas the crime in each book is solved.

Silet: In the 87th Precinct you have multiple things going on. As a writer what does that give you?

McBain: It's easier when there are more cases than when there is a single case. Obviously with a single case everything has to relate to the case, and there is a long book to write. I find sometimes that can get tiresome. It challenges you to be endlessly inventive to keep the reader on his toes. When there are a lot cases going on you can switch back and forth and the entertainment is there. The reader says, "Oh, wow, look where we are now. How'd we get here?" So it is easier in that sense. I enjoy doing them both, I suppose.

The Matthew Hope novels are very difficult to write because there is a lot of law in them. He is not an investigator so there is a stretch there making him one and making him get involved with murder and investigating it even if he uses private eyes as attorneys do. He has to get involved in it himself, he just can't let a private eye handle it. So there is a stretch but it is the stretch every private eye novelist makes every day of the week because private eyes don't investigate murders. Period. But it goes against my grain because I write realistic cop novels, and they should investgate the murders. So I have to do a little fancy footwork every time I write a Matthew Hope novel.

Silet: Where did Matthew Hope come from, and why did you start writing about him?

McBain: I had just come through a divorce and I was thinking of divorce as a kind of killing. There's a lot of fallout where people get hurt, you know—the children get hurt and relatives get hurt— other than the principals. I wanted to do a serious novel, an Evan Hunter novel, divorce and remarriage, and the effects of divorce on the lives of people who are not necessarily the principals. I got a contract with Harper and Row to do the novel and it was to be called *The Scene of the Crime*. A crime takes place, but it's a metaphor really for the divorce. I was going to tell it in terms of a brutal murder which Matthew Hope is investigating, while he himself is having an affair and contemplating divorce. Well, I wrote the book and it didn't work. It was neither fish nor fowl, neither a mystery nor a straight novel, it was just some curious hybrid. I changed the title to *Goldielocks*, which I thought sounded more mysterious than *The Scene of the Crime*.

It was published and then it was published again in England. My British paperback publishers threw a party for me, and they were lamenting the fact that Pan Books, their competitors, had all the 87th Precinct novels and they said it would be jolly good if you had *another* series *we* could publish. So I said, "Well, why don't I do Matthew Hope as a series, using fairy tale titles? Since, I've expanded into nursery rhymes.

Silet: Why did you set them in Florida?

McBain: I was living in Florida at the time and I usually would write them while we were there for the winter. But also, there was a nice change of pace—like a pitcher with a fast ball and a curve ball and a slider—setting the books in a place where one doesn't expect that sort of violence. You'd expect palm trees and sparkling beaches and balmy breezes and not that sort of violence.

Silet: They seem sexier and more graphically violent.

McBain: Yeah, they are. The sex was more concerned with the presence of sperm in a vaginal vault than a steamy sex scene, which I know how to write pretty well, by the way. There had been some sexy scenes in the 87th Precinct books, not between Carella and his wife but between Cotton and some of his women and Bert Kling and some of his women. I think there's a difference in the women in the Matthew Hope novels—who are getting more interesting for me, anyway. But you know in the 87th Precinct novels, I can have Kling's girlfriend not wanting to go to bed because she just got her period, and I haven't yet done that, get down to the nitty-gritty, in the Matthew Hope books.

Silet: What do the Hope books allow you to do that the 87th Precinct books don't?

McBain: What they really allow me to do is have a lead character who is more sophisticated than the cops of the 87th Precinct. As sensitive and as feeling as they are but more sophisticated. So he can have just come back from a trip to Paris, whereas Carella would have come back from a trip to North Carolina. Big difference. I can deal with the same upscale characters in the cases that they're investigating, because the city has very rich people in it. It's just in the difference in the personality of the lead character.

Silet: Because of the problems with your Lizzie Borden book, you said that put you off other novels and that you wanted to concentrate on the 87th Precinct books and make them the best crime novels going. What have you done differently to change them?

McBain: I think I've put more social comment in them and that may be a mistake frankly, I don't know. In *Mischief*, for example, the Deaf Man's plot is really designed to exploit racist attitudes in the city. That becomes a social problem told in terms of a diabolical scheme of the Deaf Man. In *Romance* Kling is starting an affair with the black woman from *Mischief*, the Deputy Chief Surgeon, so I get to explore what is to my mind one of America's most serious problems, the conflict between races, in terms of two leading characters starting a romance.

Also I think that the early 87th Precinct novels were pretty straight mysteries that didn't deal much with any of the social issues. Beginning with *Ice* maybe, they started to change and started to get a lot darker. *Lullaby, Vespers,* and *Kiss* are very dark novels where justice doesn't always triumph. *Mischief* is perhaps the darkest one of them. I'm not certain that the mystery novel *is* the place to explore social problems, I'm not sure of that anymore. I do know I don't like mysteries that are just shoot 'em up bang bang.

Silet: Could you expand upon that?

McBain: Yeah, I don't know how many other guys are doing it, but a lot of people have talked about this, a lot of mystery writers have talked about it as *subverting* the genre. I don't think the genre *should* be subverted. I think the genre is wide enough *not* to be subverted if you want to make social comments. But I'm not sure the average mystery reader buys a mystery to get social criticism. I'm always aware of a responsibility to the reader. I know the reader didn't buy my book to learn about the social security system in the United States of America or whatever, he bought it because he wants a *mystery*. So I'm aware of that, and if ever I see myself going too far over in another direction I say, "Hey, hey, get back to what we're supposed to be doing here. We're supposed to be solving a murder. We can't go too far astray."

Silet: How would you like to be remembered as a writer?

McBain: I feel that I can do what very few writers in America can do. I feel that I can write a really superb mystery and I feel I can write a very, very good straight novel. It's hard to change hats that easily. So I think that I'd like to be remembered for my versatility. I think that there are writers in our pantheon who are stars, and I'm not a star. I'm a good character actor. I'm the Gene Hackman; I'm the Robert Duvall. I'm not Tom Cruise; I'm not Tom Hanks. I'm just a good, solid actor that's in there doing the job and very often holding the picture together, I'm the glue. Maybe that's enough to be, I don't know. Somebody asked me what I wanted to put on my tombstone and I said all I want on my tombstone is that he wrote like an angel.

The Other Side of Those Mean Streets
Walter Mosley

Photo © Kwame Brathwaite

Walter Mosley was instantly acclaimed for his first Easy Rawlins book, *Devil in a Blue Dress* (1990). The critics loved his historical re-creation of post-war Los Angeles, and the unique voice he had captured with his characters. His second novel, *A Red Death* (1991), was also well-received by the critics. With the publication of *White Butterfly* (1992), Mosley arrived. It did not hurt his sales or recognition when the then presidential candidate Bill Clinton was seen carrying copies of his books on the campaign trail or when he told reporters that Mosley was one of his favorite mystery writers.

The paperback editions of the first two books made him more accessible to mystery readers who now eagerly awaited the next installment of the Easy Rawlins series. The fact that *Devil in a Blue Dress* was made into a well-received, major Hollywood motion picture, starring Denzel Washington, didn't hurt his reader recognition or sales either. *Black Betty* (1994), *A Little Yellow Dog*

(1996), and *Gone Fishin'* (1997), a prequel about Easy's early years, have continued the series.

Mosley has also published two non-series books: *RL's Dream* (1995), about the legendary Mississippi blues guitarist Robert (RL) Johnson, and *Always Outnumbered, Always Outgunned* (1998), a loosely connected set of stories featuring Socrates Fortlow, ex-con and philosopher of the violence and anarchy of life. Walter Mosley's latest is a science fiction novel, *Blue Light* (1998).

The following interview was conducted in 1998.

Silet: Did you begin writing when you attended the graduate writing program at CCNY?

Mosley: After I left graduate school in political theory, I moved to Boston and then later to New York, where I was a computer programmer for many years. I had written a series of letters to my wife and she said they were wonderful letters and other people in my past said I had always written wonderful letters. One Saturday I was at work when nobody else was there, and I started writing these sentences and I really loved them and I thought, "Maybe I really could be a writer." That was in 1985–86. After that I studied writing with a guy in his office for about a year. He had a little workshop behind his house. After that, I went to City College.

Silet: How did you decide you wanted to write professionally?

Mosley: Well, I never did really. What happened was I was going to City College in the writing program, and it was kind of artistic. It was not a commercial base. But I was there, and I was very serious about writing. I wrote a novel that wasn't a mystery, and nobody seemed to be very interested in that book.

Silet: Where did you get the idea for Easy Rawlins?

Mosley: Oh, it came from writing, like so many ideas. The way I write is I think you have a guy and the guy is going to the door and is about to open the door. He doesn't know what's on the other side of that door and neither do I. That's the way I write. When the door's opened, kind of magically, we both see something at the same moment, and I write it down. I was writing a short story about Mouse but from a first person point of view.

It started out: "His name was Raymond but we called him Mouse because he was small and had sharp features." It goes on and on explaining Mouse, and by page four, Mouse looks up and says, "Hey, Easy, how you doin'?" He was talking to my narrator and that's where he started. So Easy started from his relationship, his feeling for, this guy Mouse.

Silet: What is the historical progression of the Easy Rawlins series designed to do?

Mosley: One reason is to go through these moments of history of black people. Then another is the moments of history of Los Angeles itself; and then America, like with the McCarthy period. I love the mystery genre, I really do, and that's the reason that I was able to work in it, and the genre itself is in flux, it's changing. It's worthwhile to take a look at it from an intellectual or scholarly point of view. The original characters in hard-boiled detective fiction were a kind of spirit, the sad spirit of Western humanity looking at how low we've come, where we are and what kind of moral and ethical world we live in.

The characters were ageless and completely unanchored: no mother, no father, no sisters or brothers, no children, no property, no real job. All they had was their moral life. In a way, it's beautiful and most beautiful in a book like *The Maltese Falcon* and also in the series of stories by Dashiell Hammett featuring the Continental Op, because there's no progression; there's just all this terrible, insane world. But as the genre developed, it was done to death; Hammett did it, Chandler did it, Macdonald did it. I think that there's really not much left to do. What else is Sam Spade going to do? He's static.

What I'm doing with Easy is I'm making him get older and older, so the world around him is changing. His mind, to some degree, is staying the same, and to some degree, aging, and his body is getting older, his friends are dying. He's much more of an everyman in that case—rather than an overman—which is the way I see Sam Spade or Marlowe.

Silet: Obviously you don't see much distinction between what we would describe as genre or crime fiction and straight fiction or literature.

Mosley: No, I don't see any difference in it. Of course, in the genre there are certain kinds of things that you have to do, but it's the same in a coming-of-age novel, somebody has to come of age. So you have to follow the conventions. Good fiction is in the sentence and in the character and in the heart of the writer. If the writer is committed to and in love with what he or she is doing, then that's good fiction.

Silet: Who have you read both in crime fiction and in regular fiction that's had an influence on you?

Mosley: In crime fiction, I've read lots and lots of people. Charles Willeford, I just adore. Every one of his books is so deeply flawed plotwise, but it matters nothing to me because he's such a wonderful writer. I was reading one of his books the other day about some old guy and his wife; he was seventy-two but looked older and she was sixty-three and looked older than him. It was so funny; just the way he wrote it. My God, this guy is fantastic! Hoke Mosley is a real guy. It's so right. I've read everybody—Gregory MacDonald—I've read all the Fletch books. I thought they were wonderful. Parker, of course. Vachss, who I adore, because I think that he is so deeply committed to what he believes in. I feel the heart coming through it, and I compare him to Dickens. Rex Stout.

I've read almost everything Simenon ever wrote. The people I love for writing are the French: Malraux, Camus, Gide, for just the style of writing. It is almost the heart of fiction for me. Then the older guys like Proust, and tons of black poets: Gwendolyn Brooks, Derek Walcott, Amiri Baraka. It doesn't matter who writes it, no matter their sex or their race or what period of time they lived in. I mean when you read Shakespeare, it's all alive today. It's amazing what a wonderful writer he was, or whoever wrote that stuff.

Silet: You've been treated very well by the critics. How do you respond to critics?

Mosley: When they treat me well, I love them. I have been treated very well in two ways. Number one, I've been reviewed a lot; therefore a lot of people know my name, whether it's good or bad. I've also gotten a lot of very good reviews, and I'm very happy about that. I try really hard to write well; I think I know my limitations. I'm a new writer, really. I'm not young anymore, but I'm a new writer. There's a lot more that I could do a lot better, and so the fact that people overlook my flaws to see what's good about my fiction, I'm very happy about. I don't mind people criticizing, but it doesn't seem worthwhile to me to trash anybody in public no matter how successful they are. But I've been very happy about the criticism.

Silet: What are the positive and negative things about doing a series?

Mosley: It is a very difficult question to answer. There are only possibilities. It's possible for a series to be bad if you end up writing about the same character who doesn't change in time. You write your best stories about him in the beginning and after a while the stories get weaker and weaker. It's like the next wash, the next wash, until the color fades to water. That can be a problem. But the way I approach him that hasn't been a problem for me with Easy.

For instance, Rex Stout wrote what I call romances. Not romances in the sexual way or love stories. They are comical romances narrated by Archie Goodwin. It doesn't matter that Archie doesn't change because the stories are not about Archie and character development. The same is true for Simenon and his character Maigret or Sherlock Holmes. The character is set, and the stories are not about character development. But the hard-boiled genre and those genres related to the hard-boiled genre—and I think I'm in one of those—is about character development, and so you have to have the character move forward.

The wonderful thing about doing a series is you have a cast of characters that you can refer to because you've already done a lot of the work. Somebody reading the whole series can find each book more satisfying, because they already know these characters and this world very well. So when they come to a new story, they find out new things. They knew a lot of things from the previous six or seven novels and here comes another one to take them deeper and deeper.

Silet: What genre do you think you are working in?

Mosley: It's like a sub-set of the hard-boiled genre, but it's not exactly hard-boiled. As Lawrence Block says, "The hard-boiled genre is typified by the line in one of the Continental Op stories by Dashiell Hammett where the guy says, 'I hit him with the door. (Pause.) Repeatedly.'" That's hard-boiled. My stories are different. I don't adhere to the blunt irony of the hard-boiled.

Silet: Because of your success, you're breaking new ground as an African-American crime writer. How do you feel about that?

Mosley: I feel comfortable, to tell you the truth, with myself which is a nice place to be in. I don't think that I'm the last word. I'm the first one who could give you a whole bunch of criticism of my work: what it does and what it doesn't do. One of the things that I understand, like understanding Easy, I can't do everything. I think that I have a good ear for black language, not slang because slang is something that lasts for about six months and is gone. Black dialect has been with us forever.

I feel like I'm doing something that's good and I guess important. It's important for me and my sense is that it's important for a lot of black people in America and also a lot of white people who are interested in hearing and thinking and opening their minds to different things. So I guess the answer is that I feel comfortable with it.

Silet: You're opening up a whole view of a black community that has not been accessible in large measure before.

Mosley: My favorite novelists are Charles Dickens and Mark Twain and the reason is they are completely open to the reader and that's really what I want to be. I'm not going to shirk from saying what I think my character is or what I think my character's world is like, but I want to write fiction that's really embracing, that will bring in people and people will want to read it. Like E. M. Foster said in *Aspects of the Novel*, the main thing about a novel is the story and the story is what happens next.

I want my readers to say, "Oh, wow, and then what?" and I want them to turn the page because that's what is most important about writing. It just so happens that because I'm writing about black characters and black people, the thing that I'm most interested in is that they'll be wondering what happens next in these black lives, whether it's a white reader or whether it's the President, or some black person who really knows this life and is happy to read about it.

Silet: So engaging your readers is very important to you.

Mosley: I met a guy in LA—I'll never forget this—and he came to me and said, "I read your first book and I'm going to read the next, too, because I want to figure out why Easy's such a jerk!" His personal thing about what Easy did with a woman was unacceptable to him. That's real! Easy is a real character for this guy! It's very funny, but I really like that. My characters, I hope, are real enough for people to respond to. My dream is to write the series and have it treated as one of those series in crime fiction which mean something. I would love to do that.

Five Pages a Day
Robert B. Parker

Photo © John Earle

Robert B. Parker's Spenser series is now among the longest
running and most successful in the history of crime fiction. Of
writers working today Parker is also among the most knowledgeable about the history of hard-boiled detective fiction, and his
Ph.D. thesis on the American hero includes material on the classic
authors Dashiell Hammett, Raymond Chandler, and Ross
Macdonald. At the request of the Chandler estate Parker completed *Poodle Springs*, a manuscript left unfinished at the time of
Chandler's death, and later he wrote a new Philip Marlowe novel,
Perchance to Dream, a sequel to *The Long Goodbye*.

In 1998 Robert Parker contributed the introduction and chose
the stories for *The Best American Mystery Stories*, edited by Otto
Penzler (Houghton Mifflin). With the publication of *Night Passage*
he also began a second series, featuring Jesse Stone, which immediately became a best seller. The second Jesse Stone book, *Night
Passage*, was published in 1998, and the latest Spenser novel, *Hush
Money*, in 1999.

In the following interview, conducted in 1998, Parker talks about his new series, shares his thoughts on crime fiction, and discusses his own writing techniques.

Silet: You just published the first book of a new series featuring Jesse Stone. Why did you begin another series?

Parker: It seemed like a good idea at the time. It takes me about four months to write a novel. If I take more time, the novel doesn't seem to get any better. I had spent some time attempting to write entirely different kinds of novels like *All Our Yesterdays* of which I was quite proud, the reviews were quite good, but the sales were pathetic. People stayed away in droves. I thought it was a wonderful novel and in many ways the best thing I've ever done, but nobody bought it. Somehow it fell between the people who only read mysteries and people who wouldn't read a novel by a guy who usually writes mysteries. That sort of narrowed my audience.

Silet: What compelled you to write crime fiction in the first place?

Parker: I have no idea. Probably reading Raymond Chandler early and often. It wasn't a conscious decision. I remember when it came time to write the first novel, I just sat down and wrote it. I didn't think what shall I do, shall I update, shall I transfer the crime story from Southern California? I just wrote *The Godwulf Manuscript.* Once you do that and someone buys it and publishes it, you tend to write another one.

The other answer is it's what I know how to do. As I have occasionally demonstrated, I know how to write something else but the market forces tend to make that less appealing as time goes on. The experience with *All Our Yesterdays* is a case in point. This is not to say I'll never do anything but the series. I have lying around someplace a novel about Wyatt Earpe which I'm about 150 pages into. I don't even have a contract for it. It is just sort of one of my hobbies. Unless fate intervenes that will someday see the light of day. I do so well now that I can do things that aren't profitable.

Silet: Where did the character Spenser come from?

Parker: I suppose he came from Marlowe to start with. I think in *The Godwulf Manuscript* I was trying to be Raymond Chandler and make another Philip Marlowe. After a while for mostly psychological reasons you realize that you know how to do this and people will publish it. You stop trying to think what would Chandler have done here or what would Marlowe have done there? You begin to just write. I have moved away from Marlowe/Chandler. At least there is a sufficient distance between us. I'd say that is where Spenser came from. I still am a great fan of Raymond Chandler. He's a wonderful writer.

Silet: What are the advantages and disadvantages to writing a series?

Parker: The advantage is that it probably replicates, for lack of a better word, real life more than most fiction because most people have a history and know people and come and go and you have a chance to play with the characters and not just the protagonist. If you encounter a situation in which it would be useful for Vinnie Morris to show up, you can have a Vinnie Morris show up. You can go back and get him. It gives you the opportunity to develop— lapsing back into academe for a moment—a whole fictive world.

A series has some of the advantages of, and I don't mean the comparison in talent, what Yoknapatawpha County did for William Faulkner. He stayed there in much of his work. He followed the place more than the individual, but nonetheless the characters come and go and interweave. So you create this whole imaginary place. I think that's probably what a series does more for you than anything else.

Silet: Throughout your career you've done single novels outside the series, like *All Our Yesterdays*. What do they allow you to do?

Parker: Well, they allow me to write about protagonists who are different than Spenser or to write about people in the third person, which to writers means more than to readers, but the point of view for me is a large element. It's very interesting to me to play with it. I couldn't write a novel dealing with the Irish troubles over three generations like I did in *All Our Yesterdays* in Spenser's voice.

I'm of Irish ancestry, my mother's name was Murphy and my grandmother came from Cork, and having decided to do this novel, it was fascinating to me, although hard, to play with the time as I did. The time management in that novel was the most interesting of all the things I had to do and the most complicated. It's like being able to bench-press three hundred pounds when I was in my late fifties, I wanted to see if I could.

Love and Glory allowed me to play with boy meets girl, boy gets girl back, in ways once again that Spenser wouldn't permit. *Wilderness* allowed me to write a protagonist whose courage was severely suspect. By now it would be a little hard for Spenser to suddenly go yellow. I did a third-person in the Jesse Stone novel in large part because it will be interesting over the years to work with a third-person persistently in a series which I have never done before.

Silet: Do you have a writing procedure? For instance, do you outline your plots?

Parker: Yeah, I sit down every day and write five pages on my computer. I don't outline. I used to. The outlining was probably for my own peace of mind so that I wouldn't sit down some morning and have to think, "I don't know what to write." At some point I found that not outlining worked better than outlining. The outline had become something of a limitation more than a support. When I did the Raymond Chandler book, *Poodle Springs,* which was in the late eighties, I was trying to do it as Chandler did it, and since Chandler didn't outline then I thought I won't outline. If you read Chandler closely you can see that he didn't outline. What the hell happened to that chauffeur?

I would recommend to beginning writers that they should outline because they probably don't have enough self-confidence yet. But I've been writing now since 1971 and I know that I can think it up. I know it will come. Jesse Stone began with the idea of a big-city cop in a small town. I thought OK that's where we'll start. I just sat down the first day with that in my head. Each day things come as you write.

Silet: What do you think that you do best?

Parker: I guess probably I am the great economist. I don't waste much in the way of language. Was it Harold Pinter that they called the great compressionist? I would lay claim to that in my own area of expertise. It is probably what I do best. Say a lot in a little. Put the most meaning in the fewest words.

Silet: Your prose is among the smoothest in crime fiction.

Parker: It was going to be my next guess. I don't read about myself. I don't read reviews. I will not read this interview, however telling it may be, and I don't look at tapes of myself on the "Today Show" or when I'm on Larry King. It is probably not good for me as a writer because it tends to exteriorize me. So I don't know what people say. My wife Joan reads everything, not because she is avid to know but because we have agreed that someone ought to keep track. It's one thing not to pay attention to what people say; it is another thing to stick your head in the sand. So Joan prevents me from sticking my head in the sand. If every reviewer says the same thing, maybe we should look at it. So far they haven't. Reviewers say everything possible. She keeps track of what's being said in the press, but she doesn't tell me unless she thinks I need to know.

I like that old Hemingway line. If you believe the good stuff they write about you then you have to believe the bad. I've chosen not to pay attention. So I have no exterior input as to what people think, though Joan says that quite often people remark on my skills as a prose stylist, as a manager of the language or whatever expression they use. That's good. I like that. The Joe Di Maggio of prose.

Silet: You recently helped edit *The Best American Mystery Stories*. How is the state of the American mystery story?

Parker: There are a lot of people who are attracted to the form because it is nice and linear, starts at the beginning and ends at the end, and is about people who are not totally overwhelmed by a hostile environment or totally alienated from an immoral world. So I think the state of the mystery story is probably quite good.

There are a lot of good writers doing it and the environment is receptive. It is a good time when good writers can write detective stories without feeling they are debasing themselves. It used to drive Chandler crazy that he didn't get more respect because he wrote mystery stories, and his anger was probably justifiable because he was better than people gave him credit for.

Duke Ellington, I think, once said there are two kinds of music: good and bad. Duke preferred good. Well, I think you could say that about literature. I don't know that it makes a great deal of difference to anyone but the writer how his work is classified. It is convenient for someone who wants to find my books or Tony Hillerman's to look under mystery and detective or to find Stephen King's books to look under horror. But from King's point of view or Hillerman's or mine, I think we're all trying to do the same sort of thing: we're trying to write a good book.

The difference between Faulkner and me is not that I write detective stories and Faulkner didn't, but it's that he was a genius and I'm not. There's good and better. I'm good and he's better. "The Bear" is a better thing than I've ever written and it's got nothing to do whether it's about detection or not about detection. That's not the issue. For me the classification is always useful to booksellers, bookstore owners, reviewers, probably book purchasers, but it is of no particular relevance at least to the more serious practitioners.

Silet: So you would see little difference between mainstream fiction and crime fiction?

Parker: Not at its best. There is nothing going on in a Spenser novel that would prevent me from writing something as good as "The Bear," except that there is a limit on my ability. The form doesn't limit me, my ability limits me. My imagination is not as large as Faulkner's. There is nothing that happens in Elmore Leonard that would prevent him from writing "The Big Two-Hearted River," except that he probably lacks the ability to use his imagination the way Hemingway did. I'm not sure that either of us lacks the imagination to do some Hemingway, but I'm not going to bad mouth Ernie at this point.

The difference between *Small Vices* and let's say *The Great Gatsby* is once again a difference in quality not of subject matter. *Gatsby* is after all rather a mystery story, or a detective story, and if you could change Nick Caraway to a detective what would have been the difference? That's my rap on the difference between one kind and another. I don't think there is. It's good or it's not good; or it's better or it's worse.

Silet: Most of your books deal in various ways with social issues. Is the crime novel inherently a social kind of fiction?

Parker: Certainly it gives you an opportunity for an oblique social commentary whether or not it is inherent. It probably is inherent because the detective novel is imbedded in the fabric of the culture in so many ways. I suppose you could do a novel that wasn't called a detective story which would take place in some sort of ethereal plane. I'm inclined to think that most fiction is imbedded in the culture that produces it which is how it gets to be good. I refer you to T. S. Eliot and Henry James on that.

Because the detective story at the most elementary level is about human interaction, somebody kills somebody, somebody steals something belonging to somebody else, and another person tries to find out about it, and because the focus of search is into the culture and into the community and into the social fabric, it allows the protagonist to move across the full range of society. It is one of the things that I think Chandler did more that Hammett. The Black Mask school and Hammett at his best, which is the early Hammett, focused mostly on the underworld.

It was Chandler who took in the whole range of culture so that rich people were involved as well as poor people. Because the detective's search is throughout the culture, it allows you this range. It gives you the opportunity for social criticism, and it's embedded in the fabric of the society in ways a novel which was not about this search for this hidden truth might not necessarily happen to be.

Silet: In what ways are the Spencer books playing off against the traditions of the hard-boiled detective story? For example how is he different from Marlowe?

Parker: Well, Spenser has a love life, has a context, and has friends. He's not unhappy and he's not isolated. He doesn't say get me off this frozen star, as Marlowe does in one of the books. The loneliness is the price Marlowe pays for his integrity. Spenser is able to maintain it in context unlike Marlowe who has to remain separate in order to remain pure. I suppose that more than anything else separates them.

Silet: Did your thesis which included material on Hammett and Chandler influence your own writing?

Parker: None. It's the other way round. I wrote the doctoral dissertation because I'd already done all of the reading. I'd read all those guys, and of course by reading all those guys I mean I'd read them when they were still writing, except for Hammett who stopped writing when I was about two, I think. It would be a wonderful study for somebody to explore why he stopped writing in 1934 and didn't die until 1961. What the hell was he doing? I had read all that stuff and everything around it by the time I was twelve, fourteen-years-old. The pulp magazines were still flourishing in my childhood, and I was very taken with it all. So that when it came time to do a doctoral dissertation I thought, since I've done all the reading in this area, why not write on it?

It took me two weeks to write my doctoral dissertation, which is what it was worth. It was about the right amount of time. It's not terribly good, but it was sufficient to get me a Ph.D. and free me from the toils of freshman comp. The fact that I wrote this doctoral dissertation and then became who I am is far less significant than it would appear. I would have been exactly who I am had I not written that doctoral dissertation. But while I am not pro academic, I found getting the Ph.D. very useful and one of the most productive and enriching things I ever did.

To New Orleans with Love
James Sallis

Photo © Spielman, 1995

In an interview James Sallis once responded to a question about the differences between "serious" and genre fiction by stating that he has his feet firmly in both camps and that he worked toward the day when "literary" writers would stop wasting energy setting themselves apart and crime writers would stop hiding behind "fictive walls." "Literature," he continued, "is not some imposing sideboard with discrete drawers labeled poetry, mystery, serious novel, science fiction, but a long buffet table laid out with all manner of fine, diverse foods. You can go back and forth, take whatever you want or need." James Sallis has been pursuing this breakdown of writing styles in his series of crime novels featuring his African-American private investigator, Lew Griffin, which have been both fascinating and frustrating readers and reviewers alike. Depending on your point of view, Sallis is either remaking the crime novel or pushing it out of the genre.

Lew Griffin is an existentialist in the continental tradition. A part-time teacher of French literature, he is as likely to punctuate his thoughts with references to Queneau or Camus, especially *The Stranger*, as he is to Hammett or Chandler. The books also reflect the influence of a broad spectrum of other modernist writers: Borges, Nabokov, and Dostoyevsky. In Lew's world literary references are as commonplace as street violence.

Sallis paid his dues as a critic, essayist, reviewer, poet, translator, and editor as well as a writer of science fiction before turning to crime fiction. He wrote one book on blues guitar players, *The Guitar Players: One Instrument and Its Masters in American Music* (1982) and edited another, *Jazz Guitars: An Anthology* (1984). His essays on crime fiction have appeared in numerous magazines and include an Introduction to a reprint of Chester Himes's *A Case of Rape*. In his monograph, *Difficult Lives: Jim Thompson—David Goodis—Chester Himes* (1993), Sallis discusses the impact of these writers on the paperback revolution in the 1950s. He also translated Raymond Queneau's last novel *Saint Glinglin*. He has turned out numerous newspaper pieces, occasional reviews, and articles on musicology, and he has published recently a study of Samuel Delany, *Ash of Stars*, and a spy thriller, *Death Will Have Your Eyes*, which has been optioned for film and a script is underway.

This interview was conducted over a two-year period, 1996–1998.

Silet: Tell me a little bit about your past, your family, where you grew up, your education.

Sallis: I'm a Southerner, born in rural Arkansas on the banks of the Mississippi, in a town that existed only *because* of the river. In the Thirties and Forties Helena was a major blues town. Sonny Boy Williamson's from there. I grew up hearing his music every day at noon on KFFA's King Biscuit Hour. My father was a policeman for a while. He had Sonny Boy, sometimes the whole band, on the road gang. Robert Johnson lived in Helena awhile. Others came through. There was a huge black population, lots of farming, two major factories offering work.

Neither of my parents had much of an education. Dad was smart, a freethinker in his own way. I think my mother was probably schizophrenic, though no one in the family talks about it even now, with both of them dead.

My brother John is a well-known philosopher and a hell of a writer, an authority on Heidegger, hangs out with Derrida and the like when he's in Paris. Our great grandfather was French; my middle name is Chappelle, Sallis comes from Salle. There's Indian blood in there too. Look at old photos of my father and it's obvious: skin color, jet-black hair, high cheekbones. Looks a lot like Charlie Patton.

I attended Tulane on scholarship for a couple of years—that's when I fell in love with New Orleans—then got married and moved to Iowa to study journalism, dropped out and began writing stories, sold several, wound up in London editing the magazine *New Worlds*. Later on I returned to school for advanced studies in Russian and French, but I've never earned a degree.

I've lived as a writer—quite a different thing from making my living as a writer, I assure you, though sporadically I've done that as well—for some thirty years now.

Silet: When and why did you become interested in writing? Was it through reading, an inspiring teacher, another writer? Talk a bit about your early efforts to write. What did you learn from these experiences?

Sallis: It was one of those things I just knew: I was a writer. In the fourth or fifth grade I wrote a play my class performed; I was forever drawing cartoons, telling stories.

The first book I remember reading was my brother's book club edition of Heinlein's *Puppet Masters*. Soon I was reading two or three books a day: Oscar Wilde, biographies of Houdini, Dickens, every science fiction novel in the Helena library, science books, a little later, books on music and biographies of composers. My mother was furious with me. I'd stop off on the way home from school and buy a Gold Medal paperback or something by Frederic Brown. And she'd say, Not another book, you can't have read all those others. But I had. Many of them repeatedly.

Nowadays, every so often my wife and I will look up, she on the couch with her book and glass of wine or cup of tea, me in my chair with mine, and we'll say: Here we go, another hot night at the Sallis's!

As I said, I've always written, always told stories. I received encouragement from teachers, sure: high-school English teachers Mrs. Chorley and Miss Siler, most of all Joe Roppolo at Tulane, to whom *Black Hornet* is dedicated. But the serious work began in Iowa. I'd sit in the student union there drinking cup after cup of coffee and, for the first time, really *build* stories, finish them, work them over. I tell students that most of us have a certain wordage we just have to *write out* before we start getting to the good stuff. That's what I was doing. Poet James Tate was often at another table.

One day I walked by the bank in Iowa City and someone stepped out of a doorway towards me. I had this flash of paranoia, and with it, a story. All but ran to the student union to get it down. That became my first published story, "Kazoo," which begins: "Walking down the street on my way to see *The Leech*, I'm attacked by this guy who jumps out of the alley shouting..."

Mike Moorcock at *New Worlds* bought it. Then within a few weeks I wrote stories that sold to Mike, to Ed Ferman at *The Magazine of Fantasy & Science Fiction*, and to Damon Knight for his original anthology *Orbit*. Damon paid $300 for the first story he bought, an astonishing amount of money for the time. I thought I was set. Write a story a week, sell it, no problem. Never realizing that not only couldn't I go on writing a story every week, there was no way in hell they'd all sell, and only a handful would bring in anything like $300. Three years later, in fact, when the short-story market collapsed, I couldn't give them away on street corners.

But these early stories bore me across the sea to London. Mike asked me to come and edit *New Worlds*. We were publishing early work by Jimmy Ballard, D. M. Thomas, lots of fine Tom Disch and Brian Aldiss; one newspaper called us "The best magazine in Britain." I was in London for a year, and there's no way I can overstate the time's benefit to me, what I learned from it, the stimulus, remove and (for want of a better word) inspiration it afforded me. I did some of the best writing I've ever done while there. I also fell in love with French literature—and with American detective fiction.

Silet: You'd kicked around for a number of years before you wrote the first of the Lew Griffin novels. Tell me a bit about your writing career. What finally attracted you to crime fiction? Had you read a lot in the area?

Sallis: As I just said, my first sales were to science fiction publications. Exciting things were going on in science fiction then. I published several dozen stories in *F&SF, New Worlds, Galaxy, If,* and anthologies such as *Orbit* and Harry Harrison's *Nova.* Many of these were collected in my first book, *A Few Last Words.* At a signing in Philadelphia a couple of years ago a fan turned up with a copy of that book. I was amazed.

Mike introduced me to Hammett and Chandler. The opening of *Difficult Lives,* my book on Jim Thompson, David Goodis and Chester Himes, recalls this period: "Many years ago, in temporary self-exile, burrowing under covers with endless cups of tea as hot as I could bear them in my unheated two-room flat off Porto-bello Road in London, I first read the novels of Hammett and Chandler, all of them, I think, in a single week's time." I started with Hammett, read everything, moved on to Chandler, even read the letters.

I'd get up in the morning, put on tea, then go back to bed with these books. After a few hours I'd pour out a bowl of muesli, stick some pita bread in the cooker and carry *that* back to bed. Early afternoon, I'd get up and write, often a short story at a single sitting, many of them recognizably science fiction or fantasy, others (especially those written under the French influence) just very strange.

Silet: What attracted you, in *Difficult Lives,* to those particular writers: Thompson, Goodis, Himes?

Sallis: In a sense, of course, that's exactly what the book is about, why it exists at all. Let's look at this. Why *are* these writers important to me? How do they fit into my general sense of literature and commercial fiction? What's the source of the incredible *energy* these novels have? I wrote the book to find out what I thought. *Difficult Lives* well may be central to understanding what I've been up to all these years. I've turned out reams of criticism, reviews, essays on writing and literary history. A lot of it keeps circling back (like a man lost in the woods, passing the same tree again and again) to *Difficult Lives.* I like to believe the fiction and poetry, in its way, is of a piece. I'm fairly certain the criticism is.

Silet: Tell me about Lew Griffin. Who is he, what motivates him, and why did you decide to make him black? Lew has so many different parts to him, more than most detectives in crime stories: his literary background, his teaching, his understanding of music (especially jazz), his familiarity with French. What do these interests allow you to do with the character?

Sallis: First off, I didn't make Lew black. He was black from the first. It just took me a while to realize this. Thirty pages or so into a short story that eventually became *The Long-Legged Fly,* I had this character full of rage, anger, self-destructive drives, and I didn't know why. My God, I thought one day, he's black; *that's* where it comes from. I'd been reading a lot of Chester Himes, all the novels from *If He Hollers* on through the Harlem books, but also the autobiographies and whatever else I could find about him. So a lot of Lew is transposed from Himes—from his own life as much as from his fiction.

By this time I'd pretty much abandoned writing "the well-made story" where everything's plotted out: crisis, conflict, ascending action, resolution. That had come to hold absolutely no interest for me. Instead, I'd begun to improvise. Begin with a scene, a setting, a character, and let it unfold, see what was in there. I assumed my own surprise, my own sense of discovery, would be the reader's.

So Lew's character, his background and interests, unfolded organically. I never sat down and said, Okay, this guy is fifty, he's from Arkansas, he likes white women. I *discovered* his past, what he's like, in the writing. I still do, page to page, book to book. And I'm still surprised at what I find out.

In the new novel, for instance, suddenly he's back on the streets. Did I plan this? No. Did I see it coming? No, not consciously. But it's what had to happen.

I remember Rex Stout remarking how, at work on the latest Nero Wolfe, one day he found himself writing a scene in which a visitor suddenly reveals to Wolfe that he is Wolfe's son. Stout never suspected this until the very moment his fingers hit those typewriter keys. He was astonished.

Fictional characters too often are narrow, constrained. We're all composed of these astonishing contradictions, diversities, bits and pieces that never fit together. I've tried in the Lew Griffin books to be true to these baffles and trap doors, in other characters as much as in Lew himself. We all contain multitudes. And as with any democracy, there's dissent.

Silet: Let's talk a bit about the "series"—although I hate to call it that. Did you set out to write more than one book about Lew Griffin? Why the insect names? (I do detect a bit of Kafka in your work, especially the novella *Renderings*.)

Sallis: I never set out to write a series. *The Long-Legged Fly* began as a short story, insisted upon becoming a novel, and I thought that was it. Then I realized I wanted to know more about these characters and the world they lived in, and wrote *Moth*. Then *Black Hornet*, set in the sixties, with Lew just having moved to New Orleans and beginning a life there. In a way this evolution reflects the changeable nature of the novels themselves. Beginning as genre fiction, they transformed themselves—hauled themselves up by their bootstraps—into literary novels. This catalysis informs the very structure of *The Long-Legged Fly*.

At this point, I think there'll be six books. The fifth, like *Hornet*, will be set in the past, and will be more action- or plot-oriented. Again, little of this is planned out. I begin to perceive the shape of the next book as I work on the current one. There are some surprises at the end of *Eye of the Cricket*, whose final chapters closely echo sections from *Moth* and *Fly*. You *sort of* find out what happened to Lew's son David, for instance, but a lot of this is just setting you up for the *real* surprise (I only now realize) at the end of the sixth book.

There's no particular significance to the insect names. I'd chosen *The Long-Legged Fly* (from Yeats) for the first book, really a perfect title for it. Then when I decided to go on, I thought it made sense to signal the connectedness of these books. I do think the individual titles uniquely appropriate, however. Novel five will be *Bluebottle*, the last one (after Blake) *Ghost of a Flea*.

Silet: Tell me about the first Griffin book, *The Long-Legged Fly*. What did you want to do in that book? What issues does it address?

Sallis: It began with a flash of this character, a young man, killing someone. I knew he had a reason for what he was doing but I had little or no notion what that reason might be. His hard breathing, the soughing of oil pumps behind, the wind—all of this came together in my mind. All in dim light. I sat down and wrote the first chapter, which did little but make me still more curious. I wanted to have this character do something monstrous, unforgivable, then spend the rest of the story forcing you to like him.

Fly begins as fairly standard pulp fiction. Then it deepens, gains substance, circling in ever closer towards a kind of autobiography, until with the final sentences we discover that all along this "autobiography" has been every bit as fictive as the pulp fare with which *Fly* began. Only with the sixth book will we discover the "real" story, and its author.

I've always admired novels and films that cover the span of a man's life. *Fly* is in four sections, 1964, 1970, 1984, 1990, limning Lew's life from his arrival in New Orleans up, almost, to his death. When the manuscript was first making the rounds, this discontinuity bothered editors no end; now it's "structurally innovative."

Silet: *Moth* continues the series. What is the special thrust of that novel?

Sallis: Topmost in my mind was the certainty that I did not want to write the same book again and again. (Indeed, looking at *Fly*, you might paraphrase the old Heraclitean paradox and remark that I didn't want to write the same book once.) If I was going to write another novel about Lew Griffin, it had to be a *different* novel. *Moth* is probably the closest thing to a "proper" novel I'll ever write, a simple story told straight through. It's also—perhaps because of its setting outside New Orleans, in rural Mississippi, Faulkner land—decidedly Southern.

Silet: What did you want especially to say in *Black Hornet*?

Sallis: I wanted, again, a very different kind of book from *Moth* or *Fly*. Less introspection, more action. Yet at the same time I wanted to show how this bright, self-educated young black man, with no advantages whatsoever, had come down from Mississippi and started to make a place for himself (and started to destroy himself) there in New Orleans. It's set in the past (as will be the fifth novel), somewhere just before *Fly*'s first section. The sixties are a major theme. All along I had firmly in mind my admiration for Himes and for Donald Westlake's Parker books.

Silet: In another interview I know that you have said that you were not interested in changing the genre with the Lew Griffin books, yet they are very different from most other detective fiction. Can you talk about how they are different?

Sallis: I believe my comment was that I didn't wish to *subvert* the genre, and I don't. But the genre has to change if it's to endure at all. I love, embrace, and admire genre fiction. I also love, embrace, and admire what we'll call (for lack of a better designation) literature. So I've tried to combine what I love of each—the energy, thrust and immediacy of genre fiction, the substance and depth of literature—to create what, as a reader, I've been able to find nowhere else. To sum up, many pleasures in one. I'd be shocked if anyone else tried to write this way. And while I have a lot of fans among mystery readers, others consider the books utterly outside the genre and ignore them.

Silet: Other critics have commented on the centrality of New Orleans in the Griffin books, of how the city functions as more than simple place. Tell me what New Orleans means to you and to Lew?

Sallis: In many ways New Orleans is an island, cut off in time and place and not part of the larger U.S. culture at all, this incredible slurry of black, Southern, Mediterranean, Spanish and Creole influences. It's a city where shadows are sharp and hard, where you have people living in unbelievable poverty half a block from mansions. All our social problems—poverty, the rift between black and white, political corruption, urban failure—seem highlighted here. New Orleans is definitely central to the novels; they couldn't occur anywhere else.

Silet: Your writing is in so many areas: music criticism, poetry, avant-garde short fiction, translations of Raymond Queneau, literary criticism, reviewing, editing. How do all these fit together, influence one another, work in the Lew Griffin novels?

Sallis: A lot of it comes simply from thirty years of trying to make a living by writing. I began writing short stories, then, when the market for those collapsed, I sidestepped into writing about music. When I had a market for essays, I wrote essays. Criticism and reviewing seemed to me intrinsic parts of literary life.

Lurking around backstage, too, is my desire to be a true man of letters in the way that someone like Queneau was. This isn't an ordinary thing in the States, where one's expected to be a poet or a novelist, Spam or cornflakes. Queneau wrote poetry, novels, popular songs, he was a highly influential editor, a polymath. And that's become my model.

We have to remember that the critical approach is like our approach to history in general, dealing not with life as it's lived from day to day, but with life's disruptions, setting out arbitrary signs and fenceposts. I've not moved from short stories to mysteries to translation to poetry; rather, at various times I've written all these things. I'd hope there's a basic unity there, of course. Somewhere.

Silet: You've translated Raymond Queneau's novel *Saint Glinglin* for Dalkey Archive Press. What specifically attracted you to Raymond Queneau? To the art of translation?

Sallis: As I say in the introduction to *Glinglin*, when the line was drawn in the sand, I didn't step back fast enough. *Glinglin* was Queneau's last major work to be translated into English, and I soon realized there was a damned good *reason* it hadn't been translated before. It was an awesome undertaking. I could have written three or four novels in the time it took me to translate this one. But it's a book I'm inordinately proud of.

I love French literature, as you know. I'd begun reading widely in it while in London, went on to translate poetry by Apollinaire, Ponge, Du Bouchet, Cendrars, Guillevic. So far *Glinglin* is the only book-length work I've done. I'd be interested in translating more,

Boris Vian for instance, especially *L'Herbe Rouge.* But to support a habit (feed a monkey) like translation these days you have to be subsidized by a teaching job; there's no money in it. Again, things are rather different abroad, where writers such as Vian, Queneau and Pasternak supported themselves with translations. Vian's versions of Chandler, for instance, are brilliant.

Silet: Let's talk a bit about the novella *Renderings* and short-story collection *Limits of the Sensible World.* What were you striving for in these works? In both the prose is, for lack of a better word, "experimental." What were you experimenting with?

Sallis: I have no idea what that word means in relation to writing. Certainly the stories are not photorealist, mimetic, traditionally realistic fiction. But finally I see little difference between the stories in *Limits* and the Lew Griffin novels. You create a form, bring on characters, then try to get to the center of what it's all about. Same sensibility, same movements of mind, much the same resources of language. The stories in *Limits* were written over a period of twenty years or more; I do feel there's a unity to them, but it's not a preconceived one. Like *Fly, Renderings* began as a short story many years ago, eventually insisting upon becoming a novel. I've remarked that with *Renderings* I wanted to write a novel and leave out all the dull stuff. Some readers have suggested that I left all the dull stuff *in,* and took out the rest.

Silet: Over the years writers have used crime fiction as social criticism. Your novels seem especially rich in social commentary. How do you feel about the crime novel as a vehicle for social criticism?

Sallis: This is another instance in which there was really no programmatic intent. But there's no way I can have an intelligent black man moving through all levels of society, back in the sixties, on into present time, and not reflect social problems. The social commentary arises from character and setting.

I suspect that crime fiction is *the* urban fiction. D. H. Lawrence said that man murdered himself into this democracy, something we face each time we set about writing. And, with me, with the Lew Griffin books, there's always that Himes influence. No one can read a novel like Himes' *The Primitive* and remain unchallenged— on *many* levels.

Silet: Tell me about your latest Lew Griffin novel in print?

Sallis: The fourth Lew Griffin novel, *Eye of the Cricket,* is about a lot. You find out what happened to Lew's son. Lew stumbles into yet another dark night of the soul. Alouette, from *Moth,* returns. And oh, yes: it has a happy ending. My wife cried as she began fitting the manuscript back into its box.

Silet: Tell me a bit about the latest Lew Griffin book.

Sallis: The fifth Lew Griffin, *Bluebottle,* will be out in December 1998. Like *Black Hornet* it's set in the past, and is in several other ways a strange mirror image of *Hornet.* It deals with early white supremacy movements as the earlier novel did with black power movements; it begins with a rooftop sniping in which not the woman beside him but Lew himself is shot. In *Eye of the Cricket* Lew casually mentions "the holes" in his life and that once he lost almost a year of it after being shot. This is that year. The novel we are reading is Lew's attempt to reconstruct the year from fragments of memory, from what others have told him, and, finally, from imagination.

Silet: Any more in the works in the foreseeable future?

Sallis: Yes, the sixth Lew Griffin will pull all the others, for all their diversity, together.

Silet: You write prolifically. Tell me about your current projects.

Sallis: I had two books out in '97: *Cricket* in the fall, and in July, from St. Martin's, *Death Will Have Your Eyes,* "a novel about spies," which my British publisher characterized as "Le Carré meets the Coen Brothers."

Both my books in '96 were nonfiction (*The Guitar in Jazz* from University of Nebraska Press and *Ash of Stars: On the Writing of*

Samuel R. Delany from University Press of Mississippi) so it's well past time for new fiction.

Silet: You have been working on a biography of the African-American crime and protest writer Chester Himes.

Sallis: I have spent the past year and more working almost exclusively on a biography of Chester Himes to be published late in 1999 by the Scottish publisher Canongate Books/Payback Press; portions are appearing in *High Plains Literary Review,* the *Ohio Review* and *North Dakota Quarterly.*

Silet: What projects other than your crime writing are you pursuing now?

Sallis: Everything's pretty much been on hold over the past year as I worked on the Chester Himes biography. In late 1999 or possibly 2000, Michigan State University Press will bring out *Sorrow's Kitchen,* one of two major collections of my poems. This one (the other is still circulating) runs to 105 pages in manuscript and collects poems written over thirty years and originally published in *The Transatlantic Review, Poetry East, Karamu, The Chariton Review, The Dickinson Review, North Dakota Quarterly, South Dakota Review, Oasis, Negative Capability,* and others. A UK publisher plans to bring out a two-volume collection of my short stories, one of science fiction, one of mysteries, sometime in 1999. Gary Lovisi at Gryphon plans to reprint *Difficult Lives.* And Black Heron Press, which did *Renderings,* will bring out my essay collection, *Gently into the Land of Meateaters,* also sometime in 1999.

Once the Himes book is done and we are resettled on the east coast, I plan to write a longish essay on French poet Guillevic and another on British novelist Iain Sinclair; this last may be done for *The Review of Contemporary Fiction.* I'd also like to do a series of essays on forgotten or neglected writers, people such as Gerald Karsh, Marek Hlasko, Walter Tevis, Boris Vian.

I'm not sure what my next novel will be. I have, to answer your question about another non-series crime novel, one partially written, *Bottomfeeders,* a comic novel about a cop-killer and a gentle takeoff on *The Seven Samurai.* So I'll probably complete that. I've several others in mind: a realistic novel set here in Arizona, a first-person novel about Gilles de Rais. The one that's occupying my mind quite a lot just now is a kind of literary fantasy. There's a tremendous pull towards that one. I started off writing science fiction and fantasy over thirty years ago. Maybe it's time for a novel?

Silet: What is it that you think you do especially well in your crime fiction?

Sallis: I think that, here, my strong point is in uniting the pleasures and strength of the crime novel with those of the (for lack of a proper word) "literary" novel. The major strength in *all* my work is language itself: the kinetics of it, its rhythms and sounds, the way the text works to move in an almost physical manner through perception and memory towards the world, which becomes then luminous in its reality.

Lives of the Twins
Rosamond Smith
(Joyce Carol Oates)

Photo © Beth Gwinn

By the late 1980s Joyce Carol Oates was well established as a serious mainstream writer of considerable importance. She then surprised the literary world by publishing a crime novel under the pseudonym of Rosamond Smith. However, her anonymity proved to be short lived when Liz Smith, the gossip columnist for *The New York Post*, revealed her authorship. As Ms. Oates confesses in the following interview, her attempt to write under an assumed name was a desire to "begin again," to write novels that would be read freshly, unencumbered by the Joyce Carol Oates name.

Although her cover had been blown, Ms. Oates has continued to publish her Rosamond Smith books to increasing critical and public acclaim. The appearance in 1999 of *Starr Bright Will Be With You Soon* marked the seventh in the Rosamond Smith series. Beginning with *Lives of the Twins* (1987) the books have appeared steadily over the last decade: *Soul/Mate* (1989), *Nemesis* (1990), *Snake Eyes* (1992), *You Can't Catch Me* (1995), and *Double Delight*

(1997). As the titles of each of these books suggests the series is focused on twins or the twinning of the characters, often an "evil" predatory male with a "good" female victim. Of course, this theme is also a major one explored by Joyce Carol Oates in her conventional fiction, but in her crime novels, or "concept" novels as she calls them, she has been experimenting with fiction more driven by plot than character. Whether publishing under her own name or as Rosamond Smith, expanding the possibilities of the modern novel, both genre as well as mainstream, is one of the characteristics of Ms. Oates's writing. Crime fiction has become all the richer for it.

Portions of this interview appeared as "Rosamond Smith: AKA Joyce Carol Oates," *Mystery Scene*, No. 62 (1999), 60–64.

Silet: What attracted you to writing crime fiction?

Oates: Crime and mystery writing in combination with the depth of characterization and the attentiveness to language one hopes to find in "literary" fiction have always been an ideal for me. I think of mystery, if not invariably crime, as integral to human experience. Our beginnings, like our endings, are shrouded in mystery: it's natural that we should be fascinated by these forms.

Silet: Why did you decide to write your mystery/crime books under a pseudonym?

Oates: Where my ideas come from, and why, I don't know. The yearning to "begin again" for the established writer is very real; for just as we strive for identity, we're reluctant to relinquish our anonymity. I had hoped that by writing under a pseudonym I might be writing more purely, and my books, if they were read at all, might be read without recourse to any prior identity. There's romance, too, of a secret, even illicit adventure.

Silet: Would you briefly discuss the commotion that was caused when your pseudonym was unmasked?

Oates: One day shortly before the publication of my first Rosamond Smith novel, *Lives of the Twins*, an item appeared in a gossip column by Liz Smith in a New York newspaper, stating that "Rosamond Smith" was "Joyce Carol Oates." I'll never know how Liz Smith got her information, but when I was queried by reporters, as well as by my Dutton editor Billy Abrahams and my agent at that time, Blanche Gregory, of course I couldn't deny it. This was a painful episode in my life which I'd like to forget if possible.

Silet: You dedicated *Snake Eyes* to Elmore Leonard, you have written essays on crime writers (James M. Cain among others), and you occasionally review crime fiction. So obviously you are familiar with the field. When did you start reading mystery fiction, who do you like, and how has your crime reading influenced your own work?

Oates: I've been reading mystery/crime fiction and non-fiction for virtually my entire life. I'd begun reading voraciously as a young teenager, working my way through sections of the Lockport Public Library, in both mystery/crime and gothic/horror as well as in what's called mainstream literature. Mystery/crime fiction is stimulating partly because it involves problem-solving, and most of us are fascinated by this sort of mental activity. Gothic/horror excites the imagination with often bizarre dream-images; where the genre is tightly plotted, I tend to lose interest in the work. Mysteries of the sort written by A. Conan Doyle, Ellery Queen and Rex Stout are intelligent, even intellectual adventures, of particular interest to adolescents, and I remember reading these with much enjoyment.

The "hardboiled" crime/mystery novel with its usually powerful erotic subtext appeals to more mature readers; this is, on the whole, a more realistically rendered art. To search out origins is to approach repeatedly, perhaps compulsively, a primal "crime scene" accessible only through the imagination.

I can respond to virtually any writer, granted talent and commitment. So it's difficult for me to select just a few. Ruth Rendell, Elmore Leonard, P. D. James; a writer new to me, Michael Connelly; Thomas H. Cook, Edna Buchanan, Robert Parker, Sharon McCrumb, and James Ellroy, among others.

Silet: During the 1980s, starting with *Bellefleur*, you began experimenting with genre fiction, gothic romance, detective/mystery, and horror. What was the fascination with these genres? Are the Rosamond Smith books an extension of this interest? What is the relationship between genre fiction and mainstream, conventional fiction?

Oates: The relationship between "genre" and "mainstream" fiction is fluid and always shifting. In a sense, Homer's great poems are generic: *The Iliad* is action drama, *The Odyssey* is epic adventure. Shakespeare's great plays are generic: "tragedy" was a formal convention, in some hands formulaic; *Hamlet* is one of numerous revenge tragedies of the era, if also the superior example of the genre. Genre is both restraining in terms of structure (like the sonnet) yet liberating in terms of experimentation (like the sonnet—there are in fact variants of the sonnet form which allowed the individual sonneteers to display their virtuosity). As a reader, I look for only one thing in any book I pick up: originality of voice, authenticity of vision.

One of Henry James's greatest works of fiction is the "ghost story" *The Turn of the Screw*. William Faulkner's *Sanctuary* is a mystery/thriller. Joseph Conrad's *Heart of Darkness* is mystery/ adventure. Among my own novels, written under "Oates," *them, Do With Me What You Will, What I Lived For, Foxfire,* and *Man Crazy* involve mystery or crime. *Zombie* is the first-person narration of a serial killer. *We Were the Mulvaneys* explores the consequences of rape in a normal American family. *American Appetites* depicts a man tried for the murder of his wife. My long novel *My Heart Laid Bare* contains a number of crimes, ranging from the quintessentially American crime of ingenious confidence swindling to the violent crime of murder.

Silet: You have described *Lives of the Twins* (1987) as a "concept" rather than a "real" novel. Would you explain what you mean by a "concept" novel and how it differs from a "real" novel?

Oates: By "concept" I mean that I've begun with an idea, and a structure, rather than characters; my characters are then imagined to enact a story. In the traditional novel, it's more likely that we begin with characters. I tend to know my characters vividly, as if they were real individuals, and it's the ways in which they come into contact with one another that evolve into "plots." In the one case, plot is extremely important; in the other, plot may be almost incidental, or might evolve in differing ways.

Silet: How did you come to write *Lives of the Twins?* Were there any particular problems you set for yourself in that first Rosamond Smith novel?

Oates: The concept was: Do you dare explore the twinness of a man known to you, risking the revelation of evil, like Pandora recklessly opening her box? Philosophically: do we dare explore mystery, though we risk disaster in uncovering truths and precipitating actions not in our best interests?

Silet: In *Lives of the Twins* you established one of the major themes of all the Rosamond Smith novels, namely the presence of twins, the doubling of characters. Even the titles of the books refer to this doubling. What fascinates you about the subject? As a writer what does it allow you to do?

Oates: Since I have a twin-like sister born eighteen years after me, on my birthday, severely autistic, wholly without speech—very likely there's a personal reason for my fascination with twins. Otherwise, I can't explain it. Perhaps some of us were meant to be twins, but our twins died in the womb and were reabsorbed into tissue. I've been told that that's possible. So, through life, we yearn romantically for this lost self.

Silet: When you wrote the first Rosamond Smith did you plan to do others? Were you consciously beginning a series?

Oates: I'd imagined a series of novels dealing with thematic twins of one kind or another. Once the subject seizes hold of you, it's virtually impossible to let go. There is something over-the-top and melodramatic about twins that might not lend itself so readily to the subtleties of "realistic" fiction; but this is ideal for genre which thrives upon risky ventures.

Silet: In *Soul/Mate* (1989) you created in Colin Asch a serial killer who is also charming. Tell me a little about Colin Asch? Who is he? What makes him tick? What motivated you to write about such a dangerous and evil man?

Oates: I found Colin Asch "evil" only at a distance; up close, inside his skin, I found his actions to be perfectly logical. Like so many of my violent characters, who tend to be men, he's a lover of a thwarted kind. He yearns for intimacy and fulfillment—on his own terms.

I hadn't realized, years later, when I created Quentin P. (of *Zombie*) that I had already created a young male serial killer, since the two men are so different. Colin would have been disdainful of Quentin, though Quentin might well have been attracted to Colin.

Colin and Dorothea Deverell are natural "soul-mates"—from Colin's perspective at least. Though Dorothea would not wish to admit it, Colin is her dark self; the fairy-tale figure who protects her by destroying her enemies.

Silet: Throughout the Rosamond Smith books you have invented a gallery of rogues, Asch, James McEwan, Rolfe Christensen, Lee Roy Sears, but you always manage to make them three-dimensional and not just stock characters. What is it that draws you to these figures? How are you able to present them beyond their criminality?

Oates: Perhaps there is a trace of "criminality"—however we may wish to define it—in my genetic makeup. I tend to feel more sympathetic with victims of crimes. As a woman who occasionally writes about boxing, I have a natural predilection for identifying with the hurt or losing boxer for whom the crucial question is: With what grace does one "lose"? With what courage does one "survive"?

What is criminality and hurt for one is but, for another, the forging of an individual destiny. Our yearnings and appetites in collision—this is the drama of life, neutral in its Darwinian complexity and ruthlessness.

Silet: In *Snake Eyes* (1992) you center the novel on the destructive relationship between a married couple, Michael and Gina O'Meara, and the psychotic Lee Roy Sears. What did this shift away from the "woman alone" allow you to do? *Snake Eyes* reminds me of *Cape Fear*, both the films, one released in 1962 with Robert Mitchem and Gregory Peck and the second released in 1991, directed by Martin Scorsese, with Robert De Nero and Nick Nolte.

Oates: It's interesting that you should think of *Cape Fear*, of which I knew little until after finishing the novel. (The Scorsese film was released at this time.) My model for the novel's initial situation was probably the relationship between the prisoner John Henry Abbott and Norman Mailer, who was instrumental in securing the man's premature release. And there have been numerous other instances in which men of stature and influence lobby to get a convicted killer released. I don't mean to suggest that well-intentioned men like Mailer are consciously or unconsciously liberating a violent brother of sorts upon the world, as a way of channeling their own aggression; this is a "literary" idea, not a sociological one.

In *Snake Eyes*, Michael O'Meara never confronts his own yearning for violence and, eventually, revenge against his adulterous wife, and many readers, and reviewers, never identified him as his wife's assailant. Yet I didn't want to make the novel too explicit, and thus too melodramatic, preferring to suggest rather than state.

Silet: One of the other recurring motifs of the Rosamond Smith books is the unmasking of a character's dark past or the uncovering of evil in otherwise conventionally "normal" or "good" characters. What has drawn you to this theme?

Oates: To me, the unmasking or revealing of the past proceeds in a kind of systolic rhythm with the forward movement of plot. By moving into the meaningful future, in which we "know" ourselves through action, we come to know more of our past, buried selves. And this knowledge is not always welcome to us.

Silet: *You Can't Catch Me* (1995) involves a personality transfer, although this novel may present the extreme case. It also introduces a fine example of that old crime noir female figure, the "spider woman," who seduces the male protagonist into criminal behavior. Would you talk a little about the character Fleur/Zoe in that novel?

Oates: I've been fascinated by the doubleness of the female as perceived by the male, in particular the misogynist male. The rare books and anatomical drawings in Grunwald's collection of "evidence contra Woman" are all authentic, a devastating history of man's distrust and hatred of women. While non-misogynist men might contemplate such things with an air of bemusement and disdain, for a woman they're extremely upsetting, even obscene. It's as if Fleur/Zoe had materialized out of this very imagination of extremes.

Tristram Heade is drawn into evil by succumbing to temptation, out of curiosity, as many of us might in his position. Gradually the "good" Heade, a decent, gentle, soft-spoken man who respects women is overtaken by the amoral, malicious Markham. *You Can't Catch Me* is the only Rosamond Smith novel that crosses genres: its world is surreal rather that "real," and its mystery is of a gothic sort.

Silet: Let's talk about *Double Delight* (1997), which is another seduction/obsession novel. Without revealing the plot too much will you discuss what was behind writing the book? As you have said you set problems for yourself in writing. What was the "problem" here?

Oates: *Double Delight* took vivid shape for me when I was assigned a week of jury duty in Trenton, New Jersey, not many miles from Princeton and yet a radically different world from Princeton. This was several years ago. I was on a jury, and we heard a case similar to the case in the novel, in outline at least. I was fascinated by the adventure of being on a jury, emotionally involved with strangers, in a world contiguous to but not related to my own. Out of the "doubleness" of these worlds the idea of the novel arose.

Of course, in the execution, the idea became more complicated. There's a background history to my suburban Terence Greene that helps to explain the passion he comes to feel for Ava-Rose Renfrew, so like his lost mother, in his imagination at least. The challenge for me was to determine how Terence would be seduced by the family of con men of whom Ava-Rose is the most attractive yet avoid the fate of the other men who'd fallen in love with Ava-

Rose. By the novel's end, he has been transformed to a degree that allows him to survive, as his predecessors had not.

Silet: All of the Rosamond Smith books seem very filmable. Have you had any offers? Is anything under option? What has been your experience with the film world?

Oates: *Snake Eyes* was optioned for film, and, I think, actually purchased. Like so many other projects, it seems to be in a kind of limbo. *Lives of the Twins* was filmed as a TV movie (retitled *Lies of the Twins*) starring the very beautiful Isabel Rossellini. The film bears only a cursory relationship to the novel and I wasn't able to watch more than ten or fifteen minutes of it.

Two feature films have been made of my mainstream novels, *Smooth Talk* (based loosely on the story "Where Are You Going, Where Have You Been?") and *Foxfire* (based on the novel, even more loosely). I wasn't involved with these projects.

Silet: What do you think you do best in the Rosamond Smith books? What are your strengths as a writer of noir fiction?

Oates: I try to make my characters alive in psychologically immediate ways, as if I inhabited their skin; the hope is that the reader, too, will inhabit them.

Silet: How have the Rosamond Smith novels fared with the critics? Have they (you) been treated fairly?

Oates: I think the Rosamond Smith novels have been very generously treated by critics. As you mentioned, there doesn't seem to be much cross-over criticism. It's true that I've been criticized for the violence in my work, but reviewers must criticize something, and if it hadn't been violence it would perhaps have been something else. On the whole, critics have been quite sympathetic.

I'm touched and impressed by how much thoughtful analysis reviewers often give my work, even in situations in which I'd guess they receive very modest payment. These are the unsung heroes and heroines of the literary world, people who like to read, and are enthusiastic about books.

Silet: What is the place of "violence" in literature, crime or otherwise?

Oates: Realist fiction holds a mirror up to life, as both Aristotle and Stendhal have said. Art in fact mirrors only a selection of the random and pointless violence of life which is why it is "art" and not life. There is actually little violence *in* my work; often it occurs behind the scenes, or between the acts; it's the consequences of violence, often in the lives of victims, which most involve me as a writer. Of course, the Rosamond Smith novels, being mystery/crime/psychological suspense, are more likely to contain graphic violence than my other work. The mystery/crime writer who shrinks from depicting violence isn't living up to his or her contract with the reader, one might argue. The bloodless deaths and unconvincing corpses of the English "cozy" novel render that entire genre unreadable to me. This is the novel as needlepoint, not as a mirror held up to life.

Silet: In an earlier interview you said that the role of the writer is to be the conscience of his/her race. Do you still believe this? If so, how is it present in the Rosamond Smith books? On your part does the conscience take on a "feminist" perspective?

Oates: Serious artists are invariably the consciences of their cultures, intentionally or otherwise. In art, the interior is examined minutely as we might wish to examine our own souls. People tend to read fiction—and non-fiction, including memoirs and biographies—in order to see how others live. For as Nietzsche shrewdly observed, "We all pretend to ourselves that we are more simple-minded than we are." In art of an introspective, interior nature, we discover the hidden complexities of which our fellow human beings are capable.

Like most feminists, I'm not invariably and at all times "feminist." I don't write propaganda. I don't believe that men are the enemy. I don't make my women characters exemplary human beings but rather realistic women for their time and place. Still, I do have a feminist perspective, and this angle of vision informs my writing at all times.

Silet: Some critics of crime fiction feel that the form inherently contains a critique of society. How does this idea strike you?

Oates: Most works of art are critical of society because they represent individual and not communal or conformist thought. The individual spirit is one that can't be controlled, ideally. But to me, "society" is an abstraction; what exists are individuals, some of whom possess far more power than others. The will of the powerful becomes the putative will of society.

Silet: Could you talk briefly about your latest Rosamond Smith novel?

Oates: My current Rosamond Smith novel is *Starr Bright Will Be With You Soon* (1999), which involves twin sisters: one of them a woman who kills men to take revenge upon them, the other a devoted wife and mother. In writing about each sister, I felt sympathy with her. There's a duel of sorts between them in moral, and plot, terms; and a struggle for the soul of the "good" sister's adolescent daughter.

The stab of excitement I feel in contemplating the planning of any Rosamond Smith novel is very like the stab of excitement I feel when I open a mystery/crime novel in anticipation of being drawn into a world different from my own, taken to places I've never been and made to see and to feel things otherwise hidden from me. Maybe we write so that we can become ideal readers of our own work. There is a communal enterprise here, in which we are all active participants.

Choice of Evil
Andrew Vachss

Photo © Leo Sorel

Andrew Vachss is one of the pit bulls of contemporary crime fiction. His single-minded dedication to exposing the sordid world of abused children through his Burke series of crime novels has won praise from critics and readers alike. The passion with which he addresses the various ways both individuals and society exploit children—especially for sexual purposes—is evident in his novels and in his interviews. He is obviously a man on a mission.

After publishing a textbook on juvenile violence, Vachss realized that he could reach a larger audience through fiction, and in 1985, *Flood*, a novel he had written in the seventies, was released and, in his words, "just exploded." Since then he has published eleven more Burke books. The latest, *Choice of Evil*, in 1999.

Andrew Vachss also writes short fiction and has compiled three collections of it so far, the most recent being *Everybody Pays*, 1999. In his short stories, which he describes variously as being like haiku and a devastating six-inch punch, he has developed a second character, Cross. In connection with *Safe House* (1998) he released a CD, also called "Safe House," with some of his favorite jazz music, much of it featured in the Burke series. The last track by Bazza called "Ghost" has lyrics by Vachss who has been writing song lyrics for some years.

No matter whether he has been praised or damned, neither readers nor critics have ever found the crime fiction of Andrew Vachss dull or predictable. Whatever one may say about him, there is no doubt about his commitment to his cause or the passion with which he pursues it. That same sense of dedication comes through loud and clear in the following interview conducted in January 1999.

Silet: Tell me about where you were born and went to school.

Vachss: I was born in New York City in a neighborhood that has since become known as SoHo but certainly wasn't called that when I was a kid. After school, I went to what is now called Case Western Reserve University which at the time was called Western Reserve University prior to its merger with Case. I went there sporadically, but I did eventually graduate.

Silet: Did you do other things while you were going to school?

Vachss: I drove a laundry truck; I moved furniture; I did all the kinds of manual labor you could think of while I was going to school.

Silet: What did you do after you graduated from university?

Vachss: I was an investigator in a lot of places for the United States Public Health Service, investigating sexually transmitted diseases. I was in Chicago, then I was in the northern part of Ohio. Also there is a triangle between West Virginia and Ohio and Pennsylvania, where Steubenville is on one side and Wheeling, West Virginia is on the other, and that essentially was my base. The job consisted of following up on people who had tested positive for syphilis. We had to persuade these people, whoever they are and wherever they were, to disclose all of their sexual contacts in the past critical period. Then we would have to find those people and keep running the daisy chain hoping that it didn't end in somebody dying.

Silet: You are a practicing lawyer. Where did you go to law school?

Vachss: The New England School of Law in Boston.

Silet: At what point did you become interested in abused children?

Vachss: From the jump. When I first saw a baby with a prolapsed rectum while I was with the Public Health Service.

Silet: When did you first decide to write fiction?

Vachss: What you've got to understand is that after I did this job as an investigator, I became a case worker in New York City with the infamous Bureau of Welfare, and then I was in the war in Biafra. When I returned, I did everything from running a reentry center for urban migrants in Chicago to organizing a place that was supposed to be providing services to ex-convicts in Boston to managing a maximum security prison for aggressive violent youths. I spent a decade at this sort of thing, all pursuing the same sort of beast, before I went to law school. It wasn't until after all of this and after I wrote a textbook on juvenile violence and saw that wonderful reviews don't translate to reaching the public, that I decided to repackage it and call it fiction. It was a long, long period of time before I went in that direction.

Silet: Had you been writing anything before this?

Vachss: Not to speak of. The book, *Flood*, that eventually got published I wrote a dozen years before it actually got published. So I had been writing, just not publishing.

Silet: Had you been reading any crime or mystery fiction?

Vachss: I can't say none, because that would be an exaggeration, but certainly none that rings a bell with me. I really read non-fiction all through school, especially when I was a kid. There were a few, I guess you'd call them pulp writers, like Paul Cane, which I do remember reading, that I was impressed by, but not a whole lot, to be truthful.

Silet: Tell me a little about *Flood* which was published in 1985.

Vachss: That was when it got published. I had written *Flood* in the seventies, and after I had first written it, I just threw it in a drawer and paid no attention to it. A couple of years later a journalist was interviewing me about one of my trials. He said the usual about you ought to write a book, and I replied that I had written a goddamned book for all the good it had done me. He asked to see it and showed it to a guy who showed it to a guy, and I ended up getting published.

I had a wonderful agent back then who went through total hell with me, getting the same rejection from everybody: What a brilliant writer I was, what incredible power, blah, blah, blah, but gee, this topic wasn't possible. "Write about something else and we'll be happy to publish it." Finally I modified it—believe it or not what is published is toned down—and Victor, my agent, called and said, "Now you've done it. Now we're going to be on the best-seller list. We're all going to be rich. This is perfect." And he died a couple of days later. This was Victor Chapin, my first agent. I've endowed a literary prize at the University of New Mexico in his name. He was a wonderful man. The kind of agent that everybody dreams of having, and he never saw my book get published, although I dedicated it to him.

Silet: Did the publisher want another one?

Vachss: The book got released and all of a sudden it just exploded. It ended up on best-seller lists and everybody wanted it. The publisher made me an offer that I certainly was able to refuse. I subsequently went to Knopf, and I've been there ever since.

Silet: Tell me about Burke. Where did he come from?

Vachss: I wanted to show people what hell looked like. I didn't think the Chandleresque, white-knight sort of person would be an appropriate guy. I wanted him to be the prototypical abused child, hypervigilant, distrustful, but bonded beyond blood to his family of choice. He's a working criminal not a do-gooder.

Silet: Some critics have described him as an unlicensed P.I.

Vachss: An unlicensed P.I. is a lot of crap. There are plenty of heroic, white-knight, unlicensed P.I.s. I don't think that is much of a description. He's a criminal. This is something that book reviewers needed to say because of their need to make everything into a genre, but he's no more a private eye than he is an airline pilot.

Silet: He's an orphan, an ex-con, and a mercenary. What is it that motivates him?

Vachss: Number one above all else is survival. I mean, he's a survivalist in the extreme. Then the protection and safety of his family. Outside of that the world could go to hell. He's a patriot with a really tiny country.

Silet: He seems extremely paranoid.

Vachss: Paranoid is not a fair name. Remember he distrusts the government, but the government raised him. The government used, abused, and confused him. The government did everything that could be done to a child. He has no reason to believe in any benevolent system or society.

Silet: Would you describe him as a vigilante?

Vachss: I really disagree with that term. A vigilante is a person who goes out and protects the community for some higher purpose. Burke is a revenge freak. Burke is a person for whom if you cross him or cross a member of his family, homicide is not one of his inhibitions. But he doesn't get up in the morning and say, "Let's go hunt child-abusers." Unless you traverse his territory nothing is going to happen. So a vigilante who goes out there to fight "crime" doesn't fit Burke at all. Burke's out committing crimes.

Silet: This is a guy working outside the law. As a lawyer does that bother you?

Vachss: Frankly, unless you have a radically different opinion than most American citizens, I don't know why this is even a conversation.

Silet: He's a very different kind of investigator from Philip Marlowe and Sam Spade.

Vachss: He's also from a different social class from these people. Marlowe is a very erudite, intelligent, almost aristocratic person. Burke is *not.* He's a card-carrying member of whatever underclass you'd like to point to and is not interested in wry commentary about the state of affairs of society. He really feels he is at war with it and knows he can't win and so wants to stay out of the line of fire as much as he can. If he'd be left alone, which his life makes impossible, he would just go with his low-grade grifting and never get involved in much. But he is not left alone, and that's what his life is.

Silet: When *Flood* was first published did you have any idea of writing a series?

Vachss: No, my God, that's why the book is so bad. I thought it was going to be a one-round fight so I threw every punch I had. The book is a third too big. As soon as I was assured that I would be able to write other books, I went to what is a much more natural style for myself. I didn't even have a fantasy there would be another book.

Silet: But now you write about one a year.

Vachss: Because I have no need, like most writers, to look for material.

Silet: What gets you started on a book?

Vachss: I pick a particular theme that's part of my work. So one book's about internet trafficking in kiddy-porn—which of course I was writing about ten years before the press—a book's about incest, a book's about baby breeding, a book's about so-called ritual abuse, a book's about so-called false memory syndrome. I pick a topic and then bring to it the material that's already available to me and try to focus on that aspect rather than just the whole broad topic of child abuse.

Silet: Do you have a writing schedule?

Vachss: I don't have one, because I've never had the luxury of being a writer. I'm a practicing lawyer, and I also do a lot of training and consulting. So I grab time. When it's there, I'm extremely productive, and I don't need much time. I write in my head constantly, so when I sit down I'm more typing than writing.

Silet: Do you plot or plan ahead?

Vachss: Yeah, it's all done before I "write."

Silet: Tell me about the ensemble cast that appears in the on-going series, Mole, Max and so on.

Vachss: What they all have in common is that they are all "Children of the Secret" in one way or another. They're all members of a family of choice, without family of their own. They come from different parts of life and different parts of the world, but that's what they have in common. Michelle is a transsexual—which idiot book reviewers keep calling a transvestite—who has finally had the operation after many years. Mole is a person who couldn't deal with the way the world treated him and created a world of his own. Max, although he's deaf, understands very, very well and is a warrior who chose to walk his own path because he just couldn't take the ones open to him. Each of them for one reason or another hears that silent whistle that only dogs can hear. What's most important about them is the way they feel toward each other, and the fact that these are people who act on their feelings and don't just express them.

Silet: What about Pansy?

Vachss: Pansy is a Neapolitan mastiff. She's based on my dog Gussie and the portrait is completely accurate.

Silet: Why have Pansy in the books?

Vachss: The plot line is essentially a true one. I remember being a child and being so afraid of the rats that always invaded the place we lived and having my little terrier next to me and how she'd go and fight the rats that were about her size. Burke had a little terrier that he loved that was taken away from him. All he ever dreamed about while he was in prison was having some living creature that would always be glad to see him, regardless of how he was doing, how much money he was making, whether things were up or down for him. He didn't really conceive originally of bonding with a human, only with an animal. His relationship with Pansy is bone-deep. In fact, the new book literally begins with Pansy being taken from him and the chaos that results.

Silet: Burke's New York is a very selective, dark side of New York.

Vachss: Right, it is only what he sees. And I don't know if it is darker than people who plan deals in penthouses to commit the worst kind of foulness, but it's a different part of the city for sure.

Silet: How important is that environment to you as a writer?

Vachss: I don't think it is important at all, to be honest with you. I think what's important is the evil that people do, not the place where they do it. I've been all over the world, and I've been fortunate that the books have been published in so many different languages that I've had a chance to dialogue with folks everywhere, and they all think I'm writing about their place. People comment, and they're usually sort of real middle-class people, "Oh, the special world, it's like *Blade Runner*." Bullshit, you know. You can find an underbelly in any city in the world, if you know where to look. The underbelly for an abused child wouldn't matter if it were in a basement or a penthouse. I've represented children whose parents were zillionaires and who were treated just as horribly as kids from dire poverty.

Silet: You do leave the city in *Down in the Zero* when you go to Connecticut.

Vachss: To make the point that I just made to you. And I went to Indiana once too. That *is* the point. I understand that New York is a character in the books, but I know for a fact that the evils that enrage me so are not confined to a city or a state or a social class or a race or a religion or a creed or a color. Burke leaves the city to make that point. Because otherwise I think people do get lost and people in Iowa do say, "Well, these things don't happen in Iowa." So it was good to have people in upper-class Connecticut say, "Whoops," you know?

Silet: Your world is more "real" than is often true in the highly fictionalized books of traditional crime writers.

Vachss: That's right. When in my books someone gets hit in the head with a tire iron, they don't get up thirty seconds later and start looking for clues.

Silet: Your books also carry a heavy social message. Is crime fiction inherently a social form?

Vachss: That's a good question. I think because I write about crime and violence and child abuse and treachery and corruption and evil and filth that I'm a mainstream novelist as far as America in 1999 is concerned. So you can call it crime fiction if you like, but it's not racked that way in the libraries. It just depends on the individual's view. But don't get me wrong—I'm not for a second comparing myself to anybody like a Dickens or Norris or anybody like that. To generalize something is to an extent to ghettoize it, too, and say, well, this only happens here or this only happens there.

Silet: Do you see a real difference between mainstream fiction and crime fiction?

Vachss: I think there is. If you write pure genre crime fiction— where the voluptuous blonde comes into the office and you have the bottle of Jim Beam stashed in the desk and take your feet down and grind out your Lucky Strike in the ashtray and say, "What can I do for you, honey?"—you have to think that's got its own genre. No different than romance is a genre or horror. Yeah, I do. But you could certainly write horror that was not predominantly that genre, it just happens to be something that was horror and that was mainstream. I just think it depends on the individual book. But sure there is a crime genre, how could there not be?

When you have this handsome, intelligent, warm, caring, sensitive, do-the-right-thing-for-the-right-reasons hero, who does not care about minutiae like money and personal safety, then you're in a genre. But I think if you've got a person who is doing whatever it is he feels he needs to do to survive, I'm not sure that that fits. But I understand and concede that people could argue about this.

Silet: What are the strengths and drawbacks to writing a series?

Vachss: Well, the drawback is rather obvious, which is that with each book you're stuck between your loyal readers—who don't want to hear the same explanations again, because they already know—and new people—who if you don't provide some, are going to get lost. That certainly is a drawback, and it's quite a dance to get that right. The strength is that you build an audience that actually cares about the people you're writing about, and cares about what happens to them and therefore cares about what *they* care about.

Silet: Has it been difficult to work that balance?

Vachss: Yeah, it has. I mean, where you stop with the exposition is a trick with each book, sure it is. I don't have a technique. I'm just careful. I usually overwrite to begin with, say more than I need to say, and then go back with a scalpel and prune it. The only book that I've written that wasn't in the series, *Shella*—everybody talks about how skeletal that book was—wasn't stuck with any of that other baggage. It was a lot easier.

Silet: Why did you write that book?

Vachss: That's the book I wanted to write in the first place. That's as close to me as a writer—which I do not call myself—which if I was to stand before the great god of writing and he said, "All right, put up your best card," that's the one I'd deal. But there was no market, that couldn't have been published when I started writing.

Silet: Are you planning another non-series book?

Vachss: You know, the irony, my friend, is that I've gotten so much fan mail asking me when I'm going to do the next one in *that* series, that I don't even know the answer.

Silet: When writers write non-series books I wonder if that is an indication that they've grown tired of their on-going character.

Vachss: I'm not tired of him at all. I thought I would be but the support I've gotten is energizing to begin with, and at this particular stage—since I've only got this particular song that I know how to play—it would be superfluous just to create another character, simply so I could have a different character.

Silet: Tell me about the mail you get.

Vachss: The mail varies literally from death threats to "you saved my life." I couldn't give you a wider range of mail. I get a ton of it, and most of it is not about the books as books but as books about their lives. It's astounding the number of people who think I know something about their lives because of the books I've written. To me the greatest tribute that a writer, at least in my position, could get is the same one a blues musician could get, which is the audience saying, "Yeah, that's the truth." And I get that a lot.

Silet: You're obviously touching your readers in some profound way.

Vachss: Yeah, but I get it from predators as well as from prey. I get it from convicts as well as cops. I get it from everybody. NAMBLA complained about one of my books and said, "We hate this guy, he's our archenemy, but his portrait of our position is quite accurate." It should be since it is almost verbatim from a conversation I had with one of them. NAMBLA is the North American Man/Boy Love Association, a notorious pedophile organization.

Silet: *Safe House* is the last book out. Tell me about it.

Vachss: I thought that people were really misunderstanding this whole business about militias and about the radical right. I don't think they got it. I don't think they really understood it, and they don't understand what's necessary to deal with it. I don't think they see the connection between that sort of conduct and abused children. For example, skinheads. Everybody bemoans skinheads, right? If skinheads were black everybody would be trying to recruit them and come up with programs for them and divert them and everything else. But because they're working-class whites, they're just considered racist morons and they're dismissed. So they join the only club that will have them. Which is something America keeps learning to its sorrow: you can't keep rejecting and rejecting and marginalizing people without expecting them to band together at some point around whomever shows up with a banner. That was a significant point that I wanted to make in the book.

I also wanted to talk about stalking, because stalking has become too much of a goddamned sit-com joke. "Isn't it cute." I mean, I get stalked a lot and I have shown other writers, which was my mistake, some of the letters I get from women. They've said, "Gee, I wish she would stalk me." They have no idea what they're talking about when they say that. They have no idea what an erotomaniac can do to a person's life, and they have no idea what a vengeful stalker can do. There are just too many dead women found every year clutching orders of protection in their hands. A stalker is an obsessive and obsessives have the power of focus, and any martial artist will tell you that if you gather that much focus your power is increased exponentially.

Silet: Why do you think it has been trivialized?

Vachss: Because American entertainment trivializes. They trivialize every damn thing. I certainly think they trivialize child abuse. I certainly think they trivialize incest. I certainly think there are a whole lot of idiots who think Roman Polanski was mistreated. The pain of victims is generally ignored unless the victims are willing to parade themselves in some talk-show entertainment way.

Silet: Which is itself a trivialization.

Vachss: I couldn't agree with you more. I think we want stuff like—and I don't want to stigmatize any other writer—the good guy wins and he gets the girl and the bad guy gets vanquished. We don't really want to say we've got any responsibility ourselves. We have lousy child-protection systems. We have lousy juvenile-justice systems. Then we're surprised that we've got a horrible crime problem.

Silet: Is this simply a way of making ourselves feel comfortable?

Vachss: Yeah, that's right. I think entertainment is designed to entertain not to upset. Some German writer said that what I do, what I write is—and he used a French term—*littérature engagée*. He said that's the sort of stuff that makes people very angry or very sad or very *something*, and as a result people seeking entertainment would be better off avoiding it.

Silet: In *Safe House* you introduce Crystal Beth and leave us at the end wondering whether Burke and she are going to continue.

Vachss: Every woman Burke's been involved with has either left or died. So it is necessary to end a book that way because people wouldn't know what to do with him actually finding happiness. He's a doomed child. I will tell you, since this interview won't be out before the next book comes out anyway, that the new book opens with Crystal Beth getting killed.

Silet: This is *Choice of Evil*. Do you want to talk about it a bit?

Vachss: You'd have to be real familiar with the series for that one to make any sense if I spoke about it in general terms. What I am trying to do is cross into that supernatural border where there is some reality to it. It has a very interesting premise which has never been explored, that I know of, in writing before. You know all about the fag-bashing that is sweeping the nation, right? What if there was a serial killer who only killed fag-bashers? What would that do to fag-bashing? What would be the ACLU's position on it? What would gay groups want to do about it? What would happen and how would you get such a person and why?

That's what the book looks like it's about until you get much closer to the end and then you realize that it is about something else entirely. It's about understanding that the only way to become immortal is to die. This one sort of answers the question fans have been asking me for years which is, is Wesley really dead? So that's why this book is 110,000 words long instead of my usual 75,000.

Silet: How is the book about the "supernatural"?

Vachss: Have you ever heard of the myth called "reaching back"? Essentially what the myth is, and this only works for evil people, if an evil person has died and you want to bring that evil person back, generally to make them suffer, you have to find a gatekeeper and then you have to bring that gatekeeper one soul for every one that evil person took.

Silet: How will it work out in the book?

Vachss: I think it will work out great if I did my job. I think this will all make sense. One of the things I've been about is not exploding myths but explaining them. So the myth of vampires, for example. What's a predatory pedophile but a vampire? He can only reproduce by preying on others. What's a werewolf but a multiple personality disorder? I think ancients saw the same things we saw, but simply called them something different in order to explain them. So I'm not so much about myth busting as about myth explaining. I think there is a way to reach back, and if I did it right in this book, you'll see.

Silet: You did a music CD to accompany *Safe House*?

Vachss: There is a sound track to *Safe House* which has various blues cuts which I selected, because I love the blues and the blues are thematic throughout the book. I probably brought more fans to Judy Henske than any publicity effort just by having her in all the books. I get letters all the time saying is there really a Judy Henske? Is there really a Son Seals? So we just put together this CD, and it's got some of the music that is in all the books. Its title is *Safe House*.

Silet: You also have coming out another collection of short stories.

Vachss: It's going to be called *Everybody Pays*. The editor prevailed on me to change the title from *Proving It*. I love the story "Proving It," because it is the only romance I've ever written and every woman who has read it so far has broken down in tears, which I consider a great success. The novella which actually anchors the collection is called "Everybody Pays," so that's what they wanted me to do. Plus they're convinced there's going to be a Cross movie soon, and since it's a Cross story, that's what they want. By the way, there's the answer to a whole bunch of new characters. I did those in the short stories because I could go much over the top with them.

Silet: What's the attraction of short stories?

Vachss: I've always loved them. If I had my choice, I'd do nothing but short fiction. You have to be perfect with it; it is like haiku. You really don't get a margin for error. If it works, it's like one of those real six-inch punches that just is devastating. I'd rather read short stories than anything. But until I was—I guess "surprisingly" is the only fair word for it—successful no one was going to publish any collection of my short fiction.

Silet: Do you write much of it?

Vachss: Yeah, I do. Hell, that book must have forty stories in it. Again, I write plays too. I mean, it doesn't matter, I'd write any bloody thing, or do any bloody thing—if I knew how to sing I'd do that, or paint—because it's the one message. It's not really the method.

Silet: Have any of your plays been produced?

Vachss: Oh sure, in fact one play ran in New York and London and in Germany. The title was *Replay*. And we're doing that now as an audiobook.

Silet: What is the central theme of all your various work?

Vachss: Actually the central theme is simple: behavior is the truth; everything else is rhetoric. There is no biogenetic code for a child molester or a serial killer or a giggling arsonist. We make our own monsters; we build our own beasts. While some idiot book reviewers say how depressing such a thing is, I consider it the opposite, because if we create then we can correct, and we can interdict and we can change.

Silet: How would we go about doing that?

Vachss: To me the ultimate building blocks are in the child-protection system. Charles Manson wasn't wrong when he said you can see me in the eyes of a ten-year-old. Look, let's say you're a parent, right? You're constituted by whatever law you believe in— the laws of God, the laws of nature, or the laws that humans make for themselves—to protect your child. So when you don't do that, when in fact you do the opposite, you violate all those laws. If the larger parent, society, not only doesn't intervene but takes a look and goes, "Aw, so what," you've got all you need to construct a sociopath. So, if anything, I stand for the refutation of the "bad seed" theory.

Silet: What would be your recommendations for changing the system that produces sociopaths?

Vachss: Well, they're lengthy but essentially what they involve is front-ending all the money. We're spending billions and billions of dollars incarcerating people who have no business being in prison, you know, low-level dope fiends, and spending nothing, really, in protecting abused children who are in some cases the most dangerous human beings on the planet of tomorrow. For every dollar we'd invest in child-protective services, we could save a hundred thousand in criminal justice services.

Silet: So sort of preventive action?

Vachss: I don't know about preventive. I don't think you can prevent child abuse, but I think you can prevent its recurrence. I've never ever heard of or been involved in a case involving a dead baby, for example, where that kid was killed by the first attack. Over and over again we get chance after chance and we blow it.

Silet: So how do you tighten that up?

Vachss: We have to professionalize the child-protective system. It's now the garbage can of the business. In fact, people who collect garbage get paid far more and get more respect and get more training and get more supervision. We have to say this a priority as if it were a horribly communicable disease threatening the whole country. I'd like to see scholarships for young people who want to go into child-protective case work, so that they could have their college paid for if they gave x-number of years back at the other end.

There's lots and lots of things that could be done, but they're not because in every presidential campaign I've ever listened to, and I've listened to a lot, I've never heard children mentioned except in a sort of generic "I'm pro-family" way. There is no single-issue constituency for children.

Silet: You mentioned critics. Have you been well treated by them?

Vachss: No, I actually didn't say critics, I said reviewers. I don't consider them the same. Criticism is something I can learn from. Book reviewing is the expression of an individual's opinion as if anybody cares, and I've been treated every way you can be by book reviewers. I've been the next Dickens by I don't know how many book reviewers, and I've been the king of vigilante/slasher porn by I don't know how many more.

Silet: How does a critic differ from a book reviewer?

Vachss: A critic talks in terms of "why" not "what." A critic doesn't express opinion, a critic deconstructs in such a way that if I was a student in that critic's class, and I got my book back and I got a "C+" on it, I would know how to write an "A" book. That would be a critic to me.

Silet: Do you read the reviews?

Vachss: No more. I did when I first got published. I was all excited because I thought that book reviewing was criticism. No one had ever taught me how to write so I thought, "Oh, man, I'll read these book reviews and I'll learn how to make my books better." But I didn't: I learned some people liked my books and some didn't.

Silet: How would you describe your novels?

Vachss: They've been called investigative novels, and I kind of like that term, because I'm writing about stuff before you read it in the papers, not because I'm prescient or because life imitates art or any other such crap, but because we're at ground zero. We see the stuff.

Silet: And your practice is centered on this.

Vachss: My practice is exclusively representing children. You name it. Kids who have had horrible crimes committed against them; kids who have committed horrible crimes against others.

Silet: Is there any question you wanted to be asked in an interview but weren't?

Vachss: This was an unusual interview because ninety-nine percent of them are not about the books. I just don't have enough of a sense of myself as a writer that there are any sort of literary questions that I could think of that should be asked me. I believe what I say so I believe that what I do has to speak for itself, and I accept the fact that it speaks very differently to different people.

What's the Worse That Could Happen?
Donald E. Westlake

Photo © Abby Adams

Donald Westlake has written so many books over so long a period that it is almost impossible to remember them all. He even divides them into various categories when they are listed in the front of his latest novel: Novels, Comic Crime Novels, The Dortmunder Series, Crime Novels, Juvenile, Western, Reportage, Short Stories, and Anthology. *The Ax* (1997) mentions only thirtysome books; he has written well over seventy—which he admits to—and that's not counting screenplays, so even this listing is incomplete.

Many of the Crime Novels also can be subdivided by series and Westlake has written many. The first were the Parker (no first name) books which Westlake began writing under the pseudonym of Richard Stark because he was writing too fast for his publisher to keep up with him. The Parker series begat one featuring Alan Grofield, a sometime associate of Parker's, but who basically had a nicer personality. John Dortmunder was created to pull off a caper that Parker would not do. Dortmunder is long-suffering and dogged in ways that Parker is not. Mitch Tobin possesses a humanity that Parker will not allow himself to face.

Although initially he did not seek out the work, now Donald Westlake is also a highly regarded screenwriter. And after writing several movies, including a couple based on his own novels, his script for *The Grifters*, based on the classic Jim Thompson *roman noir*, won him an Academy Award nomination. The experience introduced him to Martin Scorsese, and Westlake is now working with the director/producer on other projects.

Donald Westlake was awarded the Grand Master by the Mystery Writers of America.

Portions of this interview originally appeared as "What's the Worse that Could Happen?: An Interview with Donald Westlake," *The Armchair Detective*, 29:4 (Winter 1996), 394–401.

Silet: You have had a distinguished as well as prolific career in crime fiction. How did you get started?

Westlake: When I was eleven years old I wrote a story about a gang killing in a night club. There wasn't a word in the story that I understood. Writers are always told, write about what you know, but at eleven you don't know anything, except the movies and books you've seen and read. I sold a short story when I was twenty. I wanted to be a published teenage author, but I missed it by a year.

Silet: Did you write professionally from then on?

Westlake: No, I went to New York and had a lot of different oddball jobs, including one as a manuscript reader for the Scott Meredith Agency, which read amateur manuscripts for a fee, so they hired drifting no-goods like me to do the actual reading, although the letter would be signed by Scott Meredith. I used to say, "Aren't we engaged in mail fraud here?" I worked there for six months, and it was a learning experience because it was really at the commercial level of publishing. Also because I was reading a minimum of forty short stories a week, I was learning all the mistakes writers make. After a while I had some short story sales and decided it was time to go free-lance to see what happens.

Before I left, I did a mystery novel and brought it to the guy who was running that part of the office. I thought it had hard-cover potential, but he said, "We'll try two publishers, if you want to waste the time, then we'll sell it to a paperback house." It was rejected with extreme prejudice by Simon & Schuster and then it went to Random House. Lee Wright, who's an incredible editor, called the agency and said, "I'm rejecting this book, but there're some things of interest in it, and I'd like to have a conversation with the writer." So I went over to pick up the manuscript at Random House and spent two hours talking to Lee, and it was agreed that I would rewrite it and she would look at it again. She eventually bought it. That was *The Mercenaries*.

Silet: And you did several more for Random House?

Westlake: Lee was my editor for ten years, and I did eleven or twelve books for her, the first five of which were straight mystery novels. Then the sixth one I started was in the first person, and the guy's voice was comic. I called my then agent, who told me to drop the idea because he said, "You'll never get a paperback sale, you won't get any foreign sales because nobody can translate comedy, and you're going to cut your income in half." But it was moving along pretty fast, and I decided just to do it this once and get it out of my system, and I never went back. That book was called *The Fugitive Pigeon*, which I still don't understand, and it has sold five different times so far in paperback and has had a lot of foreign sales.

Silet: You have been very successful with a number of series, the first was written under the pseudonym Richard Stark.

Westlake: After *The Mercenaries*, I did a second book for Lee, but there's always been the belief in publishing that they can't publish more than one book a year from any one author. So I thought it would be interesting to have a pen name and to have another market, to aim for a paperback original this time. So I did this book with the assumption that the bad guy has to get caught at the end. I wrote it with Gold Medal in mind, but they rejected it. Then I sent it to Bucklin Moon at Pocket Books, who said, "I like this book and I like this character. Is there any way that you could change the book so that he would escape at the end and then you could give me three books a year about him?" And I said, "I think so."

Silet: So that was the beginning of Parker?

Westlake: Yes, but I had no idea that it was going to be a series, and I had not written it that way. I'd made Parker completely remorseless, completely without redeeming characteristics, because he was going to get caught at the end. So I wound up with a truly cold leading series character, which was an interesting thing to do and try not to soften him. In a series the guy's got to be around for years and the readers have to like him. But we came in here with this son-of-a-bitch and we're going out with this son-of-a-bitch. I felt that he had to remain true to himself.

Silet: Why did you decide to discontinue the Parker series?

Westlake: I never did decide to discontinue them, I just ran dry. I was writing them regularly, and I started one more using a variation on an earlier one in which the gang goes into a building, something like a D&D building in New York where you've got wholesale jewelers, antique dealers, coin dealers on the upper floors. A lot of money in one building. The thieves would just go in, remove the building security alarm system and have the weekend to do the whole building. I started that and got sixty pages into it, and it just ran dry. I tried it a couple more times and nothing would happen.

So I thought, what's gone wrong is that I have domesticated Parker. He's now living with this woman, and he's not the character that he was. I have let him get soft, so let's start another book which begins with her getting killed. I tried that and it wouldn't work either. Eventually the idea of the building I gave to Dortmunder, and there's a female character, who I had in the segment of the book when it was a Parker novel, and I made her a little kinder and gentler and in the same job.

Then in 1989 I tried again with another idea for a specific kind of oddball robbery of an evangelical meeting where people bring their love offerings or God offerings, and you've got a stadium full of cash. In fact, I did some of it when they were shooting *The Grifters*, and I got about half of it done, and it ran dry, and I really began getting tired of this. In 1991 or 1992, I showed it to Otto Penzler, and he had a couple little suggestions for ways to clean up what was done, but I was still stuck. Recently, I was between books and I told my wife, "I don't know what I'm going to do next," and she said, "Why don't you take a look at that Richard Stark novel," and I took a look at it and I finished it.

Silet: Your current series character is Dortmunder.

Westlake: Well, Dortmunder. After I'd done about ten or eleven of the Parker novels, I was trying to think of something new for him. He handles frustration very badly, so it would annoy him if he had to steal the same thing several times because things would keep going wrong. I thought that's funny and useful, but I realized I've really got to be careful with this because the worst thing you can do with a tough guy is make him funny inadvertently, because then he isn't a tough guy anymore, he's just a jerk. So I didn't dare give Parker that job, because he wouldn't do it in the first place, and it would ruin him if he did. I still liked the idea of a guy having to constantly go back and do a robbery again in another way, so I needed another guy who couldn't be quite like Parker. He had to be more long-suffering. I was looking for a name, and in a bar I saw a German beer called "Dortmunder Actien Bier" and I said that's what I want, a guy whose "action" is wrong, and Dortmunder just has a nice gloomy sound to it.

Silet: You've had a lot of experience with the movies.

Westlake: More in the last several years. I never sought it out. I think I would have but I didn't know how. I've always lived in and around New York, and I never wanted to spend more than a week or two in California, so I didn't know people or what you did. Then in 1970 or 1971, I got a phone call from a guy who said, "Hello, I'm Elliot Kastner and I'm a movie producer, and I think it's time for another *Rififi*, and you're the guy to write it." I thought, "What the hell was that?" I called my agent and he looked into it and said he's a guy who's produced a lot of movies, and the first movie he ever did was *Harper*, the screen version of the Ross Macdonald novel, and Bill Goldman had done that screenplay. So I called Bill and asked, "Who is this guy and why is he phoning me?" Bill said, "That's Elliot. He doesn't know anything about making movies, he knows how to make the deals, and if he calls you, that means you're about to be hot. If you'd like to get into the movie business stick with Elliot. He will get the movie made with the wrong cast and the wrong director and the wrong budget, but he'll get it made, and you'll have a credit."

Jerry Bick, an assistant of Elliot's, and I had lunch, and we talked about some script ideas. I suggested a story about a couple of New York City cops who have had enough, and with their knowledge, experience, and assets could pull a major robbery to get out and retire someplace. Out of that came *Cops and Robbers*, with the wrong budget, wrong director, and wrong cast, but a credit.

Silet: You did the script for Jim Thompson's *The Grifters* which got you an Academy Award nomination.

Westlake: I had read the novel years before, and so when they came to me as a result of my having done a thing called *The Stepfather*, I read it again and thought, "Jeez, this thing is not a Disney movie." When we met for the first time, before anything was committed, I said the thing about this story is that it has a very harsh ending, but if it doesn't have that ending, it doesn't *have* an ending. I'll do this, but only if we all agree to keep the ending and everyone agreed. I remember the first time Marty Scorsese, who was producing, saw a rough cut in New York, he turned around and he smiled at us and said, "Well, one thing for sure, we don't want to do test screenings on this. We wouldn't *want* to read those cards." We were never sure what people would come out of the theater saying, but we went forward with it.

When I went out to L.A. for the last week of rehearsal, Angelica Huston, Annette Bening, and John Cusack all had the Black Lizard paperback, and they came running over to see why this and that had been cut—of course, it was all lines of theirs—but that's nice that they were defending the writer. Everybody had this feeling that we were doing something good. Back when I was working on the script Marty said, "How's it coming?" and I said, "I'm doing damage on every page," and he sort of smiled and nodded. But I was doing damage on every page, which is what the story was about.

Silet: Steven Frears, the director, likes the writer on the set during the shooting. Had you been on the set before?

Westlake: I had with *Cops and Robbers*, which was unfortunately an unhappy experience. The director was a charming man—he's now dead—but as a director he believed in consensus, and it is the nature of the beast that a director has to be a dictator. It was rather chaotic, and since it was shot in New York, I would go home every night and say, "Oh, God!" But the set on *The Grifters* was just terrific, and at the end of it I said that it was so nice to be in a boat in which everybody was rowing in the same direction instead of getting hit in the head by a lot of oars.

Silet: Isn't it frustrating to write scripts and then simply have them shelved?

Westlake: Yes, horribly. You know you've done good things and you'd like to see them. The worse thing like that in the last several years is the work I did for Roberto Grimaldi, who owns the rights to Dashiell Hammett's first novel, *Red Harvest.* He's had scripts done by tons of people—Bernardo Bertolucci did five. The German director Volker Schlondorff, who won an Academy Award for *The Tin Drum,* and I have been on a couple of doomed projects together, and Roberto came to us to do a script of the novel. We saw a couple of the other scripts and thought the wily Mr. Hammett has pulled the wool over these people's eyes. We saw how they were misled and how to do it right. At the beginning Volker talked with Bertolucci and he said, "Forget it, he's not serious." Meaning Grimaldi. We did a couple of scripts, and it turned out that it was true. He's never going to get a movie made, and it has become a way for him to have lunch with people. I know that I've solved the basic problem with the novel, and I'm never going to see the movie.

Silet: You've had about a dozen of your books made into films. Generally have you been pleased with the movies?

Westlake: It's a variety. There's a great one, *Point Blank*, with Lee Marvin, which is from the first Parker novel. And there is a quite good one from *The Outfit*, another Parker novel, with Robert Duvall as Parker. It is a good, small movie with every B-movie actor you've ever thought of in it. And *The Hot Rock* is quite good. Then there have been others that are complete disasters, and a couple I've been warned away from, told if you see this movie, you're just going to tie up the suicide hot lines.

Silet: Has your experience in Hollywood affected your writing?

Westlake: Very early on it did. Anytime a novelist is affected by film it is for the bad. It's always a mistake. There was one book that I had to go back and completely rewrite to get *Casino Royale* out of it. There is a way of telling a story in a specific kind of episodic way that the movies do, and *Casino Royale* did, very well, but in a book it just looks as if somebody has dropped a manuscript and picked it up helter-skelter. All that writing screenplays has done is confirm me in how to write a novel. Movies are just the surface of things, what it looks like and what it sounds like. Where a novel is what it means as well. Even at their best there is still that sense in movie scripts of walking down a narrow corridor. With a novel there is the sense of entering a big room where you can go anywhere.

Silet: Let's move on to your more recent fiction. What attracted you to Branson, Missouri, the setting for *Baby, Would I Lie?*

Westlake: Friends of mine who spend part of each year there described it as a real desert for anybody who has anything to do with the life of the mind. They kept saying come on down to visit, which meant come down because we need somebody to talk to. So eventually we visited, and my wife called Branson an "irony free zone." I thought there has got to be something here for me. I had already done this other book involving people from a newspaper like *The National Inquirer*, and those people are one hundred percent irony. So I felt to put the *National Inquirer* people together with Branson, Missouri should be a learning experience for both sides.

Silet: What is it about the country/western environment that attracted you?

Westlake: I wasn't really interested until then. For me the thing about a novel sometimes is that I get into its world. I got deeply interested in the whole Nashville/Branson tug of war, and I talked with some of the show biz people, who are all very bright and very knowledgeable. For guys who spent thirty years on the bus with a bottle of Jack Daniels in their hand, in Branson they can sleep in the same bed every night and play golf on Wednesday mornings. It's just a lovely retirement and more money than God.

Silet: *Smoke* is a crazy combination of sci fi and caper. Where did you come up with the idea for it?

Westlake: I was back in Anguilla for the first time in twenty years. I'd written my only non-fiction book in 1971 about their rebellion against independence. At resort places people will leave old paperback novels behind, and there was a copy of H. G. Wells' *Invisible Man,* which I had not read for many years. I read it on the beach and thought that all this is about is how much trouble it is to be invisible. I kept thinking about it, because there is nothing else to do on the beach except read and think, and I felt there must be some fun in it or people wouldn't fantasize about it. I never intended to write *The Invisible Man*—I don't write science fiction— but if I did, what would it be like?

The first thing I would do is make him a thief so that he would have some idea what to do with invisibility. The second thing I'd do would be to give him a girlfriend so there would be somebody to drive. I did the first chapter longhand down there and when I got back I looked at it. I liked the guy's style. I met a scientist years ago, a blue-sky thinker, whose job is to imagine impossible things. So I called him because I wanted to find a way to make this character invisible, and I suggested scientists who are working on melanoma, with pigmentation as the carrier, and that might be the way. He said, "It seems to me you've already got it."

Silet: Why does a tobacco company fund the research?

Westlake: That sort of just grew. The whole tobacco thing was in the air. Then I read about the human genome project. I could hear some tobacco guy saying this is for us. We've tried to make cigarettes safe for people; now let's try to make people safe for cigarettes.

Silet: Tell me about *What's the Worst That Could Happen?*

Westlake: It's different in one way: at the beginning of the book, Dortmunder is the victim. He is stolen from. Then in his efforts to get this unimportant ring back, he keeps making more and more money. He's never made a profit before. In one of the earlier chapters, he comes home and says, as he drops twenty-eight thousand dollars on the table, "I've got bad news, May. I didn't get the ring." He keeps winning, but he keeps winning the wrong stuff. He's never been on a roll before. He gets a little lighter.

Silet: He takes on a large corporate type, too.

Westlake: Somebody who is somewhere between Robert Maxwell and Rupert Murdock. Not anybody in particular. The center of the character is Maxwell, because he was supposed to be an unimportant, dead, poverty-struck child, who instead got out of Eastern Europe to England and became Robert Maxwell. But he always had fun in life, since he wasn't supposed to be here, and he didn't give a damn anyway. That devil-may-care attitude I made the heart of this guy.

5   7/06